OXFORD WORLD'S CLASSICS

JOHN KEATS
SELECTED POETRY

JOHN KEATS was born in London in 1795. Orphaned early, he studied medicine at Guy's Hospital and, in 1816, became one of a new generation of qualified apothecaries. Medicine remained for him a standard of effective action against suffering, but he soon abandoned the profession in order to live for and by his poetry. He published three volumes during his lifetime and, while many of his contemporaries were prompt to recognize his greatness, snobbery and political hostility led the Tory press to vilify and patronize him as a 'Cockney poet'. He died of TB at the age of twenty-five. Financial anxieties and the loss of those he loved most had tried him persistently, yet he dismissed the concept of life as a vale of tears and substituted the concept of a 'vale of Soul-making'. His poetry and his remarkable letters reveal a spirit of questing vitality and profound understanding, and his final volume, which contains the great odes and the unfinished *Hyperion*, attests to an astonishing maturity of power.

ELIZABETH COOK studied at Oxford and the Warburg Institute and has taught at the Universities of Essex and Leeds. She now works freelance. Her study of late Renaissance poetry *Seeing Through Words* was published by Yale University Press in 1986, and she has edited Ben Jonson's *The Alchemist*.

FRANK KERMODE, retired King Edward VII Professor of English Literature at Cambridge, is the General Editor of The Oxford Authors Series. He is the author of many books, including *Romantic Image*, *The Sense of an Ending*, *The Classic*, *The Genesis of Secrecy*, *Forms of Attention*, and *History and Value*; he is also co-editor with John Hollander of *The Oxford Anthology of English Literature*.

OXFORD WORLD'S CLASSICS

*For over 100 years Oxford World's Classics have brought
readers closer to the world's great literature. Now with over 700
titles—from the 4,000-year-old myths of Mesopotamia to the
twentieth century's greatest novels—the series makes available
lesser-known as well as celebrated writing.*

*The pocket-sized hardbacks of the early years contained
introductions by Virginia Woolf, T. S. Eliot, Graham Greene,
and other literary figures which enriched the experience of reading.
Today the series is recognized for its fine scholarship and
reliability in texts that span world literature, drama and poetry,
religion, philosophy and politics. Each edition includes perceptive
commentary and essential background information to meet the
changing needs of readers.*

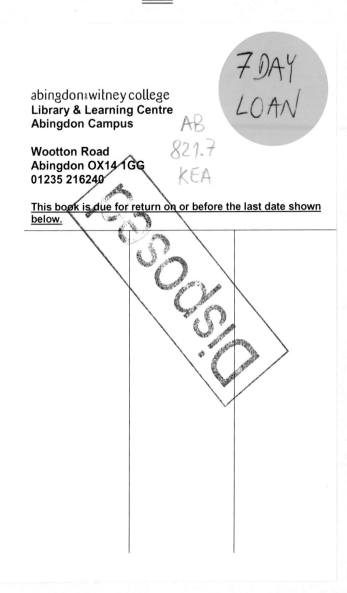

OXFORD

UNIVERSITY PRESS

Great Clarendon Street, Oxford OX2 6DP

Oxford University Press is a department of the University of Oxford.
It furthers the University's objective of excellence in research, scholarship,
and education by publishing worldwide in

Oxford New York

Athens Auckland Bangkok Bogotá Buenos Aires Calcutta
Cape Town Chennai Dar es Salaam Delhi Florence Hong Kong Istanbul
Karachi Kuala Lumpur Madrid Melbourne Mexico City Mumbai
Nairobi Paris São Paulo Shanghai Singapore Taipei Tokyo Toronto Warsaw

with associated companies in Berlin Ibadan

Oxford is a registered trade mark of Oxford University Press
in the UK and in certain other countries

Published in the United States
by Oxford University Press Inc., New York

Introduction, editorial matter, and selection © Elizabeth Cook 1994

The moral rights of the author have been asserted

Database right Oxford University Press (maker)

First published as a World's Classics paperback 1996
Reissued as an Oxford World's Classics paperback 1998
Reissued 2008

British Library Cataloguing in Publication Data

Data available

Library of Congress Cataloging in Publication Data

Keats, John, 1795–1821.
[Poems. Selections]
John Keats : selected poetry / edited with an introduction by
Elizabeth Cook.
p. cm.—(Oxford world's classics)
Includes bibliographical references and index.
I. Cook, Elizabeth, 1952– . II. Title. III. Series.
PR4832.C66 1996 821'.7—dc20 96–20898

ISBN 978–0–19–955395–2

1

Printed in Great Britain by
Clays Ltd, St Ives plc

Contents

Introduction

KEATS conceived of history as a process of realization. Collectively as well as individually the human task is to know, and bring to light by knowing, all that is latent and implicit within the creation. There is a spatial logic about this description of reality. In a letter of 1818 to his friend James Rice, Keats writes: 'as a certain bulk of Water was instituted at the Creation—so very likely a certain portion of intellect was spun forth into the thin Air for the Brains of Man to prey upon it ... That which is contained in the Pacific can't lie in the hollow of the Caspian—that which was in Miltons head could not find Room in Charles the seconds—he like a Moon attracted Intellect to its flow—it has not ebbd yet—but has left the shore pebble all bare.' The mediocrity of literary and political output (and Milton was honoured by Keats as an exponent of both) in Keats's own time is a logical consequence of Milton's 'gormandizing'.[1]

As in the history of the species, so in the progress of an individual mind. In a later letter, to J. H. Reynolds, Keats observes that the individual mind moves from the apparent biases of early life to an understanding that 'Every department of knowledge ... [is] excellent and calculated towards a great whole.'[2] The task of life, the life's work, is as nearly as is possible to realize and inform that whole. In this same letter he elaborates on his conception of human life as 'a large Mansion of Many Apartments'. In his programme for a life the whole building, 'dark Passages' included, must be experienced and known.

To Fanny Brawne, the young woman who dazzled him into vertiginous love, he expressed a wish that their life's quota of delight might be compressed within three days: 'I almost wish we were butterflies and liv'd but three summer days—three such days with you I could fill with more delight than fifty common years could ever contain.'[3]

Within twenty months of writing this Keats was dead. He had

---

[1] Letter to James Rice, 24 Mar. 1818.
[2] Letter to J. H. Reynolds, 3 May 1818.
[3] 1 July 1819.

known Fanny Brawne for little more than two years and their love had never been consummated. But when one contemplates Keats's life one is struck not only by its sad brevity but by the extraordinary and triumphant fullness of its achievement. It is as if his cells had intimation of the tuberculosis that was to kill him and his whole organism accelerated its work in response. The modest programme which he set himself in 'Sleep and Poetry' (composed in 1816) was to prove optimistic in the matter of years:

> O for ten years, that I may overwhelm
> Myself in poesy; so I may do the deed
> That my own soul has to itself decreed.

But to read Keats's poetry through in chronological sequence (the principle of this volume) is to be impressed with the astonishing speed with which it matures. Keats effectively produced his life's work in two years; the greater part of it in one.[4]

The sense of a circle having been completed is enhanced by the fact that Keats's first and last known poems were both written in imitation of the Elizabethan poet Edmund Spenser. They are, however, imitations of very different kinds and the difference says much about the journey between them. The first of these poems is derivative—not only of Spenser (himself a Middle English pasticheur) but of eighteenth-century poetry; it is the work of a young poet who is learning his craft by harnessing it to the style of one he admires. The last poem ('In after time a Sage of mickle lore') uses the Spenserian stanza and idiom with a relaxed confidence to engage not only with Spenser but with contemporary politics. In Spenser's version the egalitarian giant is destroyed by Sir Artegall and his squire. In Keats's revision, which Milton-like strikes a blow for freedom of the press, the giant now armed with wide reading and extensive knowledge, defeats his oppressors. Keats's friend Charles Brown, publishing this poem eighteen years after Keats's death, wrote that 'he died with his pen wielded in the cause of Reform'.[5]

In June 1818, when one brother, Tom, was dying of tuberculosis and the other, George, planning to sail with his new bride for America, Keats wrote to his friend Bailey: 'My love for my Brothers

---

[4] For an account of 21 Sept. 1818 to 21 Sept. 1819 see Robert Gittings, *The Living Year* (London, 1954).

[5] *Plymouth and Devenport Weekly Journal*, 4 July 1839.

from the early loss of our parents and even for earlier Misfortunes has grown into a affection "passing the Love of Women".[6] The poem 'To my Brothers', composed on Tom's birthday two years earlier, evokes a mood of tender and secure intimacy. Personal affections, necessary to all, were for Keats refuges of security and warmth in a world that had taken many away. Friendship played a large part in his life. His letters tacitly celebrate it and it is the occasion of several poems. He was clearly a nice friend to have and his friends loved him jealously and protectively. They were middle-class professional men—lawyers, business men, amateurs of literature in the sense that it was their love but not their livelihood. Only Haydon and Severn attempted (and usually failed) to live by their painting; Hunt divided his time between political journalism and literature.

Richard Abbey—the guardian whom, with misguided fore-thought, their grandmother had provided for the Keats children —was anxious to see his wards respectably and gainfully employed. Among the careers which he at various times proposed to Keats were tea-brokering (Abbey's own business), hatting, and book-selling. For his ward John to attempt to live as a poet he thought preposterous.[7]

But before the moment of 'self-will' (as he called it) when Keats, legally of age and so free to choose, declared his intention to be a poet and live by it, he had chosen the medical profession. Apprenticed first to the surgeon Thomas Hammond he became a student at Guy's Hospital. Guy's at this period was outstanding for the breadth and quality of the instruction it offered and Keats would there have come into contact with contemporary scientific ideas and issues far beyond those immediately applicable to his practice. He attended the lectures of the brilliant and tender-hearted surgeon Sir Astley Cooper and recovered some of his fees by working as a dresser. This work entailed cleaning and dressing infected wounds, attending the heart-rending operations which took place in the days before anaesthetic, and, on one day a week, standing in for a surgeon, making the rounds of the wards and deciding on admissions. It was a job bearing considerable responsibility and Keats was one of only twelve dressers taken on

[6] 10 June 1818.
[7] H. E. Rollins (ed.), *The Keats Circle: Letters and Papers 1816–1879* (Cambridge, Mass., 1965), i. 307–8.

out of a pool of about seven hundred students.[8] He worked for William Lucas, an undertrained surgeon whom Cooper described as 'neathanded but rash in the extreme'.[9] When Keats passed the exams he sat in the Apothecaries Hall in 1816 he became one of a new generation of qualified apothecaries, the forerunners of the modern general practitioner.[10]

Financial anxieties dogged Keats all his life. Had all that was due to him from his grandmother's estate materialized, he might have lived modestly without needing to earn. But the idea of living by poetry, then a highly marketable commodity, was not as far-fetched as it might be now. When he threw up the apothecary profession in 1817 Keats was reasonably hopeful that he might support himself through poetry.

Yet medicine was to remain for Keats a standard of effective action. Apollo, god of healing as well as poetry, was his tutelary deity. In the self-castigating encounter with Moneta in 'The Fall of Hyperion', the poet 'a sage| A humanist, *physician to all men*'— is distinguished from the dreamer–narrator. Keats conceived of an art which could enter the suffering world and mitigate its pain. He wrote to his friend Bailey, 'were it my choice I would reject a petrarchal coronation—on account of my dying day, and because women have Cancers'.[11] He longed for poetry to be as effective in improving the human lot as medicine. Or as politics might be. Keats's heroes were patriot champions of popular freedom: King Alfred, William Tell, Robert Burns, Robin Hood, the Polish patriot Tadeusz Kosciusko, and, among English Republicans, Algernon Sidney, Francis Vane, and John Milton. Milton, in his combination of active republicanism with great poetic achievement, was an exemplary figure for Keats. It was this combination that made Milton 'an active friend to Man all his Life and ... since his death'.[12]

These figures were held to be icons of patriotism by many who shared Keats's views. Their names occur in the liberal and radical

[8] Hermione de Almeida, *Romantic Medicine and John Keats* (Oxford, 1991), 28.

[9] Robert Gittings, *John Keats* (London, 1968), 64.

[10] The status of apothecaries had been upgraded by an Act of 1813 which ensured proper training and examination. See Llewellyn Woodward, *The Age of Reform* (Oxford, 1962), 18.

[11] 10 June 1818.

[12] Letter to James Rice, 24 Mar. 1818.

ne, would become a grand democracy of

continuous and shared is not a matter
ut fundamental to the nature of his mind

ssible to trace the route that Keats's
e it a progress outwards, widening or
ards to the 'wreath'd trellis of a working
al word for the organ, not the function).
passages, channels, windows which allow
imagination. Even death is seen in terms
As the nightingale is 'pouring forth [his]
cstasy', sending out his soul and song, so
e air my quiet breath'.

of *gradatio* by which a work of language
ression is one which Keats employs often,
or phrase of a line at the beginning of the
stone which allows a change of direction.
stanzas one and two of 'The Eve of St.
other is the step created by the repetition
t two stanzas of the 'Ode to a Nightingale'.
dymion i Keats said, 'when I wrote it it was
e Imagination towards a Truth ... It set
radations of Happiness even like a kind of
—and is my first step towards the chief
—the playing of different Natures with Joy
' in this passage seems to mean a process
ng an idea or a feeling through its various

mbitions for dramatic writing. He hoped 'to
tion in modern dramatic writing as Kean has
did in fact complete one play, *Otho the Great*,
er, *King Stephen*. But his ambitions in this
illed. *Otho,* written collaboratively with his
, is wooden Jacobethan pastiche; *King Stephen*
is only a fragment, abandoned early at the

ynolds, 19 Feb. 1818.
ylor, 30 Jan. 1818.
n Bailey, 14 Aug. 1819.

journals of the time. Hazlitt, whose brilliantly questing and rigorous mind made him Keats's most congenial living mentor, was also Keats's first anthologist. The small but choice group of poems by which Hazlitt chose to represent Keats in *Select British Poets* (1824) included 'Robin Hood', one of several poems on this subject that Keats had exchanged with his friend Reynolds. Robin Hood, who resisted the Norman yoke, is a champion of popular freedom whom it was entirely apposite to invoke at a time when 'Gagging Acts', provocateurs, and vindictive prosecutions were used in an attempt to stifle all opposition to the landed minority. Hazlitt, in choosing to represent Keats by this poem among others, is making a clear statement about Keats's alignments.

During the years that followed the French Revolution the monarchy and the ministers of the Tory government were paranoiacally fearful of a repetition in Britain.[13] Any questioning of the status quo, any request for parliamentary reform, any attempt to give the unpropertied labouring man a voice, was apt to be labelled 'sedition'. It is a word that is heard again and again in the second decade of the century—particularly in the peace that followed Waterloo when massive unemployment and poverty unmitigated by adequate parish Relief brought the country into an acute state of polarization.

In 1813 Leigh Hunt, poet and editor of the radical periodical, *The Examiner*, was imprisoned for two years, along with his brother John, on account of an attack on the Prince Regent in *The Examiner*. When he was released in February 1815 Keats, who had yet to meet Hunt, composed a poem of celebration. This poem appears in Keats's first published volume (*1817*), a volume dedicated to Hunt, by then a personal friend. This dedication ensured (as Keats must have known it would) that Keats was thereafter identified by the Tory faction with the 'seditious' enemy.

When Keats's second volume, *Endymion*, appeared in 1818 the reviewer of the *British Critic* was able to go straight for the 'jacobinical apostrophe' at the beginning of Book iii. Another who singled out this passage was John Gibson Lockhart, reviewing for *Blackwood's Edinburgh Magazine*. Lockhart was the originator of the appellation 'Cockney School of Poetry'—a phrase in which social

[13] Keats wrote to his brother and sister in law that 'They have made a handel out of this event [the French Revolution] in every way to undermine our freedom' (17–27 Sept. 1819).

snobbery thinly veils political hostility: 'We had almost forgot to mention, that Keats belongs to the Cockney School of Politics, as well as the Cockney School of Poetry.' He then refers slightingly to Keats's admiration for Hunt and suggests that he is the protégé of Hunt and *The Examiner*: 'Hear how their bantling has already learned to lisp sedition . . .'[14]—and he quotes *Endymion* iii. 1–22.

Opponents of liberty, their paranoia notwithstanding, are often obtuse in detecting subversion in all but its crudest and most explicit forms. Artists with a vocation for freedom have sometimes been driven, in a way which may seem suicidal, to declare themselves with moments of coarse spelling out which may appear greatly at variance with the rest of the work. This is the case with the poem which, more than any other piece of evidence, contributed to Osip Mandelstam's arrest and eventual death: a poem which calls Stalin 'the Kremlin mountaineer, the murderer, the peasant-slayer'.[15] It is as if Mandelstam needed to spell it out to the stupid enemy so that they would know his mettle and that the wideness and depth of the poetry which they could not understand were absolutely inimical to the world they were trying to create.

Keats's poetry is in places robustly interventionary. Of lines 105–20 of 'Isabella' Bernard Shaw wrote that they 'contain all the Factory Commission Reports that Marx read and that Keats did not read because they were not yet written in his time'.[16] They are lines that remind us that Keats wrote while the slave trade was scaldingly recent in memory and the rights of the paid labourer remained largely unwon.

There are moments of pugnacious coarseness in Keats's poetry which express his longing for poetry to be effectual—as active an agent in human healing as the medical profession he had given up. Several remarks in his letters show that he had hopes of making some direct contribution: 'I am ambitious of doing the world some good: if I should be spared that may be the work of my maturer years';[17] 'I hope sincerely I shall be able to put a Mite of help to the Liberal side of the Question before I die.'[18] After his death an

[14] *Blackwood's Edinburgh Magazine*, Aug. 1818.
[15] Nadezhda Mandelstam, *Hope against Hope* (Harmondsworth, 1975), 35.
[16] *The John Keats Memorial Volume* (London, 1921), 175.
[17] Letter to Richard Woodhouse, 27 Oct. 1818.
[18] Letter to C. W. Dilke, 22 Sept. 1819.

disheartening news that Kean would not be in the country to perform it.

Keats wrote that 'The little dramatic skill I may as yet have however badly it might show in a Drama would I think be sufficient for a Poem—I wish to diffuse the colouring of St Agnes eve throughout a Poem in which Character and Sentiment would be the figures to such a drapery—Two or three such Poems, if God should spare me, written in the course of the next six years, would be a famous gradus ad Parnassum altissimum—I mean they would nerve me up to the writing of a few fine Plays—my greatest ambition—when I do feel ambitious.'[24] Keats clearly felt that dramatic writing involved similar skills to those required by his narrative poems. He writes as if he thought of dramatic writing as a kind of denser version of narrative poetry, making similar, only greater, demands on his powers.

Though unfulfilled as a dramatist Keats used his letters, a form of implicit dialogue, to record and explore. Anyone interested in knowing Keats more deeply and in learning from his wisdom should read these letters. Their vitality suggests that the act of reaching out to other beings created in Keats a kind of energy which the more solipsistic journal form could not have provided.

The importance of friendship in Keats's life has already been mentioned. To an unusual degree Keats writes in active and conscious relationship with others. But those others are not only his contemporaries: 'I feel more and more every day, as my imagination strengthens, that I do not live in this world alone but in a thousand worlds . . . According to my state of mind I am with Achilles shouting in the Trenches or with Theocritus in the Vales of Sicily.'[25] There is nothing antiquarian about his sense of the past ('there is no *now* or *then* for the Holy Ghost', he is reported to have said).[26] While still at school he translated a large portion, if not all, of the *Aeneid*. The act of translation (etymologically a 'carrying over') is typical of Keats's relation to the past. The Elgin Marbles, Chapman's Homer, a nightingale's song, the little town on a Grecian urn provide direct access to its other countries. Like many of his contemporaries Keats thought Chatterton's medieval pastiche

---

[24] Letter to John Taylor, 17 Nov. 1819.
[25] Letter to George and Georgiana Keats, 14–31 Oct. 1818.
[26] William Sharp, *The Life and Letters of Joseph Severn* (London, 1892), 208.

to be the purest English, but his love of Chatterton (to whom he dedicated *Endymion*) must have taken in the recognition of another for whom the past was not dead.

But Keats's most joyful relationship with the past was with Shakespeare. In May 1817 he writes that he is 'very near Agreeing with Hazlit that Shakespeare is enough for us';[27] a year later, after a period of deep and delighted discovery, that he has 'great reason to be content, for thank God I can read and perhaps understand Shakespeare to his depths'.[28] While Keats was eventually, for all his admiration, to feel crowded out by Milton—that they could not breathe the same air and live[29]—the abundance of Shakespeare's achievement was a continual source of wonder and delight. Shakespeare's phrases enter Keats's writing in a way which is too intimate for them to be called quotations. He engaged with Shakespeare as with a contemporary and as an example of a 'most genuine Being'.[30] We can profit much by treating Keats in the same way.

[27] Letter to Benjamin Haydon, 11 May 1817.
[28] Letter to John Taylor, 27 Feb. 1818.
[29] 'I have lately stood on my guard against Milton. Life to him would be death to me.' (Letter to George and Georgiana Keats, 24 Sept. 1819.)
[30] Letter to Benjamin Bailey, 14 Aug. 1819.

journals of the time. Hazlitt, whose brilliantly questing and rigorous mind made him Keats's most congenial living mentor, was also Keats's first anthologist. The small but choice group of poems by which Hazlitt chose to represent Keats in *Select British Poets* (1824) included 'Robin Hood', one of several poems on this subject that Keats had exchanged with his friend Reynolds. Robin Hood, who resisted the Norman yoke, is a champion of popular freedom whom it was entirely apposite to invoke at a time when 'Gagging Acts', provocateurs, and vindictive prosecutions were used in an attempt to stifle all opposition to the landed minority. Hazlitt, in choosing to represent Keats by this poem among others, is making a clear statement about Keats's alignments.

During the years that followed the French Revolution the monarchy and the ministers of the Tory government were para-noiacally fearful of a repetition in Britain.[13] Any questioning of the status quo, any request for parliamentary reform, any attempt to give the unpropertied labouring man a voice, was apt to be labelled 'sedition'. It is a word that is heard again and again in the second decade of the century—particularly in the peace that followed Waterloo when massive unemployment and poverty unmitigated by adequate parish Relief brought the country into an acute state of polarization.

In 1813 Leigh Hunt, poet and editor of the radical periodical, *The Examiner*, was imprisoned for two years, along with his brother John, on account of an attack on the Prince Regent in *The Examiner*. When he was released in February 1815 Keats, who had yet to meet Hunt, composed a poem of celebration. This poem appears in Keats's first published volume (*1817*), a volume dedicated to Hunt, by then a personal friend. This dedication ensured (as Keats must have known it would) that Keats was thereafter identified by the Tory faction with the 'seditious' enemy.

When Keats's second volume, *Endymion*, appeared in 1818 the reviewer of the *British Critic* was able to go straight for the 'jacobinical apostrophe' at the beginning of Book iii. Another who singled out this passage was John Gibson Lockhart, reviewing for *Blackwood's Edinburgh Magazine*. Lockhart was the originator of the appellation 'Cockney School of Poetry'—a phrase in which social

---

[13] Keats wrote to his brother and sister in law that 'They have made a handel out of this event [the French Revolution] in every way to undermine our freedom' (17–27 Sept. 1819).

snobbery thinly veils political hostility: 'We had almost forgot to mention, that Keats belongs to the Cockney School of Politics, as well as the Cockney School of Poetry.' He then refers slightingly to Keats's admiration for Hunt and suggests that he is the protégé of Hunt and *The Examiner*: 'Hear how their bantling has already learned to lisp sedition . . .'[14]—and he quotes *Endymion* iii. 1–22.

Opponents of liberty, their paranoia notwithstanding, are often obtuse in detecting subversion in all but its crudest and most explicit forms. Artists with a vocation for freedom have sometimes been driven, in a way which may seem suicidal, to declare themselves with moments of coarse spelling out which may appear greatly at variance with the rest of the work. This is the case with the poem which, more than any other piece of evidence, contributed to Osip Mandelstam's arrest and eventual death: a poem which calls Stalin 'the Kremlin mountaineer, the murderer, the peasant-slayer'.[15] It is as if Mandelstam needed to spell it out to the stupid enemy so that they would know his mettle and that the wideness and depth of the poetry which they could not understand were absolutely inimical to the world they were trying to create.

Keats's poetry is in places robustly interventionary. Of lines 105–20 of 'Isabella' Bernard Shaw wrote that they 'contain all the Factory Commission Reports that Marx read and that Keats did not read because they were not yet written in his time'.[16] They are lines that remind us that Keats wrote while the slave trade was scaldingly recent in memory and the rights of the paid labourer remained largely unwon.

There are moments of pugnacious coarseness in Keats's poetry which express his longing for poetry to be effectual—as active an agent in human healing as the medical profession he had given up. Several remarks in his letters show that he had hopes of making some direct contribution: 'I am ambitious of doing the world some good: if I should be spared that may be the work of my maturer years';[17] 'I hope sincerely I shall be able to put a Mite of help to the Liberal side of the Question before I die.'[18] After his death an

---

[14] *Blackwood's Edinburgh Magazine*, Aug. 1818.
[15] Nadezhda Mandelstam, *Hope against Hope* (Harmondsworth, 1975), 35.
[16] *The John Keats Memorial Volume* (London, 1921), 175.
[17] Letter to Richard Woodhouse, 27 Oct. 1818.
[18] Letter to C. W. Dilke, 22 Sept. 1819.

anonymous correspondent in the *Morning Chronicle* wrote that 'His love of freedom was ardent and grand. He once said, that if he should live a few years, he would go over to South America, and write a Poem on Liberty.'[19]

While there are moments when Keats shows his hand and makes explicit his political and humanitarian principles these principles are also implicit in the very nature and dynamic of his thought. He exhibits what might now be called a 'continuous' mind: as opposed to a discontinuous mind which seeks to make arbitrary divisions absolute. Richard Dawkins, the contemporary zoologist, links the discontinuous and 'speciesist' thinking which would, for example, see as absolute the divide between ape and human, with the activities in apartheid SouthAfrican courts adjudicating the colour of people of mixed parentage. Discontinuous thinking is especially prevalent, says Dawkins, among politicans, members of the legal profession, and the Church.[20] These are the targets of *Endymion* iii. 1–22. The continuous mind conceives of differences of intensity and degree which admit of no absolute distinctions between kinds, though complete transformations of things into their opposites may occur by degrees. To the continuous mind boundaries are provisional: they enable thought but are not absolute limits. Continuous thinking is inherently more democratic than discontinuous for it sees each individual as participating in and benefiting from the evolution of the whole.

Keats, who admired Wordsworth but disliked the self-importance with which he projected himself, expresses a vision of human life in which 'almost Man may like the Spider spin from his own inwards his own airy Citadel' and, though each mind is distinct and bent on its own journey:

Minds would leave each other in contrary directions, traverse each other in Numberless points, and [at] last greet each other at the Journeys end— A old Man and a child would talk together and the old Man be led on his Path, and the child left thinking—Man should not dispute or assert but whisper results to his neighbour, and thus by every germ of Spirit sucking the Sap from mould ethereal every human might become great, and Humanity instead of being a wide heath of Furse and Briars with here

[19] *Morning Chronicle*, 27 July 1821. The correspondent may have been Charles Cowden Clarke, Keats's old schoolmaster and friend.

[20] 'Meet my Cousin, the chimpanzee', *New Scientist*, 5 June 1993, pp. 36–8.

and there a remote Oak or Pine, would become a grand democracy of Forest Trees.[21]

This vision of experience as continuous and shared is not a matter of willed opinion to Keats but fundamental to the nature of his mind and imagination.

It is almost always possible to trace the route that Keats's imagination is following, be it a progress outwards, widening or enlarging, or a moving inwards to the 'wreath'd trellis of a working brain' (that material, medical word for the organ, not the function). His poetry is full of steps, passages, channels, windows which allow us to follow the path of his imagination. Even death is seen in terms of a continuity outwards. As the nightingale is 'pouring forth [his] soul abroad | In such an ecstasy', sending out his soul and song, so death would 'take into the air my quiet breath'.

The rhetorical figure of *gradatio* by which a work of language proceeds by stepped progression is one which Keats employs often, repeating the final word or phrase of a line at the beginning of the next to create a stepping stone which allows a change of direction. The movement between stanzas one and two of 'The Eve of St. Agnes' is an example; another is the step created by the repetition of 'forlorn' to link the last two stanzas of the 'Ode to a Nightingale'.

Of lines 777–81 of *Endymion* i Keats said, 'when I wrote it it was a regular stepping of the Imagination towards a Truth ... It set before me at once the gradations of Happiness even like a kind of Pleasure Thermometer—and is my first step towards the chief Attempt in the Drama—the playing of different Natures with Joy and Sorrow.'[22] 'Playing' in this passage seems to mean a process of playing out, following an idea or a feeling through its various pitches and gradations.

Keats had strong ambitions for dramatic writing. He hoped 'to make as great a revolution in modern dramatic writing as Kean has done in acting'.[23] He did in fact complete one play, *Otho the Great*, and embark on another, *King Stephen*. But his ambitions in this direction were unfulfilled. *Otho*, written collaboratively with his friend Charles Brown, is wooden Jacobethan pastiche; *King Stephen* has great energy but is only a fragment, abandoned early at the

---

[21] Letter to J. H. Reynolds, 19 Feb. 1818.
[22] Letter to John Taylor, 30 Jan. 1818.
[23] Letter to Benjamin Bailey, 14 Aug. 1819.

to be the purest English, but his love of Chatterton (to whom he
dedicated *Endymion*) must have taken in the recognition of another
for whom the past was not dead.

But Keats's most joyful relationship with the past was with
Shakespeare. In May 1817 he writes that he is 'very near Agreeing
with Hazlit that Shakespeare is enough for us';[27] a year later,
after a period of deep and delighted discovery, that he has 'great
reason to be content, for thank God I can read and perhaps
understand Shakespeare to his depths'.[28] While Keats was even-
tually, for all his admiration, to feel crowded out by Milton—that
they could not breathe the same air and live[29]—the abundance of
Shakespeare's achievement was a continual source of wonder and
delight. Shakespeare's phrases enter Keats's writing in a way which
is too intimate for them to be called quotations. He engaged with
Shakespeare as with a contemporary and as an example of a 'most
genuine Being'.[30] We can profit much by treating Keats in the same
way.

[27] Letter to Benjamin Haydon, 11 May 1817.
[28] Letter to John Taylor, 27 Feb. 1818.
[29] 'I have lately stood on my guard against Milton. Life to him would be
death to me.' (Letter to George and Georgiana Keats, 24 Sept. 1819.)
[30] Letter to Benjamin Bailey, 14 Aug. 1819.

disheartening news that Kean would not be in the country to perform it.

Keats wrote that 'The little dramatic skill I may as yet have however badly it might show in a Drama would I think be sufficient for a Poem—I wish to diffuse the colouring of St Agnes eve throughout a Poem in which Character and Sentiment would be the figures to such a drapery—Two or three such Poems, if God should spare me, written in the course of the next six years, would be a famous gradus ad Parnassum altissimum—I mean they would nerve me up to the writing of a few fine Plays—my greatest ambition—when I do feel ambitious.'[24] Keats clearly felt that dramatic writing involved similar skills to those required by his narrative poems. He writes as if he thought of dramatic writing as a kind of denser version of narrative poetry, making similar, only greater, demands on his powers.

Though unfulfilled as a dramatist Keats used his letters, a form of implicit dialogue, to record and explore. Anyone interested in knowing Keats more deeply and in learning from his wisdom should read these letters. Their vitality suggests that the act of reaching out to other beings created in Keats a kind of energy which the more solipsistic journal form could not have provided.

The importance of friendship in Keats's life has already been mentioned. To an unusual degree Keats writes in active and conscious relationship with others. But those others are not only his contemporaries: 'I feel more and more every day, as my imagination strengthens, that I do not live in this world alone but in a thousand worlds ... According to my state of mind I am with Achilles shouting in the Trenches or with Theocritus in the Vales of Sicily.'[25] There is nothing antiquarian about his sense of the past ('there is no *now* or *then* for the Holy Ghost', he is reported to have said).[26] While still at school he translated a large portion, if not all, of the *Aeneid.* The act of translation (etymologically a 'carrying over') is typical of Keats's relation to the past. The Elgin Marbles, Chapman's Homer, a nightingale's song, the little town on a Grecian urn provide direct access to its other countries. Like many of his contemporaries Keats thought Chatterton's medieval pastiche

---

[24] Letter to John Taylor, 17 Nov. 1819.
[25] Letter to George and Georgiana Keats, 14–31 Oct. 1818.
[26] William Sharp, *The Life and Letters of Joseph Severn* (London, 1892), 208.

Chronology

1795   Keats born at Swan and Hoop Livery Stables, Moorfields Pavement, London (31 October); Thomas Carlyle born.

1797   George Keats born (28 February).

1799   Tom Keats born (18 November). The Keats family move to Craven Street, off City Road.

1801   Edward Keats born (28 April).

1802   Death of Edward Keats. *Edinburgh Review* founded.

1802   Peace at Amiens. Fanny Keats born (3 June). Keats attends Clarke's school at Enfield (George and Tom attend later).

1804   Keats's father Thomas Keats is killed in a riding accident (16 April). Napoleon is crowned Emperor. Keats's mother marries William Rawlings (June). The Keats children move in with their maternal grandparents, John and Alice Jennings, at Ponders End, Enfield.

1805   Death of John Jennings (8 March). The family move to Lower Edmonton. Battle of Trafalgar.

1809   *Quarterly Review* founded.

1810   Keats's mother dies (10 March).

1811   Prince of Wales made Regent. Keats is apprenticed to the surgeon Thomas Hammond of Edmonton.

1812   Lord Liverpool becomes Prime Minister with Castlereagh as Leader of the Commons and Foreign Secretary.

1813   Leigh Hunt and his brother John imprisoned for libelling the Regent.

1814   Keats composes his earliest known poems. Napoleon resigns as Emperor. Death of Alice Jennings (19 December). Richard Abbey becomes official guardian of the Keats children. Wordsworth's *Excursion* published.

1815   Keats enters Guy's Hospital as a student. Leigh Hunt released from prison. Napoleon Emperor again for a 'hundred days'. Battle of Waterloo. Keats becomes a dresser.

1816   'To Solitude' ('O Solitude! if I must with thee dwell')
        published in the *Examiner*. Keats passes qualifying examina-
        tions and, when of age in October, is licensed to practise as
        an apothecary. Holiday in Margate. By mid-November is
        living at 76 Cheapside with Tom and George. Meets Leigh
        Hunt, Haydon, and Reynolds. Writes 'On First Looking
        into Chapman's Homer' and 'Sleep and Poetry'. Spa Fields
        meetings for parliamentary reform (December).

1817   *1817* published by C. and J. Ollier. Suspension of Habeas
        Corpus. Trial and acquittal of the publisher William Hone.
        Keats and brothers move to 1 Well Walk, Hampstead
        (March). Keats composes *Endymion* while at Carisbrooke on
        the Isle of Wight (15–24 April), Margate (till mid-May),
        Canterbury (mid-May), Hastings (late May), Hampstead
        (from 10 June), Oxford (early September until early October)
        —where he was Bailey's guest. He completes Book iv at
        Burford Bridge, Surrey (late November). Reads Shakespeare
        deeply all year. Reviews theatre for the *Indicator* in Reynolds's
        absence.

1818   Habeas Corpus restored. Revises *Endymion*. Attends Hazlitt's
        lectures on the English Poets at the Surrey Institution (13
        January–3 March). Joins Tom at Teignmouth (March–
        April). Composes 'Isabella'. George marries Georgiana
        Wylie (May). *Endymion* published by Taylor and Hessey: it
        is harshly reviewed by *Blackwood's* in May. The *British Critic*
        in June, and the *Quarterly* in October. Accompanies George
        and Georgiana to Liverpool from where they depart for
        America (23 June). Keats sets off on a walking tour of the
        North—the Lakes, Scotland, and Northern Ireland—with
        Brown. Returns to London from Inverness because of ill
        health (8 August). Finds Tom very ill. Meets Fanny Brawne
        during summer. Begins *Hyperion* (November). Tom Keats
        dies (1 December). Keats moves into Wentworth Place as
        Brown's tenant. Spends Christmas day with the Brawnes.

1819   Visits Chichester and Bedhampton (January). Writes 'St
        Agnes Eve'. The publisher Richard Carlile is arrested in
        February (tried in October). Wordsworth publishes *Peter
        Bell*. Byron publishes Cantos i–ii of *Don Juan*. Keats
        composes 'La belle dame sans merci' (April). Acute financial
        worries lead him to consider work as a ship's surgeon.

Composes odes on Grecian Urn, Melancholy, Nightingale, and Indolence. Accompanies Rice to Isle of Wight (late June). Begins work on verse tragedy *Otho the Great* and on 'Lamia'. Accompanies Brown to Winchester (mid-August). Works on the 'Fall of Hyperion'. Peterloo Massacre (16 August). Keats returns briefly to London in mid-September and witnesses Henry Hunt's arrival for trial (13 September). Composes 'To Autumn'. Returns to Hampstead and visits Fanny Brawne. Plans to work as a journalist and briefly (mid-October) lodges at 25 College Street, Westminster. Back in Wentworth Place by 22 October. Parliament passes the 'Six Acts'. Keats is engaged to Fanny Brawne by end of the year.

1820   Thomas Wooler (editor of the *Black Dwarf*) imprisoned. George Keats returns to London to raise funds (leaves 28 January). Death of George III. Keats returns to Hampstead from London by stage-coach and has a severe haemorrhage (3 February). Arrest of 'Cato Street Conspirators' (set up by government *provocateur* Edwards). Keats declared 'out of danger' (March). Revises 'Lamia'. Brown lets Wentworth Place for the summer and Keats moves to 2 Wesleyan Place, Kentish Town. Queen Caroline (absent since 1814) returns to England (6 June). Keats moves into Leigh Hunt's house in Mortimer Terrace, Kentish Town (23 June). *1820* published by Taylor and Hessey (1 or 2 July). It is thought another English winter would kill Keats and his doctor orders him to go to Italy. Coronation of George IV (19 July). Bill of Pains and Penalties (to deprive Queen Caroline of title of Consort) debated between July and November. Keats leaves Hunt's house (12 August) and stays with the Brawnes at Wentworth Place. *1820* favourably reviewed though public interest in the Queen's affairs leads to neglect of all other publications. Keats and Severn sail from Gravesend in the *Maria Crowther* (18 September), reach Naples harbour (21 October), and are kept in quarantine on board for ten days because of a typhus epidemic in London. 31 October (Keats's birthday) Keats and Severn take rooms above a trattoria in Vico S. Giuseppe, Naples. Keats and Severn travel (6 or 7 November) by carriage to Rome, arriving 15 November. They take rooms at No. 26

Piazza di Spagna. Keats writes his last known letter (10 December).

1821   23 February, Keats dies at 11 p.m. News of his death reaches London on 17 March.

Note on Text

ONLY a third of the 150 or so poems written by Keats were published during his lifetime. The other two-thirds—which includes much of his politically explicit verse—he decided against offering for publication. These latter have come down to us from a variety of sources, including transcripts by friends and relatives of varying reliability. In the case of those poems published during Keats's life my choice of text has been the latest published form in which Keats saw the poem. I have extended this rule to journal publication as well as to the three volumes, *1817*, *Endymion*, and *1820*. The only instance in which this rule has not been followed is 'La belle dame sans merci'. Keats's draft of this poem, and not the version printed in the *Indicator*, is (justly in my opinion) the better known. This is the text I give here.

I have not attempted to tidy up with editorial punctuation those other poems, which, for a variety of reasons, Keats did not smarten up for publication. Instead I have left them in their rawer states (unless the only surviving transcript had already received the officious editing of the transcriber). Detailed notes as to my choice of texts can be found in the Oxford Authors *John Keats*.

Now Morning from her orient chamber came,
And her first footsteps touch'd a verdant hill;
Crowning its lawny crest with amber flame,
Silv'ring the untainted gushes of its rill;
Which, pure from mossy beds, did down distill,
And after parting beds of simple flowers,
By many streams a little lake did fill,
Which round its marge reflected woven bowers,
And, in its middle space, a sky that never lowers.

There the king-fisher saw his plumage bright   10
Vieing with fish of brilliant dye below;
Whose silken fins, and golden scales light
Cast upward, through the waves, a ruby glow:
There saw the swan his neck of arched snow,
And oar'd himself along with majesty;
Sparkled his jetty eyes; his feet did show
Beneath the waves like Afric's ebony,
And on his back a fay reclined voluptuously.

Ah! could I tell the wonders of an isle
That in that fairest lake had placed been,   20
I could e'en Dido of her grief beguile;
Or rob from aged Lear his bitter teen:
For sure so fair a place was never seen,
Of all that ever charm'd romantic eye:
It seem'd an emerald in the silver sheen
Of the bright waters; or as when on high,
Through clouds of fleecy white, laughs the cœrulean sky.

And all around it dipp'd luxuriously
Slopings of verdure through the glossy tide,
Which, as it were in gentle amity,   30
Rippled delighted up the flowery side;
As if to glean the ruddy tears, it tried,
Which fell profusely from the rose-tree stem!
Haply it was the workings of its pride,
In strife to throw upon the shore a gem
Outvieing all the buds in Flora's diadem.

Written on the Day that Mr. Leigh Hunt Left Prison

What though, for showing truth to flatter'd state,
  Kind Hunt was shut in prison, yet has he,
  In his immortal spirit, been as free
As the sky-searching lark, and as elate.
Minion of grandeur! think you he did wait?
  Think you he nought but prison walls did see,
  Till, so unwilling, thou unturn'dst the key?
Ah, no! far happier, nobler was his fate!
In Spenser's halls he strayed, and bowers fair,
  Culling enchanted flowers; and he flew   10
With daring Milton through the fields of air:
  To regions of his own his genius true
Took happy flights. Who shall his fame impair
  When thou art dead, and all thy wretched crew?

To Hope

When by my solitary hearth I sit,
  And hateful thoughts enwrap my soul in gloom;
When no fair dreams before my 'mind's eye' flit,
  And the bare heath of life presents no bloom;
    Sweet Hope, ethereal balm upon me shed,
    And wave thy silver pinions o'er my head.

Whene'er I wander, at the fall of night,
  Where woven boughs shut out the moon's bright ray,
Should sad Despondency my musings fright,
  And frown, to drive fair Cheerfulness away,   10
    Peep with the moon-beams through the leafy roof,
    And keep that fiend Despondence far aloof.

Should Disappointment, parent of Despair,
  Strive for her son to seize my careless heart;
When, like a cloud, he sits upon the air,
  Preparing on his spell-bound prey to dart:
    Chace him away, sweet Hope, with visage bright,
    And fright him as the morning frightens night!

Whene'er the fate of those I hold most dear
  Tells to my fearful breast a tale of sorrow,   20
O bright-eyed Hope, my morbid fancy cheer;
  Let me awhile thy sweetest comforts borrow:
    Thy heaven-born radiance around me shed,
    And wave thy silver pinions o'er my head!

Should e'er unhappy love my bosom pain,
  From cruel parents, or relentless fair;
O let me think it is not quite in vain
  To sigh out sonnets to the midnight air!
    Sweet Hope, ethereal balm upon me shed,
    And wave thy silver pinions o'er my head!   30

In the long vista of the years to roll,
  Let me not see our country's honour fade:
O let me see our land retain her soul,
  Her pride, her freedom; and not freedom's shade.
    From thy bright eyes unusual brightness shed—
    Beneath thy pinions canopy my head!

Let me not see the patriot's high bequest,
  Great Liberty! how great in plain attire!
With the base purple of a court oppress'd,
  Bowing her head, and ready to expire: 40
    But let me see thee stoop from heaven on wings
    That fill the skies with silver glitterings!

And as, in sparkling majesty, a star
  Gilds the bright summit of some gloomy cloud;
Brightening the half veil'd face of heaven afar:
  So, when dark thoughts my boding spirit shroud,
    Sweet Hope, celestial influence round me shed,
    Waving thy silver pinions o'er my head.

Ode to Apollo

I

In thy Western Halls of gold
  When thou sittest in thy state,
Bards, that erst sublimely told
  Heroic deeds, and sung of Fate,
With fervour seize their adamantine lyres,
Whose cords are solid rays, and twinkle radiant fires.

2

There Homer with his nervous arms
  Strikes the twanging harp of war,
And even the Western splendour warms
  While the trumpets sound afar;   10
But, what creates the most intense surprize,
His soul looks out through renovated eyes.

3

Then, through thy Temple wide, melodious swells
  The sweet majestic tone of Maro's lyre;
The soul delighted on each accent dwells,—
  Enraptured dwells,—not daring to respire,
The while he tells of grief, around a funeral pyre.

4

'Tis awful silence then again:
  Expectant stand the spheres;
  Breathless the laurel'd peers;   20
Nor move, till ends the lofty strain,
Nor move till Milton's tuneful thunders cease,
And leave once more the ravish'd heavens in peace.

5

Thou biddest Shakspeare wave his hand,
  And quickly forward spring
The Passions—a terrific band—

And each vibrates the string
That with its tyrant temper best accords,
While from their Master's lips pour forth the inspiring words.

6

A silver trumpet Spenser blows, 30
And as its martial notes to silence flee,
From a virgin Chorus flows
A hymn in praise of spotless Chastity.
'Tis still!—Wild warblings from the Æolian lyre
Enchantment softly breathe, and tremblingly expire.

7

Next, thy Tasso's ardent Numbers
Float along the pleased air,
Calling Youth from idle Slumbers,
Rousing them from pleasure's lair:—
Then o'er the strings his fingers gently move, 40
And melt the soul to pity and to love.

8

But when *Thou* joinest with the Nine,
And all the Powers of Song combine,
We listen here on earth:
The dying tones that fill the air,
And charm the ear of Evening fair,
From thee, great God of Bards, receive their heavenly birth.

Lines Written on 29 May, the Anniversary of Charles's Restoration, on Hearing the Bells Ringing

Infatuate Britons, will you still proclaim
His memory, your direst, foulest shame?
Nor Patriots revere?
Ah! when I hear each traitorous lying bell,
'Tis gallant Sydney's, Russell's, Vane's sad knell,
That pains my wounded ear—

'O Solitude! if I must with thee dwell'

O Solitude! if I must with thee dwell,
　　Let it not be among the jumbled heap
　　Of murky buildings; climb with me the steep,—
Nature's observatory—whence the dell,
Its flowery slopes, its river's crystal swell,
　　May seem a span; let me thy vigils keep
　　'Mongst boughs pavillion'd, where the deer's swift leap
Startles the wild bee from the fox-glove bell.
But though I'll gladly trace these scenes with thee,
　　Yet the sweet converse of an innocent mind,   10
　　Whose words are images of thoughts refin'd,
Is my soul's pleasure; and it sure must be
　　Almost the highest bliss of human-kind,
When to thy haunts two kindred spirits flee.

'Give me women wine and snuff'

Give me women wine and snuff
Untill I cry out hold enough!
You may do so sans objection
Till ye day of resurrection
For bless my beard they aye shall be
My beloved Trinity—

'I am as brisk'

I am as brisk
As a bottle of Wisk-
Ey and as nimble
As a Milliner's thimble—

'O grant that like to Peter I'

O grant that like to Peter I
May like to Peter B.
And tell me lovely Jesus Y
Old Jonah went to C.

To My Brother George

Full many a dreary hour have I past
My brain bewilder'd, and my mind o'ercast
With heaviness; in seasons when I've thought
No spherey strains by me could e'er be caught
From the blue dome, though I to dimness gaze
On the far depth where sheeted lightning plays;
Or, on the wavy grass outstretch'd supinely,
Pry 'mong the stars, to strive to think divinely:
That I should never hear Apollo's song.
Though feathery clouds were floating all along   10
The purple west, and, two bright streaks between,
The golden lyre itself were dimly seen:
That the still murmur of the honey bee
Would never teach a rural song to me:
That the bright glance from beauty's eyelids slanting
Would never make a lay of mine enchanting,
Or warm my breast with ardour to unfold
Some tale of love and arms in time of old.

But there are times, when those that love the bay,
Fly from all sorrowing far, far away;   20
A sudden glow comes on them, nought they see
In water, earth, or air, but poesy.
It has been said, dear George, and true I hold it,
(For knightly Spenser to Libertas told it,)
That when a Poet is in such a trance,
In air he sees white coursers paw, and prance,
Bestridden of gay knights, in gay apparel,
Who at each other tilt in playful quarrel,

And what we, ignorantly, sheet-lightning call,
Is the swift opening of their wide portal,   30
When the bright warder blows his trumplet clear,
Whose tones reach nought on earth but Poet's ear.
When these enchanted portals open wide,
And through the light the horsemen swiftly glide,
The Poet's eye can reach those golden halls,
And view the glory of their festivals:
Their ladies fair, that in the distance seem
Fit for the silv'ring of a seraph's dream;
Their rich brimm'd goblets, that incessant run
Like the bright spots that move about the sun;   40
And, when upheld, the wine from each bright jar
Pours with the lustre of a falling star.
Yet further off, are dimly seen their bowers,
Of which no mortal eye can reach the flowers;
And 'tis right just, for well Apollo knows
'Twould make the Poet quarrel with the rose.
All that's reveal'd from that far seat of blisses,
Is, the clear fountains' interchanging kisses,
As gracefully descending, light and thin,
Like silver streaks across a dolphin's fin,   50
When he upswimmeth from the coral caves,
And sports with half his tail above the waves.

These wonders strange he sees, and many more,
Whose head is pregnant with poetic lore.
Should he upon an evening ramble fare
With forehead to the soothing breezes bare,
Would he naught see but the dark, silent blue
With all its diamonds trembling through and through?
Or the coy moon, when in the waviness
Of whitest clouds she does her beauty dress,   60
And staidly paces higher up, and higher,
Like a sweet nun in holy-day attire?
Ah yes! much more would start into his sight—
The revelries, and mysteries of night:
And should I ever see them, I will tell you
Such tales as needs must with amazement spell you.

These are the living pleasures of the bard:
But richer far posterity's award.
What does he murmur with his latest breath,
While his proud eye looks through the film of death? 70
'What though I leave this dull, and earthly mould,
Yet shall my spirit lofty converse hold
With after times.—The patriot shall feel
My stern alarum, and unsheath his steel;
Or, in the senate thunder out my numbers
To startle princes from their easy slumbers.
The sage will mingle with each moral theme
My happy thoughts sententious; he will teem
With lofty periods when my verses fire him,
And then I'll stoop from heaven to inspire him. 80
Lays have I left of such a dear delight
That maids will sing them on their bridal night.
Gay villagers, upon a morn of May,
When they have tired their gentle limbs with play,
And form'd a snowy circle on the grass,
And plac'd in midst of all that lovely lass
Who chosen is their queen,—with her fine head
Crowned with flowers purple, white, and red:
For there the lily, and the musk-rose, sighing,
Are emblems true of hapless lovers dying: 90
Between her breasts, that never yet felt trouble,
A bunch of violets full blown, and double,
Serenely sleep:—she from a casket takes
A little book,—and then a joy awakes
About each youthful heart,—with stifled cries,
And rubbing of white hands, and sparkling eyes:
For she's to read a tale of hopes, and fears;
One that I foster'd in my youthful years:
The pearls, that on each glist'ning circlet sleep,
Gush ever and anon with silent creep, 100
Lured by the innocent dimples. To sweet rest
Shall the dear babe, upon its mother's breast,
Be lull'd with songs of mine. Fair world, adieu!
Thy dales, and hills, are fading from my view:
Swiftly I mount, upon wide spreading pinions,
From the narrow bounds of thy dominions.

Full joy I feel, while thus I cleave the air,
That my soft verse will charm thy daughters fair,
And warm thy sons!' Ah, my dear friend and brother,
Could I, at once, my mad ambition smother,   110
For tasting joys like these, sure I should be
Happier, and dearer to society.
At times, 'tis true, I've felt relief from pain
When some bright thought has darted through my brain:
Through all that day I've felt a greater pleasure
Than if I'd brought to light a hidden treasure.
As to my sonnets, though none else should heed them,
I feel delighted, still, that you should read them.
Of late, too, I have had much calm enjoyment,
Stretch'd on the grass at my best lov'd employment   120
Of scribbling lines for you. These things I thought
While, in my face, the freshest breeze I caught.
E'en now I'm pillowed on a bed of flowers
That crowns a lofty clift, which proudly towers
Above the ocean-waves. The stalks, and blades,
Chequer my tablet with their quivering shades.
On one side is a field of drooping oats,
Through which the poppies show their scarlet coats;
So pert and useless, that they bring to mind
The scarlet coats that pester human-kind.   130
And on the other side, outspread, is seen
Ocean's blue mantle streak'd with purple, and green.
Now 'tis I see a canvass'd ship, and now
Mark the bright silver curling round her prow.
I see the lark down-dropping to his nest,
And the broad winged sea-gull never at rest;
For when no more he spreads his feathers free,
His breast is dancing on the restless sea.
Now I direct my eyes into the west,
Which at this moment is in sunbeams drest: 140
Why westward turn? 'Twas but to say adieu!
'Twas but to kiss my hand, dear George, to you!

To Charles Cowden Clarke

Oft have you seen a swan superbly frowning,
And with proud breast his own white shadow crowning;
He slants his neck beneath the waters bright
So silently, it seems a beam of light
Come from the galaxy: anon he sports,—
With outspread wings the Naiad Zephyr courts
Or ruffles all the surface of the lake
In striving from its crystal face to take
Some diamond water drops, and them to treasure
In milky nest, and sip them off at leisure.   10
But not a moment can he there insure them,
Nor to such downy rest can he allure them;
For down they rush as though they would be free,
And drop like hours into eternity.
Just like that bird am I in loss of time,
Whene'er I venture on the stream of rhyme;
With shatter'd boat, oar snapt, and canvass rent,
I slowly sail, scarce knowing my intent;
Still scooping up the water with my fingers,
In which a trembling diamond never lingers.   20

By this, friend Charles, you may full plainly see
Why I have never penn'd a line to thee:
Because my thoughts were never free, and clear,
And little fit to please a classic ear;
Because my wine was of too poor a savour
For one whose palate gladdens in the flavour
Of sparkling Helicon:—small good it were
To take him to a desert rude, and bare,
Who had on Baiæ's shore reclin'd at ease,
While Tasso's page was floating in a breeze   30
That gave soft music from Armida's bowers,
Mingled with fragrance from her rarest flowers:
Small good to one who had by Mulla's stream
Fondled the maidens with the breasts of cream;
Who had beheld Belphœbe in a brook,
And lovely Una in a leafy nook,
And Archimago leaning o'er his book:

Who had of all that's sweet tasted, and seen,
From silv'ry ripple, up to beauty's queen;
From the sequester'd haunts of gay Titania,   40
To the blue dwelling of divine Urania:
One who, of late, had ta'en sweet forest walks
With him who elegantly chats, and talks—
The wrong'd Libertas,—who has told you stories
Of laurel chaplets, and Apollo's glories;
Of troops chivalrous prancing through a city,
And tearful ladies made for love, and pity:
With many else which I have never known.
Thus have I thought; and days on days have flown
Slowly, or rapidly—unwilling still   50
For you to try my dull, unlearned quill.
Nor should I now, but that I've known you long;
That you first taught me all the sweets of song:
The grand, the sweet, the terse, the free, the fine;
What swell'd with pathos, and what right divine:
Spenserian vowels that elope with ease,
And float along like birds o'er summer seas;
Miltonian storms, and more, Miltonian tenderness;
Michael in arms, and more, meek Eve's fair slenderness.
Who read for me the sonnet swelling loudly   60
Up to its climax and then dying proudly?
Who found for me the grandeur of the ode,
Growing, like Atlas, stronger from its load?
Who let me taste that more than cordial dram,
The sharp, the rapier-pointed epigram?
Shew'd me that epic was of all the king,
Round, vast, and spanning all like Saturn's ring?
You too upheld the veil from Clio's beauty,
And pointed out the patriot's stern duty;
The might of Alfred, and the shaft of Tell;   70
The hand of Brutus, that so grandly fell
Upon a tyrant's head. Ah! had I never seen,
Or known your kindness, what might I have been?
What my enjoyments in my youthful years,
Bereft of all that now my life endears?
And can I e'er these benefits forget?
And can I e'er repay the friendly debt?
No, doubly no;—yet should these rhymings please,

I shall roll on the grass with two-fold ease:
For I have long time been my fancy feeding 80
With hopes that you would one day think the reading
Of my rough verses not an hour misspent;
Should it e'er be so, what a rich content!
Some weeks have pass'd since last I saw the spires
In lucent Thames reflected:—warm desires
To see the sun o'er peep the eastern dimness,
And morning shadows streaking into slimness
Across the lawny fields, and pebbly water;
To mark the time as they grow broad, and shorter;
To feel the air that plays about the hills, 90
And sips its freshness from the little rills;
To see high, golden corn wave in the light
When Cynthia smiles upon a summer's night,
And peers among the cloudlet's jet and white,
As though she were reclining in a bed
Of bean blossoms, in heaven freshly shed.
No sooner had I stepp'd into these pleasures
Than I began to think of rhymes and measures:
The air that floated by me seem'd to say
'Write! thou wilt never have a better day.' 100
And so I did. When many lines I'd written,
Though with their grace I was not oversmitten,
Yet, as my hand was warm, I thought I'd better
Trust to my feelings, and write you a letter.
Such an attempt required an inspiration
Of a peculiar sort,—a consummation;—
Which, had I felt, these scribblings might have been
Verses from which the soul would never wean:
But many days have past since last my heart
Was warm'd luxuriously by divine Mozart; 110
By Arne delighted, or by Handel madden'd;
Or by the song of Erin pierc'd and sadden'd:
What time you were before the music sitting,
And the rich notes to each sensation fitting;
Since I have walk'd with you through shady lanes
That freshly terminate in open plains,
And revel'd in a chat that ceased not
When at night-fall among your books we got:
No, nor when supper came, nor after that,—

Nor when reluctantly I took my hat;   120
No, nor till cordially you shook my hand
Mid-way between our homes:—your accents bland
Still sounded in my ears, when I no more
Could hear your footsteps touch the grav'ly floor.
Sometimes I lost them, and then found again;
You chang'd the footpath for the grassy plain.
In those still moments I have wish'd you joys
That well you know to honour:—'Life's very toys
With him,' said I, 'will take a pleasant charm;
It cannot be that ought will work him harm.'   130
These thoughts now come o'er me with all their might:—
Again I shake your hand,—friend Charles, good night.

On First Looking into Chapman's Homer

Much have I travell'd in the realms of gold,
    And many goodly states and kingdoms seen;
    Round many western islands have I been
Which bards in fealty to Apollo hold.
Oft of one wide expanse had I been told
    That deep-brow'd Homer ruled as his demesne;
    Yet did I never breathe its pure serene
Till I heard Chapman speak out loud and bold:
Then felt I like some watcher of the skies
    When a new planet swims into his ken;   10
Or like stout Cortez when with eagle eyes
    He star'd at the Pacific—and all his men
Look'd at each other with a wild surmise—
    Silent, upon a peak in Darien.

Sleep and Poetry

As I lay in my bed slepe full unmete
Was unto me, but why that I ne might
Rest I ne wist, for there n'as erthly wight
(As I suppose) had more of hertis ese
Than I, for I n'ad sicknesse nor disease.
                                CHAUCER

What is more gentle than a wind in summer?
What is more soothing that the pretty hummer
That stays one moment in an open flower,
And buzzes cheerily from bower to bower?
What is more tranquil than a musk-rose blowing
In a green island, far from all men's knowing?
More healthful than the leafiness of dales?
More secret than a nest of nightingales?
More serene than Cordelia's countenance?
More full of visions than a high romance?   10
What, but thee Sleep? Soft closer of our eyes!
Low murmurer of tender lullabies!
Light hoverer around our happy pillows!
Wreather of poppy buds, and weeping willows!
Silent entangler of a beauty's tresses!
Most happy listener! when the morning blesses
Thee for enlivening all the cheerful eyes
That glance so brightly at the new sun-rise.

But what is higher beyond thought than thee?
Fresher than berries of a mountain tree?   20
More strange, more beautiful, more smooth, more regal,
Than wings of swans, than doves, than dim-seen eagle?
What is it? And to what shall I compare it?
It has a glory, and nought else can share it:
The thought thereof is awful, sweet, and holy,
Chacing away all worldliness and folly;
Coming sometimes like fearful claps of thunder,
Or the low rumblings earth's regions under;
And sometimes like a gentle whispering
Of all the secrets of some wond'rous thing   30
That breathes about us in the vacant air;
So that we look around with prying stare,
Perhaps to see shapes of light, aerial lymning,
And catch soft floatings from a faint-heard hymning;
To see the laurel wreath, on high suspended,
That is to crown our name when life is ended.
Sometimes it gives a glory to the voice,
And from the heart up-springs, rejoice! rejoice!
Sounds which will reach the Framer of all things,
And die away in ardent mutterings.   40

No one who once the glorious sun has seen,
And all the clouds, and felt his bosom clean
For his great Maker's presence, but must know
What 'tis I mean, and feel his being glow:
Therefore no insult will I give his spirit,
By telling what he sees from native merit.

O Poesy! for thee I hold my pen
That am not yet a glorious denizen
Of thy wide heaven—Should I rather kneel
Upon some mountain-top until I feel   50
A glowing splendour round about me hung,
And echo back the voice of thine own tongue?
O Poesy! for thee I grasp my pen
That am not yet a glorious denizen
Of thy wide heaven; yet, to my ardent prayer,
Yield from thy sanctuary some clear air,
Smoothed for intoxication by the breath
Of flowering bays, that I may die a death
Of luxury, and my young spirit follow
The morning sun-beams to the great Apollo   60
Like a fresh sacrifice; or, if I can bear
The o'erwhelming sweets, 'twill bring to me the fair
Visions of all places: a bowery nook
Will be elysium—an eternal book
Whence I may copy many a lovely saying
About the leaves, and flowers—about the playing
Of nymphs in woods, and fountains; and the shade
Keeping a silence round a sleeping maid;
And many a verse from so strange influence
That we must ever wonder how, and whence   70
It came. Also imaginings will hover
Round my fire-side, and haply there discover
Vistas of solemn beauty, where I'd wander
In happy silence, like the clear Meander
Through its lone vales; and where I found a spot
Of awfuller shade, or an enchanted grot,
Or a green hill o'erspread with chequered dress
Of flowers, and fearful from its loveliness,
Write on my tablets all that was permitted,

All that was for our human senses fitted.   80
Then the events of this wide world I'd seize
Like a strong giant, and my spirit teaze
Till at its shoulders it should proudly see
Wings to find out an immortality.

Stop and consider! life is but a day;
A fragile dew-drop on its perilous way
From a tree's summit; a poor Indian's sleep
While his boat hastens to the monstrous steep
Of Montmorenci. Why so sad a moan?
Life is the rose's hope while yet unblown;   90
The reading of an ever-changing tale;
The light uplifting of a maiden's veil;
A pigeon tumbling in clear summer air;
A laughing school-boy, without grief or care,
Riding the springy branches of an elm.

O for ten years, that I may overwhelm
Myself in poesy; so I may do the deed
That my own soul has to itself decreed.
Then will I pass the countries that I see
In long perspective, and continually   100
Taste their pure fountains. First the realm I'll pass
Of Flora, and old Pan: sleep in the grass,
Feed upon apples red, and strawberries,
And choose each pleasure that my fancy sees;
Catch the white-handed nymphs in shady places,
To woo sweet kisses from averted faces,—
Play with their fingers, touch their shoulders white
Into a pretty shrinking with a bite
As hard as lips can make it: till agreed,
A lovely tale of human life we'll read.   110
And one will teach a tame dove how it best
May fan the cool air gently o'er my rest;
Another, bending o'er her nimble tread,
Will set a green robe floating round her head,
And still will dance with ever varied ease,
Smiling upon the flowers and the trees:
Another will entice me on, and on
Through almond blossoms and rich cinnamon;

Till in the bosom of a leafy world
We rest in silence, like two gems upcurl'd
In the recesses of a pearly shell.   120

And can I ever bid these joys farewell?
Yes, I must pass them for a nobler life,
Where I may find the agonies, the strife
Of human hearts: for lo! I see afar,
O'er sailing the blue cragginess, a car
And steeds with streamy manes—the charioteer
Looks out upon the winds with glorious fear:
And now the numerous tramplings quiver lightly
Along a huge cloud's ridge; and now with sprightly   130
Wheel downward come they into fresher skies,
Tipt round with silver from the sun's bright eyes.
Still downward with capacious whirl they glide;
And now I see them on a green-hill's side
In breezy rest among the nodding stalks.
The charioteer with wond'rous gesture talks
To the trees and mountains; and there soon appear
Shapes of delight, of mystery, and fear,
Passing along before a dusky space
Made by some mighty oaks: as they would chase   140
Some ever-fleeting music on they sweep.
Lo! how they murmur, laugh, and smile, and weep:
Some with upholden hand and mouth severe;
Some with their faces muffled to the ear
Between their arms; some, clear in youthful bloom,
Go glad and smilingly athwart the gloom;
Some looking back, and some with upward gaze;
Yes, thousands in a thousand different ways
Flit onward—now a lovely wreath of girls
Dancing their sleek hair into tangled curls;   150
And now broad wings. Most awfully intent
The driver of those steeds is forward bent,
And seems to listen: O that I might know
All that he writes with such a hurrying glow.

The visions all are fled—the car is fled
Into the light of heaven, and in their stead
A sense of real things comes doubly strong,

And, like a muddy stream, would bear along
My soul to nothingness: but I will strive
Against all doubtings, and will keep alive   160
The thought of that same chariot, and the strange
Journey it went.

        Is there so small a range
In the present strength of manhood, that the high
Imagination cannot freely fly
As she was wont of old? prepare her steeds,
Paw up against the light, and do strange deeds
Upon the clouds? Has she not shewn us all?
From the clear space of ether, to the small
Breath of new buds unfolding? From the meaning
Of Jove's large eye-brow, to the tender greening   170
Of April meadows? Here her altar shone,
E'en in this isle; and who could paragon
The fervid choir that lifted up a noise
Of harmony, to where it aye will poise
Its mighty self of convoluting sound,
Huge as a planet, and like that roll round,
Eternally around a dizzy void?
Ay, in those days the Muses were nigh cloy'd
With honors; nor had any other care
Than to sing out and sooth their wavy hair.   180

Could all this be forgotten? Yes, a scism
Nurtured by foppery and barbarism,
Made great Apollo blush for this his land.
Men were thought wise who could not understand
His glories: with a puling infant's force
They sway'd about upon a rocking horse,
And thought it Pegasus. Ah dismal soul'd!
The winds of heaven blew, the ocean roll'd
Its gathering waves—ye felt it not. The blue
Bared its eternal bosom, and the dew   190
Of summer nights collected still to make
The morning precious: beauty was awake!
Why were ye not awake? But ye were dead
To things ye knew not of,—were closely wed
To musty laws lined out with wretched rule

And compass vile: so that ye taught a school
Of dolts to smooth, inlay, and clip, and fit,
Till, like the certain wands of Jacob's wit,
Their verses tallied. Easy was the task:
A thousand handicraftsmen wore the mask   200
Of Poesy. Ill-fated, impious race!
That blasphemed the bright Lyrist to his face,
And did not know it,—no, they went about,
Holding a poor, decrepid standard out
Mark'd with most flimsy mottos, and in large
The name of one Boileau!

                    O ye whose charge
It is to hover round our pleasant hills!
Whose congregated majesty so fills
My boundly reverence, that I cannot trace
Your hallowed names, in this unholy place,   210
So near those common folk; did not their shames
Affright you? Did our old lamenting Thames
Delight you? Did ye never cluster round
Delicious Avon, with a mournful sound,
And weep? Or did ye wholly bid adieu
To regions where no more the laurel grew?
Or did ye stay to give a welcoming
To some lone spirits who could proudly sing
Their youth away, and die? 'Twas even so:
But let me think away those times of woe: 220
Now 'tis a fairer season; ye have breathed
Rich benedictions o'er us; ye have wreathed
Fresh garlands: for sweet music has been heard
In many places;—some has been upstirr'd
From out its crystal dwelling in a lake,
By a swan's ebon bill; from a thick brake
Nested and quiet in a valley mild,
Bubbles a pipe; fine sounds are floating wild
About the earth: happy are ye and glad.

These things are doubtless: yet in truth we've had   230
Strange thunders from the potency of song;
Mingled indeed with what is sweet and strong,
From majesty: but in clear truth the themes
Are ugly clubs, the Poets Polyphemes

Disturbing the grand sea. A drainless shower
Of light is poesy; 'tis the supreme of power;
'Tis might half slumb'ring on its own right arm.
The very archings of her eye-lids charm
A thousand willing agents to obey,
And still she governs with the mildest sway: 240
But strength alone though of the Muses born
Is like a fallen angel: trees uptorn,
Darkness, and worms, and shrouds, and sepulchres
Delight it; for it feeds upon the burrs,
And thorns of life; forgetting the great end
Of poesy, that it should be a friend
To sooth the cares, and lift the thoughts of man.

Yet I rejoice: a myrtle fairer than
E'er grew in Paphos, from the bitter weeds
Lifts its sweet head into the air, and feeds 250
A silent space with ever sprouting green.
All tenderest birds there find a pleasant screen,
Creep through the shade with jaunty fluttering,
Nibble the little cupped flowers and sing.
Then let us clear away the choaking thorns
From round its gentle stem; let the young fawns,
Yeaned in after times, when we are flown,
Find a fresh sward beneath it, overgrown
With simple flowers: let there nothing be
More boisterous than a lover's bended knee; 260
Nought more ungentle than the placid look
Of one who leans upon a closed book;
Nought more untranquil than the grassy slopes
Between two hills. All hail delightful hopes!
As she was wont, th' imagination
Into most lovely labyrinths will be gone,
And they shall be accounted poet kings
Who simply tell the most heart-easing things.
O may these joys be ripe before I die.

Will not some say that I presumptuously 270
Have spoken? that from hastening disgrace
'Twere better far to hide my foolish face?
That whining boyhood should with reverence bow

Ere the dread thunderbolt could reach? How!
If I do hide myself, it sure shall be
In the very fane, the light of Poesy:
If I do fall, at least I will be laid
Beneath the silence of a poplar shade;
And over me the grass shall be smooth shaven;
And there shall be a kind of memorial graven.   280
But off Despondence! miserable bane!
They should not know thee, who athirst to gain
A noble end, are thirsty every hour.
What though I am not wealthy in the dower
Of spanning wisdom; though I do not know
The shiftings of the mighty winds that blow
Hither and thither all the changing thoughts
Of man: though no great minist'ring reason sorts
Out the dark mysteries of human souls
To clear conceiving: yet there ever rolls   290
A vast idea before me, and I glean
Therefrom my liberty; thence too I've seen
The end and aim of Poesy. 'Tis clear
As any thing most true; as that the year
Is made of the four seasons—manifest
As a large cross, some old cathedral's crest,
Lifted to the white clouds. Therefore should I
Be but the essence of deformity,
A coward, did my very eye-lids wink
At speaking out what I have dared to think.   300
Ah! rather let me like a madman run
Over some precipice; let the hot sun
Melt my Dedalian wings, and drive me down
Convuls'd and headlong! Stay! an inward frown
Of conscience bids me be more calm awhile.
An ocean dim, sprinkled with many an isle,
Spreads awfully before me. How much toil!
How many days! what desperate turmoil!
Ere I can have explored its widenesses.
Ah, what a task! upon my bended knees,   310
I could unsay those—no, impossible!
Impossible!

         For sweet relief I'll dwell
On humbler thoughts, and let this strange assay
Begun in gentleness die so away.
E'en now all tumult from my bosom fades:
I turn full hearted to the friendly aids
That smooth the path of honour; brotherhood,
And friendliness the nurse of mutual good;
The hearty grasp that sends a pleasant sonnet
Into the brain ere one can think upon it;   320
The silence when some rhymes are coming out;
And when they're come, the very pleasant rout:
The message certain to be done to-morrow—
'Tis perhaps as well that it should be to borrow
Some precious book from out its snug retreat,
To cluster round it when we next shall meet.
Scarce can I scribble on; for lovely airs
Are fluttering round the room like doves in pairs;
Many delights of that glad day recalling,
When first my senses caught their tender falling.   330
And with these airs come forms of elegance
Stooping their shoulders o'er a horse's prance,
Careless, and grand—fingers soft and round
Parting luxuriant curls;—and the swift bound
Of Bacchus from his chariot, when his eye
Made Ariadne's cheek look blushingly.
Thus I remember all the pleasant flow
Of words at opening a portfolio.

Things such as these are ever harbingers
To trains of peaceful images: the stirs   340
Of a swan's neck unseen among the rushes:
A linnet starting all about the bushes:
A butterfly, with golden wings broad parted,
Nestling a rose, convuls'd as though it smarted
With over pleasure—many, many more,
Might I indulge at large in all my store
Of luxuries: yet I must not forget
Sleep, quiet with his poppy coronet:
For what there may be worthy in these rhymes
I partly owe to him: and thus, the chimes   350

Of friendly voices had just given place
To as sweet a silence, when I 'gan retrace
The pleasant day, upon a couch at ease.
It was a poet's house who keeps the keys
Of pleasure's temple. Round about were hung
The glorious features of the bards who sung
In other ages—cold and sacred busts
Smiled at each other. Happy he who trusts
To clear Futurity his darling fame!
Then there were fauns and satyrs taking aim   360
At swelling apples with a frisky leap
And reaching fingers, 'mid a luscious heap
Of vine leaves. Then there rose to view a fane
Of liny marble, and thereto a train
Of nymphs approaching fairly o'er the sward:
One, loveliest, holding her white hand toward
The dazzling sun-rise: two sisters sweet
Bending their graceful figures till they meet
Over the trippings of a little child:
And some are hearing, eagerly, the wild   370
Thrilling liquidity of dewy piping.
See, in another picture, nymphs are wiping
Cherishingly Diana's timorous limbs;—
A fold of lawny mantle dabbling swims
At the bath's edge, and keeps a gentle motion
With the subsiding crystal: as when ocean
Heaves calmly its broad swelling smoothiness o'er
Its rocky marge, and balances once more
The patient weeds; that now unshent by foam
Feel all about their undulating home.   380

Sappho's meek head was there half smiling down
At nothing; just as though the earnest frown
Of over thinking had that moment gone
From off her brow, and left her all alone.

Great Alfred's too, with anxious, pitying eyes,
As if he always listened to the sighs
Of the goaded world; and Kosciusko's worn
By horrid suffrance—mightily forlorn.

Petrarch, outstepping from the shady green,
Starts at the sight of Laura; nor can wean 390
His eyes from her sweet face. Most happy they!
For over them was seen a free display
Of out-spread wings, and from between them shone
The face of Poesy: from off her throne
She overlook'd things that I scarce could tell.
The very sense of where I was might well
Keep Sleep aloof: but more than that there came
Thought after thought to nourish up the flame
Within my breast; so that the morning light
Surprised me even from a sleepless night; 400
And up I rose refresh'd, and glad, and gay,
Resolving to begin that very day
These lines; and howsoever they be done,
I leave them as a father does his son.

To My Brothers

Small, busy flames play through the fresh laid coals,
   And their faint cracklings o'er our silence creep
   Like whispers of the household gods that keep
A gentle empire o'er fraternal souls.
And while, for rhymes, I search around the poles,
   Your eyes are fix'd, as in poetic sleep,
   Upon the lore so voluble and deep,
That aye at fall of night our care condoles.
This is your birth-day Tom, and I rejoice
   That thus it passes smoothly, quietly. 10
Many such eves of gently whisp'ring noise
   May we together pass, and calmly try
What are this world's true joys,—ere the great voice,
   From its fair face, shall bid our spirits fly.

Addressed to [Haydon]

Great spirits now on earth are sojourning;
  He of the cloud, the cataract, the lake,
  Who on Helvellyn's summit, wide awake,
Catches his freshness from Archangel's wing:
He of the rose, the violet, the spring,
  The social smile, the chain for Freedom's sake:
And lo!—whose stedfastness would never take
A meaner sound than Raphael's whispering.
And other spirits there are standing apart
  Upon the forehead of the age to come;   10
These, these will give the world another heart,
  And other pulses. Hear ye not the hum
Of mighty workings?—
    Listen awhile ye nations, and be dumb.

To Kosciusko

Good Kosciusko, thy great name alone
  Is a full harvest whence to reap high feeling;
  It comes upon us like the glorious pealing
Of the wide spheres—an everlasting tone.
And now it tells me, that in worlds unknown,
  The names of heroes, burst from clouds concealing,
  And change to harmonies, for ever stealing
Through cloudless blue, and round each silver throne.
It tells me too, that on a happy day,
  When some good spirit walks upon the earth,   10
    Thy name with Alfred's and the great of yore
  Gently commingling, gives tremendous birth
To a loud hymn, that sounds far, far away
    To where the great God lives for evermore.

'I stood tip-toe upon a little hill'

Places of nestling green for Poets made.

Story of Rimini

I stood tip-toe upon a little hill,
The air was cooling, and so very still,
That the sweet buds which with a modest pride
Pull droopingly, in slanting curve aside,
Their scantly leaved, and finely tapering stems,
Had not yet lost those starry diadems
Caught from the early sobbing of the morn.
The clouds were pure and white as flocks new shorn,
And fresh from the clear brook; sweetly they slept
On the blue fields of heaven, and then there crept   10
A little noiseless noise among the leaves,
Born of the very sigh that silence heaves:
For not the faintest motion could be seen
Of all the shades that slanted o'er the green.
There was wide wand'ring for the greediest eye,
To peer about upon variety;
Far round the horizon's crystal air to skim,
And trace the dwindled edgings of its brim;
To picture out the quaint, and curious bending
Of a fresh woodland alley, never ending;   20
Or by the bowery clefts, and leafy shelves,
Guess where the jaunty streams refresh themselves.
I gazed awhile, and felt as light, and free
As though the fanning wings of Mercury
Had played upon my heels: I was light-hearted,
And many pleasures to my vision started;
So I straightway began to pluck a posey
Of luxuries bright, milky, soft and rosy.

A bush of May flowers with the bees about them;
Ah, sure no tasteful nook would be without them;   30
And let a lush laburnum oversweep them,
And let long grass grow round the roots to keep them
Moist, cool and green; and shade the violets,
That they may bind the moss in leafy nets.

A filbert hedge with wild briar overtwined,
And clumps of woodbine taking the soft wind
Upon their summer thrones; there too should be
The frequent chequer of a youngling tree,
That with a score of light green brethren shoots
From the quaint mossiness of aged roots: 40
Round which is heard a spring-head of clear waters
Babbling so wildly of its lovely daughters
The spreading blue bells: it may haply mourn
That such fair clusters should be rudely torn
From their fresh beds, and scattered thoughtlessly
By infant hands, left on the path to die.

Open afresh your round of starry folds
Ye ardent marigolds!
Dry up the moisture from your golden lids,
For great Apollo bids   50
That in these days your praises should be sung
On many harps, which he has lately strung;
And when again your dewiness he kisses,
Tell him, I have you in my world of blisses:
So haply when I rove in some far vale,
His mighty voice may come upon the gale.

Here are sweet peas, on tip-toe for a flight:
With wings of gentle flush o'er delicate white,
And taper fingers catching at all things,
To bind them all about with tiny rings.   60

Linger awhile upon some bending planks
That lean against a streamlet's rushy banks,
And watch intently Nature's gentle doings:
They will be found softer than ring-dove's cooings.
How silent comes the water round that bend;
Not the minutest whisper does it send
To the o'erhanging sallows: blades of grass
Slowly across the chequer'd shadows pass.
Why, you might read two sonnets, ere they reach
To where the hurrying freshnesses aye preach   70
A natural sermon o'er their pebbly beds;

Where swarms of minnows show their little heads,
Staying their wavy bodies 'gainst the streams,
To taste the luxury of sunny beams
Temper'd with coolness. How they ever wrestle
With their own sweet delight, and never nestle
Their silver bellies on the pebbly sand.
If you but scantily hold out the hand,
That very instant not one will remain;
But turn your eye, and they are there again.   80
The ripples seem right glad to reach those cresses,
And cool themselves among the em'rald tresses;
The while they cool themselves, they freshness give,
And moisture, that the bowery green may live:
So keeping up an interchange of favours,
Like good men in the truth of their behaviours,
Sometimes goldfinches one by one will drop
From low hung branches; little space they stop;
But sip, and twitter, and their feathers sleek;
Then off at once, as in a wanton freak: 90
Or perhaps, to show their black, and golden wings,
Pausing upon their yellow flutterings.
Were I in such a place, I sure should pray
That nought less sweet might call my thoughts away,
Than the soft rustle of a maiden's gown
Fanning away the dandelion's down;
Than the light music of her nimble toes
Patting against the sorrel as she goes.
How she would start, and blush, thus to be caught
Playing in all her innocence of thought.   100
O let me lead her gently o'er the brook,
Watch her half-smiling lips, and downward look;
O let me for one moment touch her wrist;
Let me one moment to her breathing list;
And as she leaves me may she often turn
Her fair eyes looking through her locks auburne.

What next? A tuft of evening primroses,
O'er which the mind may hover till it dozes;
O'er which it well might take a pleasant sleep,
But that 'tis ever startled by the leap   110
Of buds into ripe flowers; or by the flitting

Of diverse moths, that aye their rest are quitting;
Or by the moon lifting her silver rim
Above a cloud, and with a gradual swim
Coming into the blue with all her light.
O Maker of sweet poets, dear delight
Of this fair world, and all its gentle livers;
Spangler of clouds, halo of crystal rivers,
Mingler with leaves, and dew and tumbling streams,
Closer of lovely eyes to lovely dreams,   120
Lover of loneliness, and wandering,
Of upcast eye, and tender pondering!
Thee must I praise above all other glories
That smile us on to tell delightful stories.
For what has made the sage or poet write
But the fair paradise of Nature's light?
In the calm grandeur of a sober line,
We see the waving of the mountain pine;
And when a tale is beautifully staid,
We feel the safety of a hawthorn glade: 130
When it is moving on luxurious wings,
The soul is lost in pleasant smotherings:
Fair dewy roses brush against our faces,
And flowering laurels spring from diamond vases;
O'er head we see the jasmine and sweet briar,
And bloomy grapes laughing from green attire;
While at our feet, the voice of crystal bubbles
Charms us at once away from all our troubles:
So that we feel uplifted from the world,
Walking upon the white clouds wreath'd and curl'd.   140
So felt he, who first told, how Psyche went
On the smooth wind to realms of wonderment;
What Psyche felt, and Love, when their full lips
First touch'd; what amorous, and fondling nips
They gave each other's cheeks; with all their sighs,
And how they kist each other's tremulous eyes:
The silver lamp,—the ravishment,—the wonder—
The darkness,—loneliness,—the fearful thunder;
Their woes gone by, and both to heaven upflown,
To bow for gratitude before Jove's throne.   150
So did he feel, who pull'd the boughs aside,
That we might look into a forest wide,

To catch a glimpse of Fawns, and Dryades
Coming with softest rustle through the trees;
And garlands woven of flowers wild, and sweet,
Upheld on ivory wrists, or sporting feet:
Telling us how fair, trembling Syrinx fled
Arcadian Pan, with such a fearful dread.
Poor nymph,—poor Pan,—how he did weep to find,
Nought but a lovely sighing of the wind   160
Along the reedy stream; a half heard strain,
Full of sweet desolation—balmy pain.

What first inspired a bard of old to sing
Narcissus pining o'er the untainted spring?
In some delicious ramble, he had found
A little space, with boughs all woven round;
And in the midst of all, a clearer pool
Than e'er reflected in its pleasant cool,
The blue sky here, and there, serenely peeping
Through tendril wreaths fantastically creeping.   170
And on the bank a lonely flower he spied,
A meek and forlorn flower, with naught of pride,
Drooping its beauty o'er the watery clearness,
To woo its own sad image into nearness:
Deaf to light Zephyrus it would not move;
But still would seem to droop, to pine, to love.
So while the Poet stood in this sweet spot,
Some fainter gleamings o'er his fancy shot;
Nor was it long ere he had told the tale
Of young Narcissus, and sad Echo's bale.   180

Where had he been, from whose warm head out-flew
That sweetest of all songs, that ever new,
That aye refreshing, pure deliciousness,
Coming ever to bless
The wanderer by moonlight? to him bringing
Shapes from the invisible world, unearthly singing
From out the middle air, from flowery nests,
And from the pillowy silkiness that rests
Full in the speculation of the stars.
Ah! surely he had burst our mortal bars;   190

Into some wond'rous region he had gone,
To search for thee, divine Endymion!

He was a Poet, sure a lover too,
Who stood on Latmus' top, what time there blew
Soft breezes from the myrtle vale below;
And brought in faintness solemn, sweet, and slow
A hymn from Dian's temple; while upswelling,
The incense went to her own starry dwelling.
But though her face was clear as infant's eyes,
Though she stood smiling o'er the sacrifice,   200
The Poet wept at her so piteous fate,
Wept that such beauty should be desolate:
So in fine wrath some golden sounds he won,
And gave meek Cynthia her Endymion.

Queen of the wide air; thou most lovely queen
Of all the brightness that mine eyes have seen!
As thou exceedest all things in thy shine,
So every tale, does this sweet tale of thine.
O for three words of honey, that I might
Tell but one wonder of thy bridal night!   210

Where distant ships do seem to show their keels,
Phœbus awhile delayed his mighty wheels,
And turned to smile upon thy bashful eyes,
Ere he his unseen pomp would solemnize.
The evening weather was so bright, and clear,
That men of health were of unusual cheer;
Stepping like Homer at the trumpet's call,
Or young Apollo on the pedestal:
And lovely women were as fair and warm,
As Venus looking sideways in alarm.   220
The breezes were ethereal, and pure,
And crept through half closed lattices to cure
The languid sick; it cool'd their fever'd sleep,
And soothed them into slumbers full and deep.
Soon they awoke clear eyed: nor burnt with thirsting,
Nor with hot fingers, nor with temples bursting:
And springing up, they met the wond'ring sight
Of their dear friends, nigh foolish with delight;

Who feel their arms, and breasts, and kiss and stare,
And on their placid foreheads part the hair.   230
Young men, and maidens at each other gaz'd
With hands held back, and motionless, amaz'd
To see the brightness in each other's eyes;
And so they stood, fill'd with a sweet surprise,
Until their tongues were loos'd in poesy.
Therefore no lover did of anguish die:
But the soft numbers, in that moment spoken,
Made silken ties, that never may be broken.
Cynthia! I cannot tell the greater blisses,
That follow'd thine, and thy dear shepherd's kisses: 240
Was there a Poet born?—but now no more,
My wand'ring spirit must no further soar.—

Written in Disgust of Vulgar Superstition

The Church bells toll a melancholy round,
  Calling the people to some other prayers,
  Some other gloominess, more dreadfull cares,
More heark'ning to the Sermon's horrid sound—
Surely the mind of Man is closely bound
  In some black spell; seeing that each one tears
  Himself from fireside joys and Lydian airs,
And converse high of those with glory crown'd—
Still, still they toll, and I should feel a damp,—
  A chill as from a tomb, did I not know   10
That they are dying like an outburnt lamp;
  That 'tis their sighing, wailing ere they go
  Into oblivion;—that fresh flowers will grow,
And many glories of immortal stamp—

'After dark vapors have oppress'd our plains'

After dark vapors have oppress'd our plains
  For a long dreary season, comes a day
  Born of the gentle SOUTH, and clears away
From the sick heavens all unseemly stains,

The anxious Month, relieving of its pains,
  Takes as a long lost right the feel of May:
  The eyelids with the passing coolness play
Like Rose leaves with the drip of Summer rains.
And calmest thoughts come round us; as of leaves
  Budding—fruit ripening in stillness—Autumn Suns   10
Smiling at Eve upon the quiet sheaves—
    Sweet Sappho's Cheek—a sleeping infant's breath—
    The gradual Sand that through an hour-glass runs—
    A woodland Rivulet—a Poet's death.

On seeing the Elgin Marbles

My spirit is too weak—mortality
  Weighs heavily on me like unwilling sleep,
  And each imagined pinnacle and steep
Of godlike hardship, tells me I must die
Like a sick eagle looking at the sky.
  Yet 'tis a gentle luxury to weep
  That I have not the cloudy winds to keep,
Fresh for the opening of the morning's eye.
Such dim-conceived glories of the brain
  Bring round the heart an undescribable feud;   10
So do these wonders a most dizzy pain,
  That mingles Grecian grandeur with the rude
Wasting of old time—with a billowy main—
  A sun—a shadow of a magnitude.

On a Leander which Miss Reynolds my kind friend gave me

Come hither all sweet Maidens soberly
  Downlooking—aye and with a chastened Light
  Hid in the fringes of your eyelids white—
And meekly let your fair hands joined be.
So gentle are ye that ye could not see
  Untouch'd a Victim of your beauty bright—
  Sinking away to his young spirit's Night,

Sinking bewilder'd mid the dreary Sea—
'Tis young Leander toiling to his Death.
  Nigh swooning he doth purse his weary Lips   10
    For Hero's cheek and smiles against her smile.
  O horrid dream—see how his body dips
    Dead heavy—Arms and shoulders gleam awhile—
He's gone—upbubbles all his amourous breath—

On the Sea

It keeps eternal whisperings around
Desolate shores,—and with its mighty swell
Gluts twice ten thousand caverns,—till the spell
Of Hecate leaves them their old shadowy sound.
Often 'tis in such gentle temper found,
That scarcely will the very smallest shell
Be lightly moved, from where it sometime fell,
When last the winds of heaven were unbound.
Ye, that have your eye-balls vex'd and tired,
Feast them upon the wideness of the sea;—   10
Or are your hearts disturb'd with uproar rude,
Or fed too much with cloying melody,—
Sit ye near some old cavern's mouth and brood
Until ye start, as if the sea nymphs quired.

'Hither hither Love'

Hither hither Love
  'Tis a shady Mead.
Hither, hither Love
  Let us feed and feed.

Hither hither sweet
  'Tis a cowslip bed,
Hither hither sweet
  'Tis with dew bespread.

Hither hither dear
  By the breath of Life,   10
Hither hither dear
  Be the summer's wife.

Though one moment's pleasure
  In one moment flies,
Though the passion's treasure
  In one moment dies;

Yet it has not pass'd
  Think how near, how near,
And while it doth last
  Think how dear how dear—   20

Hither hither hither
  Love this boon has sent,
If I die and wither
  I shall die content—

Endymion: A Poetic Romance

'The stretched metre of an antique song'

Inscribed to the memory of Thomas Chatterton

Preface

Knowing within myself the manner in which this Poem has been produced, it is not without a feeling of regret that I make it public.

What manner I mean, will be quite clear to the reader, who must soon perceive great inexperience, immaturity, and every error denoting a feverish attempt, rather than a deed accomplished. The two first books, and indeed the two last, I feel sensible are not of such completion as to warrant their passing the press; nor should they if I thought a year's castigation would do them any good;—it will not: the foundations are too sandy. It is just that this youngster should die away: a sad thought for me, if I had not some hope that

while it is dwindling I may be plotting, and fitting myself for verses
fit to live.

This may be speaking too presumptuously, and may deserve a
punishment: but no feeling man will be forward to inflict it: he will
leave me alone, with the conviction that there is not a fiercer hell
than the failure in a great object. This is not written with the least
atom of purpose to forestall criticisms of course, but from the desire
I have to conciliate men who are competent to look, and who do
look with a zealous eye, to the honour of English literature.

The imagination of a boy is healthy, and the mature imagination
of a man is healthy; but there is a space of life between, in which
the soul is in a ferment, the character undecided, the way of life
uncertain, the ambition thick-sighted: thence proceeds mawkish-
ness, and all the thousand bitters which those men I speak of must
necessarily taste in going over the following pages.

I hope I have not in too late a day touched the beautiful
mythology of Greece, and dulled its brightness: for I wish to try
once more, before I bid it farewel.

Teignmouth, April 10, 1818

Book I

A thing of beauty is a joy for ever:
Its loveliness increases; it will never
Pass into nothingness; but still will keep
A bower quiet for us, and a sleep
Full of sweet dreams, and health, and quiet breathing.
Therefore, on every morrow, are we wreathing
A flowery band to bind us to the earth,
Spite of despondence, of the inhuman dearth
Of noble natures, of the gloomy days,
Of all the unhealthy, and o'er-darkened ways   10
Made for our searching: yes, in spite of all,
Some shape of beauty moves away the pall
From our dark spirits. Such the sun, the moon,
Trees old, and young sprouting a shady boon
For simple sheep; and such are daffodils
With the green world they live in; and clear rills
That for themselves a cooling covert make
'Gainst the hot season; the mid forest brake,

Rich with a sprinkling of fair musk-rose blooms:
And such too is the grandeur of the dooms   20
We have imagined for the mighty dead;
All lovely tales that we have heard or read:
An endless fountain of immortal drink,
Pouring unto us from the heaven's brink.

Nor do we merely feel these essences
For one short hour; no, even as the trees
That whisper round a temple become soon
Dear as the temple's self, so does the moon,
The passion poesy, glories infinite,
Haunt us till they become a cheering light   30
Unto our souls, and bound to us so fast,
That, whether there be shine, or gloom o'ercast,
They always must be with us, or we die.

Therefore, 'tis with full happiness that I
Will trace the story of Endymion
The very music of the name has gone
Into my being, and each pleasant scene
Is growing fresh before me as the green
Of our own vallies: so I will begin
Now while I cannot hear the city's din;   40
Now while the early budders are just new,
And run in mazes of the youngest hue
About old forests; while the willow trails
Its delicate amber; and the dairy pails
Bring home increase of milk. And, as the year
Grows lush in juicy stalks, I'll smoothly steer
My little boat, for many quiet hours,
With streams that deepen freshly into bowers.
Many and many a verse I hope to write,
Before the daisies, vermeil rimm'd and white,   50
Hide in deep herbage; and ere yet the bees
Hum about globes of clover and sweet peas,
I must be near the middle of my story.
O may no wintry season, bare and hoary,
See it half finished: but let Autumn bold,
With universal tinge of sober gold,
Be all about me when I make an end.

And now at once, adventuresome, I send
My herald thought into a wilderness:
There let its trumpet blow, and quickly dress   60
My uncertain path with green, that I may speed
Easily onward, thorough flowers and weed.

Upon the sides of Latmos was outspread
A mighty forest; for the moist earth fed
So plenteously all weed-hidden roots
Into o'er-hanging boughs, and precious fruits.
And it had gloomy shades, sequestered deep,
Where no man went; and if from shepherd's keep
A lamb strayed far a-down those inmost glens,
Never again saw he the happy pens   70
Whither his brethren, bleating with content,
Over the hills at every nightfall went.
Among the shepherds, 'twas believed ever,
That not one fleecy lamb which thus did sever
From the white flock, but pass'd unworried
By angry wolf, or pard with prying head,
Until it came to some unfooted plains
Where fed the herds of Pan: ay great his gains
Who thus one lamb did lose. Paths there were many,
Winding through palmy fern, and rushes fenny,   80
And ivy banks; all leading pleasantly
To a wide lawn, whence one could only see
Stems thronging all around between the swell
Of turf and slanting branches: who could tell
The freshness of the space of heaven above,
Edg'd round with dark tree tops? through which a dove
Would often beat its wings, and often too
A little cloud would move across the blue.

Full in the middle of this pleasantness
There stood a marble altar, with a tress   90
Of flowers budded newly; and the dew
Had taken fairy phantasies to strew
Daisies upon the sacred sward last eve,
And so the dawned light in pomp receive.
For 'twas the morn: Apollo's upward fire
Made every eastern cloud a silvery pyre

Of brightness so unsullied, that therein
A melancholy spirit well might win
Oblivion, and melt out his essence fine
Into the winds: rain-scented eglantine   100
Gave temperate sweets to that well-wooing sun;
The lark was lost in him; cold springs had run
To warm their chilliest bubbles in the grass;
Man's voice was on the mountains; and the mass
Of nature's lives and wonders puls'd tenfold,
To feel this sun-rise and its glories old.

Now while the silent workings of the dawn
Were busiest, into that self-same lawn
All suddenly, with joyful cries, there sped
A troop of little children garlanded;   110
Who gathering round the altar, seemed to pry
Earnestly round as wishing to espy
Some folk of holiday: nor had they waited
For many moments, ere their ears were sated
With a faint breath of music, which ev'n then
Fill'd out its voice, and died away again.
Within a little space again it gave
Its airy swellings, with a gentle wave,
To light-hung leaves, in smoothest echoes breaking
Through copse-clad vallies,—ere their death, o'ertaking   120
The surgy murmurs of the lonely sea.

And now, as deep into the wood as we
Might mark a lynx's eye, there glimmered light
Fair faces and a rush of garments white,
Plainer and plainer shewing, till at last
Into the widest alley they all past,
Making directly for the woodland altar.
O kindly muse! let not my weak tongue faulter
In telling of this goodly company,
Of their old piety, and of their glee: 130
But let a portion of ethereal dew
Fall on my head, and presently unmew
My soul; that I may dare, in wayfaring,
To stammer where old Chaucer used to sing.

Leading the way, young damsels danced along,
Bearing the burden of a shepherd song;
Each having a white wicker over brimm'd
With April's tender younglings: next, well trimm'd,
A crowd of shepherds with as sunburnt looks
As may be read of in Arcadian books;   140
Such as sat listening round Apollo's pipe,
When the great deity, for earth too ripe,
Let his divinity o'er-flowing die
In music, through the vales of Thessaly:
Some idly trailed their sheep-hooks on the ground,
And some kept up a shrilly mellow sound
With ebon-tipped flutes: close after these,
Now coming from beneath the forest trees,
A venerable priest full soberly,
Begirt with ministring looks: alway his eye   150
Stedfast upon the matted turf he kept,
And after him his sacred vestments swept.
From his right hand there swung a vase, milk-white,
Of mingled wine, out-sparkling generous light;
And in his left he held a basket full
Of all sweet herbs that searching eye could cull:
Wild thyme, and valley-lilies whiter still
Than Leda's love, and cresses from the rill.
His aged head, crowned with beechen wreath,
Seem'd like a poll of ivy in the teeth   160
Of winter hoar. Then came another crowd
Of shepherds, lifting in due time aloud
Their share of the ditty. After them appear'd,
Up-followed by a multitude that rear'd
Their voices to the clouds, a fair wrought car,
Easily rolling so as scarce to mar
The freedom of three steeds of dapple brown:
Who stood therein did seem of great renown
Among the throng. His youth was fully blown,
Shewing like Ganymede to manhood grown;   170
And, for those simple times, his garments were
A chieftain king's: beneath his breast, half bare,
Was hung a silver bugle, and between
His nervy knees there lay a boar-spear keen.

A smile was on his countenance; he seem'd,
To common lookers on, like one who dream'd
Of idleness in groves Elysian:
But there were some who feelingly could scan
A lurking trouble in his nether lip,
And see that oftentimes the reins would slip   180
Through his forgotten hands: then would they sigh,
And think of yellow leaves, of owlet's cry,
Of logs piled solemnly.—Ah, well-a-day,
Why should our young Endymion pine away!

    Soon the assembly, in a circle rang'd
Stood silent round the shrine: each look was chang'd
To sudden veneration: women meek
Beckon'd their sons to silence; while each cheek
Of virgin bloom paled gently for slight fear.
Endymion too, without a forest peer,   190
Stood, wan, and pale, and with an awed face,
Among his brothers of the mountain chase.
In midst of all, the venerable priest
Eyed them with joy from greatest to the least,
And, after lifting up his aged hands,
Thus spake he: 'Men of Latmos! shepherd bands!
Whose care it is to guard a thousand flocks:
Whether descended from beneath the rocks
That overtop your mountains; whether come
From vallies where the pipe is never dumb;   200
Or from your swelling downs, where sweet air stirs
Blue hair-bells lightly, and where prickly furze
Buds lavish gold; or ye, whose precious charge
Nibble their fill at ocean's very marge,
Whose mellow reeds are touch'd with sounds forlorn
By the dim echoes of old Triton's horn:
Mothers and wives! who day by day prepare
The scrip, with needments, for the mountain air;
And all ye gentle girls who foster up
Udderless lambs, and in a little cup   210
Will put choice honey for a favoured youth:
Yea, every one attend! for in good truth
Our vows are wanting to our great god Pan.
Are not our lowing heifers sleeker than

Night-swollen mushrooms? Are not our wide plains
Speckled with countless fleeces? Have not rains
Green'd over April's lap? No howling sad
Sickens our fearful ewes; and we have had
Great bounty from Endymion our lord.
The earth is glad: the merry lark has pour'd   220
His early song against yon breezy sky,
That spreads so clear o'er our solemnity.'

    Thus ending, on the shrine he heap'd a spire
Of teeming sweets, enkindling sacred fire;
Anon he stain'd the thick and spongy sod
With wine, in honour of the shepherd-god.
Now while the earth was drinking it, and while
Bay leaves were crackling in the fragrant pile,
And gummy frankincense was sparkling bright
'Neath smothering parsley, and a hazy light   230
Spread greyly eastward, thus a chorus sang:

    'O thou, whose mighty palace roof doth hang
From jagged trunks, and overshadoweth
Eternal whispers, glooms, the birth, life, death
Of unseen flowers in heavy peacefulness;
Who lov'st to see the hamadryads dress
Their ruffled locks where meeting hazels darken;
And through whole solemn hours dost sit, and hearken
The dreary melody of bedded reeds—
In desolate places, where dank moisture breeds   240
The pipy hemlock to strange overgrowth;
Bethinking thee, how melancholy loth
Thou wast to lose fair Syrinx—do thou now,
By thy love's milky brow!
By all the trembling mazes that she ran,
Hear us, great Pan!

    'O thou, for whose soul-soothing quiet, turtles
Passion their voices cooingly 'mong myrtles,
What time thou wanderest at eventide
Through sunny meadows, that outskirt the side   250
Of thine enmossed realms: O thou, to whom
Broad leaved fig trees even now foredoom

Their ripen'd fruitage; yellow girted bees
Their golden honeycombs; our village leas
Their fairest blossom'd beans and poppied corn;
The chuckling linnet its five young unborn,
To sing for thee; low creeping strawberries
Their summer coolness; pent up butterflies
Their freckled wings; yea, the fresh budding year
All its completions—be quickly near,   260
By every wind that nods the mountain pine,
O forester divine!

'Thou, to whom every fawn and satyr flies
For willing service; whether to surprise
The squatted hare while in half sleeping fit;
Or upward ragged precipices flit
To save poor lambkins from the eagle's maw;
Or by mysterious enticement draw
Bewildered shepherds to their path again;
Or to tread breathless round the frothy main,   270
And gather up all fancifullest shells
For thee to tumble into Naiad's cells,
And, being hidden, laugh at their out-peeping;
Or to delight thee with fantastic leaping,
The while they pelt each other on the crown
With silvery oak apples, and fir cones brown—
By all the echoes that about thee ring,
Hear us, O satyr king!

'O Hearkener to the loud clapping shears,
While ever and anon to his shorn peers   280
A ram goes bleating: Winder of the horn,
When snouted wild-boars routing tender corn
Anger our huntsmen: Breather round our farms,
To keep off mildews, and all weather harms:
Strange ministrant of undescribed sounds,
That come a swooning over hollow grounds,
And wither drearily on barren moors:
Dread opener of the mysterious doors
Leading to universal knowledge—see,
Great son of Dryope,   290

The many that are come to pay their vows
With leaves about their brows!

   'Be still the unimaginable lodge
For solitary thinkings; such as dodge
Conception to the very bourne of heaven,
Then leave the naked brain: be still the leaven,
That spreading in this dull and clodded earth
Gives it a touch ethereal—a new birth:
Be still a symbol of immensity;
A firmament reflected in a sea;   300
An element filling the space between;
An unknown—but no more: we humbly screen
With uplift hands our foreheads, lowly bending,
And giving out a shout most heaven rending,
Conjure thee to receive our humble pæan,
Upon thy Mount Lycean!'

   Even while they brought the burden to a close,
A shout from the whole multitude arose,
That lingered in the air like dying rolls
Of abrupt thunder, when Ionian shoals   310
Of dolphins bob their noses through the brine.
Meantime, on shady levels, mossy fine,
Young companies nimbly began dancing
To the swift treble pipe, and humming string.
Aye, those fair living forms swam heavenly
To tunes forgotten—out of memory:
Fair creatures! whose young children's children bred
Thermopylæ its heroes—not yet dead,
But in old marbles ever beautiful.
High genitors, unconscious did they cull   320
Time's sweet first-fruits—they danc'd to weariness,
And then in quiet circles did they press
The hillock turf, and caught the latter end
Of some strange history, potent to send
A young mind from its bodily tenement.
Or they might watch the quoit-pitchers, intent
On either side; pitying the sad death
Of Hyacinthus, when the cruel breath
Of Zephyr slew him,—Zephyr penitent,

Who now, ere Phœbus mounts the firmament,   330
Fondles the flower amid the sobbing rain.
The archers too, upon a wider plain,
Beside the feathery whizzing of the shaft,
And the dull twanging bowstring, and the raft
Branch down sweeping from a tall ash top,
Call'd up a thousand thoughts to envelope
Those who would watch. Perhaps, the trembling knee
And frantic gape of lonely Niobe,
Poor, lonely Niobe! when her lovely young
Were dead and gone, and her caressing tongue   340
Lay a lost thing upon her paly lip,
And very, very deadliness did nip
Her motherly cheeks. Arous'd from this sad mood
By one, who at a distance loud halloo'd,
Uplifting his strong bow into the air,
Many might after brighter visions stare:
After the Argonauts, in blind amaze
Tossing about on Neptune's restless ways,
Until, from the horizon's vaulted side,
There shot a golden splendour far and wide,   350
Spangling those million poutings of the brine
With quivering ore: 'twas even an awful shine
From the exaltation of Apollo's bow;
A heavenly beacon in their dreary woe.
Who thus were ripe for high contemplating,
Might turn their steps towards the sober ring
Where sat Endymion and the aged priest
'Mong shepherds gone in eld, whose looks increas'd
The silvery setting of their mortal star.
There they discours'd upon the fragile bar   360
That keeps us from our homes ethereal;
And what our duties there: to nightly call
Vesper, the beauty-crest of summer weather;
To summon all the downiest clouds together
For the sun's purple couch; to emulate
In ministring the potent rule of fate
With speed of fire-tailed exhalations;
To tint her pallid cheek with bloom, who cons
Sweet poesy by moonlight: besides these,
A world of other unguess'd offices.   370

Anon they wander'd, by divine converse,
Into Elysium; vieing to rehearse
Each one his own anticipated bliss.
One felt heart-certain that he could not miss
His quick gone love, among fair blossom'd boughs,
Where every zephyr-sigh pouts, and endows
Her lips with music for the welcoming.
Another wish'd, mid that eternal spring,
To meet his rosy child, with feathery sails,
Sweeping, eye-earnestly, through almond vales: 380
Who, suddenly, should stoop through the smooth wind,
And with the balmiest leaves his temples bind;
And, ever after, through those regions be
His messenger, his little Mercury.
Some were athirst in soul to see again
Their fellow huntsmen o'er the wide champaign
In times long past; to sit with them, and talk
Of all the chances in their earthly walk;
Comparing, joyfully, their plenteous stores
Of happiness, to when upon the moors,   390
Benighted, close they huddled from the cold,
And shar'd their famish'd scrips. Thus all out-told
Their fond imaginations,—saving him
Whose eyelids curtain'd up their jewels dim,
Endymion: yet hourly had he striven
To hide the cankering venom, that had riven
His fainting recollections. Now indeed
His senses had swoon'd off: he did not heed
The sudden silence, or the whispers low,
Or the old eyes dissolving at this woe,   400
Or anxious calls, or close of trembling palms,
Or maiden's sigh, that grief itself embalms:
But in the self-same fixed trance he kept,
Like one who on the earth had never stept,
Aye, even as dead-still as a marble man,
Frozen in that old tale Arabian.

    Who whispers him so pantingly and close?
Peona, his sweet sister: of all those,
His friends, the dearest. Hushing signs she made,
And breath'd a sister's sorrow to persuade   410

A yielding up, a cradling on her care.
Her eloquence did breathe away the curse:
She led him, like some midnight spirit nurse
Of happy changes in emphatic dreams,
Along a path between two little streams,—
Guarding his forehead, with her round elbow,
From low-grown branches, and his footsteps slow
From stumbling over stumps and hillocks small;
Until they came to where these streamlets fall,
With mingled bubblings and a gentle rush,   420
Into a river, clear, brimful, and flush
With crystal mocking of the trees and sky.
A little shallop, floating there hard by,
Pointed its beak over the fringed bank;
And soon it lightly dipt, and rose, and sank,
And dipt again, with the young couple's weight,—
Peona guiding, through the water straight,
Towards a bowery island opposite;
Which gaining presently, she steered light
Into a shady, fresh, and ripply cove,   430
Where nested was an arbour, overwove
By many a summer's silent fingering;
To whose cool bosom she was used to bring
Her playmates, with their needle broidery,
And minstrel memories of times gone by.

　　So she was gently glad to see him laid
Under her favourite bower's quiet shade,
On her own couch, new made of flower leaves,
Dried carefully on the cooler side of sheaves
When last the sun his autumn tresses shook,   440
And the tann'd harvesters rich armfuls took.
Soon was he quieted to slumbrous rest:
But, ere it crept upon him, he had prest
Peona's busy hand against his lips,
And still, a sleeping, held her finger-tips
In tender pressure. And as a willow keeps
A patient watch over the stream that creeps
Windingly by it, so the quiet maid
Held her in peace: so that a whispering blade
Of grass, a wailful gnat, a bee bustling   450

Down in the blue-bells, or a wren light rustling
Among sere leaves and twigs, might all be heard.

  O magic sleep! O comfortable bird,
That broodest o'er the troubled sea of the mind
Till it is hush'd and smooth! O unconfin'd
Restraint! imprisoned liberty! great key
To golden palaces, strange minstrelsy,
Fountains grotesque, new trees, bespangled caves,
Echoing grottos, full of tumbling waves
And moonlight; aye, to all the mazy world   460
Of silvery enchantment!—who, upfurl'd
Beneath thy drowsy wing a triple hour,
But renovates and lives?—Thus, in the bower,
Endymion was calm'd to life again.
Opening his eyelids with a healthier brain,
He said: 'I feel this thine endearing love
All through my bosom: thou art as a dove
Trembling its closed eyes and sleeked wings
About me; and the pearliest dew not brings
Such morning incense from the fields of May,   470
As do those brighter drops that twinkling stray
From those kind eyes,—the very home and haunt
Of sisterly affection. Can I want
Aught else, aught nearer heaven, than such tears?
Yet dry them up, in bidding hence all fears
That, any longer, I will pass my days
Alone and sad. No, I will once more raise
My voice upon the mountain-heights; once more
Make my horn parley from their foreheads hoar:
Again my trooping hounds their tongues shall loll   480
Around the breathed boar: again I'll poll
The fair-grown yew tree, for a chosen bow:
And, when the pleasant sun is getting low,
Again I'll linger in a sloping mead
To hear the speckled thrushes, and see feed
Our idle sheep. So be thou cheered sweet,
And, if thy lute is here, softly intreat
My soul to keep in its resolved course.'

  Hereat Peona, in their silver source,
Shut her pure sorrow drops with glad exclaim,   490

And took a lute, from which there pulsing came
A lively prelude, fashioning the way
In which her voice should wander. 'Twas a lay
More subtle cadenced, more forest wild
Than Dryope's lone lulling of her child;
And nothing since has floated in the air
So mournful strange. Surely some influence rare
Went, spiritual, through the damsel's hand;
For still, with Delphic emphasis, she spann'd
The quick invisible strings, even though she saw   500
Endymion's spirit melt away and thaw
Before the deep intoxication.
But soon she came, with sudden burst, upon
Her self-possession—swung the lute aside,
And earnestly said: 'Brother, 'tis vain to hide
That thou dost know of things mysterious,
Immortal, starry; such alone could thus
Weigh down thy nature. Hast thou sinn'd in aught
Offensive to the heavenly powers? Caught
A Paphian dove upon a message sent?   510
Thy deathful bow against some deer-herd bent,
Sacred to Dian? Haply, thou hast seen
Her naked limbs among the alders green;
And that, alas! is death. No, I can trace
Something more high perplexing in thy face!'

Endymion look'd at her, and press'd her hand,
And said, 'Art thou so pale, who wast so bland
And merry in our meadows? How is this?
Tell me thine ailment: tell me all amiss!—
Ah! thou hast been unhappy at the change   520
Wrought suddenly in me. What indeed more strange?
Or more complete to overwhelm surmise?
Ambition is no sluggard: 'tis no prize,
That toiling years would put within my grasp,
That I have sigh'd for: with so deadly gasp
No man e'er panted for a mortal love.
So all have set my heavier grief above
These things which happen. Rightly have they done:
I, who still saw the horizontal sun
Heave his broad shoulder o'er the edge of the world,   530

Out-facing Lucifer, and then had hurl'd
My spear aloft, as signal for the chace—
I, who, for very sport of heart, would race
With my own steed from Araby; pluck down
A vulture from his towery perching; frown
A lion into growling, loth retire—
To lose, at once, all my toil breeding fire,
And sink thus low! but I will ease my breast
Of secret grief, here in this bowery nest.

'This river does not see the naked sky,   540
Till it begins to progress silverly
Around the western border of the wood,
Whence, from a certain spot, its winding flood
Seems at the distance like a crescent moon:
And in that nook, the very pride of June,
Had I been used to pass my weary eves;
The rather for the sun unwilling leaves
So dear a picture of his sovereign power,
And I could witness his most kingly hour,
When he doth tighten up the golden reins,   550
And paces leisurely down amber plains
His snorting four. Now when his chariot last
Its beams against the zodiac-lion cast,
There blossom'd suddenly a magic bed
Of sacred ditamy, and poppies red:
At which I wondered greatly, knowing well
That but one night had wrought this flowery spell;
And, sitting down close by, began to muse
What it might mean. Perhaps, thought I, Morpheus,
In passing here, his owlet pinions shook;   560
Or, it may be, ere matron Night uptook
Her ebon urn, young Mercury, by stealth,
Had dipt his rod in it: such garland wealth
Came not by common growth. Thus on I thought,
Until my head was dizzy and distraught.
Moreover, through the dancing poppies stole
A breeze, most softly lulling to my soul;
And shaping visions all about my sight
Of colours, wings, and bursts of spangly light;
The which became more strange, and strange, and dim,   570
And then were gulph'd in a tumultuous swim:

And then I fell asleep. Ah, can I tell
The enchantment that afterwards befel?
Yet it was but a dream: yet such a dream
That never tongue, although it overteem
With mellow utterance, like a cavern spring,
Could figure out and to conception bring
All I beheld and felt. Methought I lay
Watching the zenith, where the milky way
Among the stars in virgin splendour pours;   580
And travelling my eye, until the doors
Of heaven appear'd to open for my flight,
I became loth and fearful to alight
From such high soaring by a downward glance:
So kept me stedfast in that airy trance,
Spreading imaginary pinions wide.
When, presently, the stars began to glide,
And faint away, before my eager view:
At which I sigh'd that I could not pursue,
And dropt my vision to the horizon's verge;   590
And lo! from opening clouds, I saw emerge
The loveliest moon, that ever silver'd o'er
A shell for Neptune's goblet: she did soar
So passionately bright, my dazzled soul
Commingling with her argent spheres did roll
Through clear and cloudy, even when she went
At last into a dark and vapoury tent—
Whereat, methought, the lidless-eyed train
Of planets all were in the blue again.
To commune with those orbs, once more I rais'd   600
My sight right upward: but it was quite dazed
By a bright something, sailing down apace,
Making me quickly veil my eyes and face:
Again I look'd, and, O ye deities,
Who from Olympus watch our destinies!
Whence that completed form of all completeness?
Whence came that high perfection of all sweetness?
Speak stubborn earth, and tell me where, O where
Hast thou a symbol of her golden hair?
Not oat-shaves drooping in the western sun;   610
Not—thy soft hand, fair sister! let me shun
Such follying before thee—yet she had,

Indeed, locks bright enough to make me mad;
And they were simply gordian'd up and braided,
Leaving, in naked comeliness, unshaded,
Her pearl round ears, white neck, and orbed brow;
The which were blended in, I know not how,
With such a paradise of lips and eyes,
Blush-tinted cheeks, half smiles, and faintest sighs,
That, when I think thereon, my spirit clings   620
And plays about its fancy, till the stings
Of human neighbourhood envenom all.
Unto what awful power shall I call?
To what high fane?—Ah! see her hovering feet,
More bluely vein'd, more soft, more whitely sweet
Than those of sea-born Venus, when she rose
From out her cradle shell. The wind out-blows
Her scarf into a fluttering pavilion;
'Tis blue, and over-spangled with a million
Of little eyes, as though thou wert to shed,   630
Over the darkest, lushest blue-bell bed,
Handfuls of daises.'—'Endymion, how strange!
Dream within dream!'—'She took an airy range,
And then, towards me, like a very maid,
Came blushing, waning, willing, and afraid,
And press'd me by the hand: Ah! 'twas too much;
Methought I fainted at the charmed touch,
Yet held my recollection, even as one
Who dives three fathoms where the waters run
Gurgling in beds of coral: for anon,   640
I felt upmounted in that region
Where falling stars dart their artillery forth,
And eagles struggle with the buffeting north
That balances the heavy meteor-stone;—
Felt too, I was not fearful, nor alone,
But lapp'd and lull'd along the dangerous sky.
Soon, as it seem'd, we left our journeying high,
And straightway into frightful eddies swoop'd;
Such as ay muster where grey time has scoop'd
Huge dens and caverns in a mountain's side: 650
There hollow sounds arous'd me, and I sigh'd
To faint once more by looking on my bliss—
I was distracted; madly did I kiss

The wooing arms which held me, and did give
My eyes at once to death: but 'twas to live,
To take in draughts of life from the gold fount
Of kind and passionate looks; to count, and count
The moments, by some greedy help that seem'd
A second self, that each might be redeem'd
And plunder'd of its load of blessedness.   660
Ah, desperate mortal! I ev'n dar'd to press
Her very cheek against my crowned lip,
And, at that moment, felt my body dip
Into a warmer air: a moment more,
Our feet were soft in flowers. There was store
Of newest joys upon that alp. Sometimes
A scent of violets, and blossoming limes,
Loiter'd around us; then of honey cells,
Made delicate from all white-flower bells;
And once, above the edges of our nest,   670
An arch face peep'd,—an Oread as I guess'd.

  'Why did I dream that sleep o'er-powered me
In midst of all this heaven? Why not see,
Far off, the shadows of his pinions dark,
And stare them from me? But no, like a spark
That needs must die, although its little beam
Reflects upon a diamond, my sweet dream
Fell into nothing—into stupid sleep.
And so it was, until a gentle creep,
A careful moving caught my waking ears,   680
And up I started: Ah! my sighs, my tears,
My clenched hands;—for lo! the poppies hung
Dew-dabbled on their stalks, the ouzel sung
A heavy ditty, and the sullen day
Had chidden herald Hesperus away,
With leaden looks: the solitary breeze
Bluster'd, and slept, and its wild self did teaze
With wayward melancholy; and I thought,
Mark me, Peona! that sometimes it brought
Faint fare-thee-wells, and sigh-shrilled adieus!—   690
Away I wander'd—all the pleasant hues
Of heaven and earth had faded: deepest shades
Were deepest dungeons; heaths and sunny glades

Were full of pestilent light; our taintless rills
Seem'd sooty, and o'er-spread with upturn'd gills
Of dying fish; the vermeil rose had blown
In frightful scarlet, and its thorns out-grown
Like spiked aloe. If an innocent bird
Before my heedless footsteps stirr'd, and stirr'd
In little journeys, I beheld in it   700
A disguis'd demon, missioned to knit
My soul with under darkness; to entice
My stumblings down some monstrous precipice:
Therefore I eager followed, and did curse
The disappointment. Time, that aged nurse,
Rock'd me to patience. Now, thank gentle heaven!
These things, with all their comfortings, are given
To my down-sunken hours, and with thee,
Sweet sister, help to stem the ebbing sea
Of weary life.'

           Thus ended he, and both   710
Sat silent: for the maid was very loth
To answer; feeling well that breathed words
Would all be lost, unheard, and vain as swords
Against the enchased crocodile, or leaps
Of grasshoppers against the sun. She weeps,
And wonders; struggles to devise some blame;
To put on such a look as would say, *Shame
On this poor weakness!* but, for all her strife,
She could as soon have crush'd away the life
From a sick dove. At length, to break the pause,   720
She said with trembling chance: 'Is this the cause?
This all? Yet it is strange, and sad, alas!
That one who through this middle earth should pass
Most like a sojourning demi-god, and leave
His name upon the harp-string, should achieve
No higher bard than simple maidenhood,
Singing alone, and fearfully,—how the blood
Left his young cheek; and how he used to stray
He knew not where; and how he would say, *nay*,
If any said 'twas love: and yet 'twas love;   730
What could it be but love? How a ring-dove
Let fall a sprig of yew tree in his path;

And how he died: and then, that love doth scathe
The gentle heart, as northern blasts do roses;
And then the ballad of his sad life closes
With sighs, and an alas!—Endymion!
Be rather in the trumpet's mouth,—anon
Among the winds at large—that all may hearken!
Although, before the crystal heavens darken,
I watch and dote upon the silver lakes   740
Pictur'd in western cloudiness, that takes
The semblance of gold rocks and bright gold sands,
Islands, and creeks, and amber-fretted strands
With horses prancing o'er them, palaces
And towers of amethyst,—would I so tease
My pleasant days, because I could not mount
Into those regions? The Morphean fount
Of that fine element that visions, dreams,
And fitful whims of sleep are made of, streams
Into its airy channels with so subtle,   750
So thin a breathing, not the spider's shuttle,
Circled a million times within the space
Of a swallow's nest-door, could delay a trace,
A tinting of its quality: how light
Must dreams themselves be; seeing they're more slight
Than the mere nothing that engenders them!
Then wherefore sully the entrusted gem
Of high and noble life with thoughts so sick?
Why pierce high-fronted honour to the quick
For nothing but a dream?' Hereat the youth   760
Look'd up: a conflicting of shame and ruth
Was in his plaited brow: yet, his eyelids
Widened a little, as when Zephyr bids
A little breeze to creep between the fans
Of careless butterflies: amid his pains
He seem'd to taste a drop of manna-dew,
Full palatable; and a colour grew
Upon his cheek, while thus he lifeful spake.

'Peona! ever have I long'd to slake
My thirst for the world's praises: nothing base,   770
No merely slumberous phantasm, could unlace
The stubborn canvas for my voyage prepar'd—

Though now 'tis tatter'd; leaving my bark bar'd
And sullenly drifting: yet my higher hope
Is of too wide, too rainbow-large a scope,
To fret at myriads of earthly wrecks.
Wherein lies happiness? In that which becks
Our ready minds to fellowship divine,
A fellowship with essence; till we shine,
Full alchemiz'd, and free of space. Behold   780
The clear religion of heaven! Fold
A rose leaf round thy finger's taperness,
And soothe thy lips: hist, when the airy stress
Of music's kiss impregnates the free winds,
And with a sympathetic touch unbinds
Eolian magic from their lucid wombs:
The old songs waken from enclouded tombs;
Old ditties sigh above their father's grave;
Ghosts of melodious prophecyings rave
Round every spot where trod Apollo's foot;   790
Bronze clarions awake, and faintly bruit,
Where long ago a giant battle was;
And, from the turf, a lullaby doth pass
In every place where infant Orpheus slept.
Feel we these things?—that moment have we stept
Into a sort of oneness, and our state
Is like a floating spirit's. But there are
Richer entanglements, enthralments far
More self-destroying, leading, by degrees,
To the chief intensity: the crown of these   800
Is made of love and friendship, and sits high
Upon the forehead of humanity.
All its more ponderous and bulky worth
Is friendship, whence there ever issues forth
A steady splendour; but at the tip-top,
There hangs by unseen film, an orbed drop
Of light, and that is love: its influence,
Thrown in our eyes, genders a novel sense,
At which we start and fret; till in the end,
Melting into its radiance, we blend,   810
Mingle, and so become a part of it,—
Nor with aught else can our souls interknit
So wingedly: when we combine therewith,

Life's self is nourish'd by its proper pith,
And we are nurtur'd like a pelican brood.
Aye, so delicious is the unsating food,
That men, who might have tower'd in the van
Of all the congregated world, to fan
And winnow from the coming step of time
All chaff of custom, wipe away all slime   820
Left by men-slugs and human serpentry,
Have been content to let occasion die,
Whilst they did sleep in love's elysium.
And, truly, I would rather be struck dumb,
Than speak against this ardent listlessness:
For I have ever thought that it might bless
The world with benefits unknowingly;
As does the nightingale, upperched high,
And cloister'd among cool and bunched leaves—
She sings but to her love, nor e'er conceives   830
How tiptoe Night holds back her dark-grey hood.
Just so may love, although 'tis understood
The mere commingling of passionate breath,
Produce more than our searching witnesseth:
What I know not: but who, of men, can tell
That flowers would bloom, or that green fruit would swell
To melting pulp, that fish would have bright mail,
The earth its dower of river, wood, and vale,
The meadows runnels, runnels pebble-stones,
The seed its harvest, or the lute its tones,   840
Tones ravishment, or ravishment its sweet,
If human souls did never kiss and greet?

'Now, if this earthly love has power to make
Men's being mortal, immortal; to shake
Ambition from their memories, and brim
Their measure of content; what merest whim,
Seems all this poor endeavour after fame,
To one, who keeps within his stedfast aim
A love immortal, an immortal too.
Look not so wilder'd; for these things are true,   850
And never can be born of atomies
That buzz about our slumbers, like brain-flies,
Leaving us fancy-sick. No, no, I'm sure,

My restless spirit never could endure
To brood so long upon one luxury,
Unless it did, though fearfully, espy
A hope beyond the shadow of a dream.
My sayings will the less obscured seem,
When I have told thee how my waking sight
Has made me scruple whether that same night   860
Was pass'd in dreaming. Hearken, sweet Peona!
Beyond the matron-temple of Latona,
Which we should see but for these darkening boughs,
Lies a deep hollow, from whose ragged brows
Bushes and trees do lean all round athwart,
And meet so nearly, that with wings outraught,
And spreaded tail, a vulture could not glide
Past them, but he must brush on every side.
Some moulder'd steps lead into this cool cell,
Far as the slabbed margin of a well,   870
Whose patient level peeps its crystal eye
Right upward, through the bushes, to the sky.
Oft have I brought thee flowers, on their stalks set
Like vestal primroses, but dark velvet
Edges them round, and they have golden pits:
'Twas there I got them, from the gaps and slits
In a mossy stone, that sometimes was my seat,
When all above was faint with mid-day heat.
And there in strife no burning thoughts to heed,
I'd bubble up the water through a reed;   880
So reaching back to boy-hood: make me ships
Of moulted feathers, touchwood, alder chips,
With leaves stuck in them; and the Neptune be
Of their petty ocean. Oftener, heavily,
When love-lorn hours had left me less a child,
I sat contemplating the figures wild
Of o'er-head clouds melting the mirror through.
Upon a day, while thus I watch'd, by flew
A cloudy Cupid, with his bow and quiver;
So plainly character'd, no breeze would shiver   890
The happy chance: so happy, I was fain
To follow it upon the open plain,
And, therefore, was just going; when, behold!
A wonder, fair as any I have told—

The same bright face I tasted in my sleep,
Smiling in the clear well. My heart did leap
Through the cool depth.—It moved as if to flee—
I started up, when lo! refreshfully,
There came upon my face, in plenteous showers,
Dew-drops, and dewy buds, and leaves, and flowers,   900
Wrapping all objects from my smothered sight,
Bathing my spirit in a new delight.
Aye, such a breathless honey-feel of bliss
Alone preserved me from the drear abyss
Of death, for the fair form had gone again.
Pleasure is oft a visitant; but pain
Clings cruelly to us, like the gnawing sloth
On the deer's tender haunches: late, and loth,
'Tis scar'd away by slow returning pleasure.
How sickening, how dark the dreadful leisure   910
Of weary days, made deeper exquisite,
By a fore-knowledge of unslumbrous night!
Like sorrow came upon me, heavier still,
Than when I wander'd from the poppy hill:
And a whole age of lingering moments crept
Sluggishly by, ere more contentment swept
Away at once the deadly yellow spleen.
Yes, thrice have I this fair enchantment seen;
Once more been tortured with renewed life.
When last the wintry gusts gave over strife   920
With the conquering sun of spring, and left the skies
Warm and serene, but yet with moistened eyes
In pity of the shatter'd infant buds,—
That time thou didst adorn, with amber studs,
My hunting cap, because I laugh'd and smil'd,
Chatted with thee, and many days exil'd
All torment from my breast;—'twas even then,
Straying about, yet, coop'd up in the den
Of helpless discontent,—hurling my lance
From place to place, and following at chance,   930
At last, by hap, through some young trees it struck,
And, plashing among bedded pebbles, stuck
In the middle of a brook,—whose silver ramble
Down twenty little falls, through reeds and bramble,
Tracing along, it brought me to a cave,

Whence it ran brightly forth, and white did lave
The nether sides of mossy stones and rock,—
'Mong which it gurgled blythe adieus, to mock
Its own sweet grief at parting. Overhead,
Hung a lush screen of drooping weeds, and spread 940
Thick, as to curtain up some wood-nymph's home.
"Ah! impious mortal, whither do I roam?"
Said I, low voic'd: "Ah, whither! 'Tis the grot
Of Proserpine, when Hell, obscure and hot,
Doth her resign; and where her tender hands
She dabbles, on the cool and sluicy sands:
Or 'tis the cell of Echo, where she sits,
And babbles thorough silence, till her wits
Are gone in tender madness, and anon,
Faints into sleep, with many a dying tone 950
Of sadness. O that she would take my vows,
And breathe them sighingly among the boughs,
To sue her gentle ears for whose fair head,
Daily, I pluck sweet flowerets from their bed,
And weave them dyingly—send honey-whispers
Round every leaf, that all those gentle lispers
May sigh my love unto her pitying!
O charitable echo! hear, and sing
This ditty to her!—tell her"—so I stay'd
My foolish tongue, and listening, half afraid, 960
Stood stupefied with my own empty folly,
And blushing for the freaks of melancholy.
Salt tears were coming, when I heard my name
Most fondly lipp'd, and then these accents came:
"Endymion! the cave is secreter
Than the isle of Delos. Echo hence shall stir
No sighs but sigh-warm kisses, or light noise
Of thy combing hand, the while it travelling cloys
And trembles through my labyrinthine hair."
At that oppress'd I hurried in.—Ah! where 970
Are those swift moments? Whither are they fled?
I'll smile no more, Peona; nor will wed
Sorrow the way to death; but patiently
Bear up against it: so farewel, sad sigh;
And come instead demurest meditation,
To occupy me wholly, and to fashion

My pilgrimage for the world's dusky brink.
No more will I count over, link by link,
My chain of grief: no longer strive to find
A half-forgetfulness in mountain wind   980
Blustering about my ears: aye, thou shalt see,
Dearest of sisters, what my life shall be;
What a calm round of hours shall make my days.
There is a paly flame of hope that plays
Where'er I look: but yet, I'll say 'tis naught—
And here I bid it die. Have not I caught,
Already, a more healthy countenance?
By this the sun is setting; we may chance
Meet some of our near-dwellers with my car.'

    This said, he rose, faint-smiling like a star   990
Through autumn mists, and took Peona's hand:
They stept into the boat, and launch'd from land.

Book III

There are who lord it o'er their fellow-men
With most prevailing tinsel: who unpen
Their baaing vanities, to browse away
The comfortable green and juicy hay
From human pastures; or, O torturing fact!
Who, through an idiot blink, will see unpack'd
Fire-branded foxes to sear up and singe
Our gold and ripe-ear'd hopes. With not one tinge
Of sanctuary splendour, not a sight
Able to face an owl's, they still are dight   10
By the blear-eyed nations in empurpled vests,
And crowns, and turbans. With unladen breasts,
Save of blown self-applause, they proudly mount
To their spirit's perch, their being's high account,
Their tiptop nothings, their dull skies, their thrones—
Amid the fierce intoxicating tones
Of trumpets, shoutings, and belabour'd drums,
And sudden cannon. Ah! how all this hums,
In wakeful ears, like uproar past and gone—
Like thunder clouds that spake to Babylon,   20
And set those old Chaldeans to their tasks.—

Are then regalities all gilded masks?
No, there are throned seats unscalable
But by a patient wing, a constant spell,
Or by ethereal things that, unconfin'd,
Can make a ladder of the eternal wind,
And poise about in cloudy thunder-tents
To watch the abysm-birth of elements.
Aye, 'bove the withering of old-lipp'd Fate
A thousand Powers keep religious state,   30
In water, fiery realm, and airy bourne;
And, silent as a consecrated urn,
Hold sphery sessions for a season due.
Yet few of these far majesties, ah, few!
Have bared their operations to this globe—
Few, who with gorgeous pageantry enrobe
Our piece of heaven—whose benevolence
Shakes hand with our own Ceres; every sense
Filling with spiritual sweets to plenitude,
As bees gorge full their cells. And, by the feud   40
'Twixt Nothing and Creation, I here swear,
Eterne Apollo! that thy Sister fair
Is of all these the gentlier-mightiest.
When thy gold breath is misting in the west,
She unobserved steals unto her throne,
And there she sits most meek and most alone;
As if she had not pomp subservient;
As if thine eye, high Poet! was not bent
Towards her with the Muses in thine heart;
As if the ministring stars kept not apart,   50
Waiting for silver-footed messages.
O Moon! the oldest shades 'mong oldest trees
Feel palpitations when thou lookest in:
O Moon! old boughs lisp forth a holier din
The while they feel thine airy fellowship.
Thou dost bless every where, with silver lip
Kissing dead things to life. The sleeping kine,
Couched in thy brightness, dream of fields divine:
Innumerable mountains rise, and rise,
Ambitious for the hallowing of thine eyes;   60
And yet thy benediction passeth not
One obscure hiding-place, one little spot

Where pleasure may be sent: the nested wren
Has thy fair face within its tranquil ken,
And from beneath a sheltering ivy leaf
Takes glimpses of thee; thou art a relief
To the poor patient oyster, where it sleeps
Within its pearly house.—The mighty deeps,
The monstrous sea is thine—the myriad sea!
O Moon! far-spooming Ocean bows to thee,   70
And Tellus feels his forehead's cumbrous load.

Cynthia! where art thou now? What far abode
Of green or silvery bower doth enshrine
Such utmost beauty? Alas, thou dost pine
For one as sorrowful: thy cheek is pale
For one whose cheek is pale: thou dost bewail
His tears, who weeps for thee. Where dost thou sigh?
Ah! surely that light peeps from Vesper's eye,
Or what a thing is love! 'Tis She, but lo!
How chang'd, how full of ache, how gone in woe!   80
She dies at the thinnest cloud; her loveliness
Is wan on Neptune's blue: yet there's a stress
Of love-spangles, just off yon cape of trees,
Dancing upon the waves, as if to please
The curly foam with amorous influence.
O, not so idle: for down-glancing thence
She fathoms eddies, and runs wild about
O'erwhelming water-courses; scaring out
The thorny sharks from hiding-holes, and fright'ning
Their savage eyes with unaccustomed lightning.   90
Where will the splendour be content to reach?
O love! how potent hast thou been to teach
Strange journeyings! Wherever beauty dwells,
In gulf or aerie, mountains or deep dells,
In light, in gloom, in star or blazing sun,
Thou pointest out the way, and straight 'tis won.
Amid his toil thou gav'st Leander breath;
Thou leddest Orpheus through the gleams of death;
Thou madest Pluto bear thin element;
And now, O winged Chieftain! thou hast sent   100
A moon-beam to the deep, deep water-world,
To find Endymion.

. . . .

'What is there in thee, Moon! that thou shouldst move
My heart so potently? When yet a child
I oft have dried my tears when thou hast smil'd.
Thou seem'dst my sister: hand in hand we went
From eve to morn across the firmament.
No apples would I gather from the tree,
Till thou hadst cool'd their cheeks deliciously:
No tumbling water ever spake romance,
But when my eyes with thine thereon could dance: 150
No woods were green enough, no bower divine,
Until thou liftedst up thine eyelids fine:
In sowing time ne'er would I dibble take,
Or drop a seed, till thou wast wide awake;
And, in the summer tide of blossoming,
No one but thee hath heard me blithly sing
And mesh my dewy flowers all the night.
No melody was like a passing spright
If it went not to solemnize thy reign.
Yes, in my boyhood, every joy and pain   160
By thee were fashion'd to the self-same end;
And as I grew in years, still didst thou blend
With all my ardours: thou wast the deep glen;
Thou wast the mountain-top—the sage's pen—
The poet's harp—the voice of friends—the sun;
Thou wast the river—thou wast glory won;
Thou wast my clarion's blast—thou wast my steed—
My goblet full of wine—my topmost deed:—
Thou wast the charm of women, lovely Moon!
O what a wild and harmonized tune   170
My spirit struck from all the beautiful!
On some bright essence could I lean, and lull
Myself to immortality: I prest
Nature's soft pillow in a wakeful rest.
But, gentle Orb! there came a nearer bliss—
My strange love came—Felicity's abyss!
She came, and thou didst fade, and fade away—
Yet not entirely; no, thy starry sway
Has been an under-passion to this hour.
Now I begin to feel thine orby power   180

Is coming fresh upon me: O be kind,
Keep back thine influence, and do not blind
My sovereign vision.—Dearest love, forgive
That I can think away from thee and live!—
Pardon me, airy planet, that I prize
One thought beyond thine argent luxuries!
How far beyond!' At this a surpris'd start
Frosted the springing verdure of his heart;
For as he lifted up his eyes to swear
How his own goddess was past all things fair,   190
He saw far in the concave green of the sea
An old man sitting calm and peacefully.
Upon a weeded rock this old man sat,
And his white hair was awful, and a mat
Of weeds were cold beneath his cold thin feet;
And, ample as the largest winding-sheet,
A cloak of blue wrapp'd up his aged bones,
O'erwrought with symbols by the deepest groans
Of ambitious magic: every ocean-form
Was woven in with black distinctness; storm,   200
And calm, and whispering, and hideous roar
Quicksand and whirlpool, and deserted shore
Were emblem'd in the woof; with every shape
That skims, or dives, or sleeps, 'twixt cape and cape.
The gulphing whale was like a dot in the spell,
Yet look upon it, and 'twould size and swell
To its huge self; and the minutest fish
Would pass the very hardest gazer's wish,
And shew his little eye's anatomy.
Then there was pictur'd the regality   210
Of Neptune; and the sea nymphs round his state,
In beauteous vassalage, look up and wait.
Beside this old man lay a pearly wand,
And in his lap a book, the which he conn'd
So stedfastly, that the new denizen
Had time to keep him in amazed ken,
To mark these shadowings, and stand in awe.

The old man rais'd his hoary head and saw
The wilder'd stranger—seeming not to see,
His features were so lifeless. Suddenly   220

He woke as from a trance; his snow-white brows
Went arching up, and like two magic ploughs
Furrow'd deep wrinkles in his forehead large,
Which kept as fixedly as rocky marge,
Till round his wither'd lips had gone a smile.
Then up he rose, like one whose tedious toil
Had watch'd for years in forlorn hermitage,
Who had not from mid-life to utmost age
Eas'd in one accent his o'er-burdened soul,
Even to the trees. He rose: he grasp'd his stole,   230
With convuls'd clenches waving it abroad,
And in a voice of solemn joy, that aw'd
Echo into oblivion, he said:—

'Thou art the man! Now shall I lay my head
In peace upon my watery pillow: now
Sleep will come smoothly to my weary brow.
O Jove! I shall be young again, be young!
O shell-borne Neptune, I am pierc'd and stung
With new-born life! What shall I do? Where go,
When I have cast this serpent-skin of woe?—   240
I'll swim to the syrens, and one moment listen
Their melodies, and see their long hair glisten;
Anon upon that giant's arm I'll be,
That writhes about the roots of Sicily:
To northern seas I'll in a twinkling sail,
And mount upon the snortings of a whale
To some black cloud; thence down I'll madly sweep
On forked lightning, to the deepest deep,
Where through some sucking pool I will be hurl'd
With rapture to the other side of the world!   250
O, I am full of gladness! Sisters three,
I bow full hearted to your old decree!
Yes, every god be thank'd, and power benign,
For I no more shall wither, droop, and pine.
Thou art the man!' Endymion started back
Dismay'd; and, like a wretch from whom the rack
Tortures hot breath, and speech of agony,
Mutter'd: 'What lonely death am I to die
In this cold region? Will he let me freeze,
And float my brittle limbs o'er polar seas?   260

Or will he touch me with his searing hand,
And leave a black memorial on the sand?
Or tear me piece-meal with a bony saw,
And keep me as a chosen food to draw
His magian fish through hated fire and flame?
O misery of hell! resistless, tame,
Am I to be burnt up? No, I will shout,
Until the gods through heaven's blue look out!—
O Tartarus! but some few days agone
Her soft arms were entwining me, and on   270
Her voice I hung like fruit among green leaves:
Her lips were all my own, and—ah, ripe sheaves
Of happiness! ye on the stubble droop,
But never may be garner'd. I must stoop
My head, and kiss death's foot. Love! love, farewell!
Is there no hope from thee? This horrid spell
Would melt at thy sweet breath.—By Dian's hind
Feeding from her white fingers, on the wind
I see thy streaming hair! and now, by Pan,
I care not for this old mysterious man!'   280

.   .   .   .

Book IV

Muse of my native land! loftiest Muse!
O first-born on the mountains! by the hues
Of heaven on the spiritual air begot:
Long didst thou sit alone in northern grot,
While yet our England was a wolfish den;
Before our forests heard the talk of men;
Before the first of Druids was a child;—
Long didst thou sit amid our regions wild
Rapt in a deep prophetic solitude.
There came an eastern voice of solemn mood:—   10
Yet wast thou patient. Then sang forth the Nine,
Apollo's garland:—yet didst thou divine
Such home-bred glory, that they cry'd in vain,
'Come hither, Sister of the Island!' Plain
Spake fair Ausonia; and once more she spake
A higher summons:—still didst thou betake
Thee to thy native hopes. O thou hast won

A full accomplishment! The thing is done,
Which undone, these our latter days had risen
On barren souls. Great Muse, thou know'st what prison,   20
Of flesh and bone, curbs, and confines, and frets
Our spirit's wings: despondency besets
Our pillows; and the fresh to-morrow morn
Seems to give forth its light in very scorn
Of our dull, uninspired, snail-paced lives.
Long have I said, how happy he who shrives
To thee! But then I thought on poets gone,
And could not pray: nor can I now—so on
I move to the end in lowliness of heart.—

   'Ah, woe is me! that I should fondly part   30
From my dear native land! Ah, foolish maid!
Glad was the hour, when, with thee, myriads bade
Adieu to Ganges and their pleasant fields!
To one so friendless the clear freshet yields
A bitter coolness; the ripe grape is sour:
Yet I would have, great gods! but one short hour
Of native air—let me but die at home.'

   Endymion to heaven's airy dome
Was offering up a hecatomb of vows,
When these words reach'd him. Whereupon he bows   40
His head through thorny-green entanglement
Of underwood, and to the sound is bent,
Anxious as hind towards her hidden fawn.

   'Is no one near to help me? No fair dawn
Of life from charitable voice? No sweet saying
To set my dull and sadden'd spirit playing?
No hand to toy with mine? No lips so sweet
That I may worship them? No eyelids meet
To twinkle on my bosom? No one dies
Before me, till from these enslaving eyes   50
Redemption sparkles!—I am sad and lost.'

   Thou, Carian lord, hadst better have been tost
Into a whirlpool. Vanish into air,
Warm mountaineer! for canst thou only bear

A woman's sigh alone and in distress?
See not her charms! Is Phœbe passionless?
Phœbe is fairer far—O gaze no more:—
Yet if thou wilt behold all beauty's store,
Behold her panting in the forest grass!
Do not those curls of glossy jet surpass   60
For tenderness the arms so idly lain
Amongst them? Feelest not a kindred pain,
To see such lovely eyes in swimming search
After some warm delight, that seems to perch
Dovelike in the dim cell lying beyond
Their upper lids?—Hist!

      'O for Hermes' wand,
To touch this flower into human shape!
That woodland Hyacinthus could escape
From his green prison, and here kneeling down
Call me his queen, his second life's fair crown!   70
Ah me, how I could love!—My soul doth melt
For the unhappy youth—Love! I have felt
So faint a kindness, such a meek surrender
To what my own full thoughts had made too tender,
That but for tears my life had fled away!—
Ye deaf and senseless minutes of the day,
And thou, old forest, hold ye this for true,
There is no lightning, no authentic dew
But in the eye of love: there's not a sound,
Melodious howsoever, can confound   80
The heavens and earth in one to such a death
As doth the voice of love: there's not a breath
Will mingle kindly with the meadow air,
Till it has panted round, and stolen a share
Of passion from the heart!'—

      Upon a bough
He leant, wretched. He surely cannot now
Thirst for another love: O impious,
That he can even dream upon it thus!—
Thought he, 'Why am I not as are the dead,
Since to a woe like this I have been led   90
Through the dark earth, and through the wondrous sea?

Goddess! I love thee not the less: from thee
By Juno's smile I turn not—no, no, no—
While the great waters are at ebb and flow.—
I have a triple soul! O fond pretence—
For both, for both my love is so immense,
I feel my heart is cut for them in twain.'

And so he groan'd, as one by beauty slain.
The lady's heart beat quick, and he could see
Her gentle bosom heave tumultuously.   100
He sprang from his green covert: there she lay,
Sweet as a muskrose upon new-made hay;
With all her limbs on tremble, and her eyes
Shut softly up alive. To speak he tries.
'Fair damsel, pity me! Forgive that I
Thus violate thy bower's sanctity!
O pardon me, for I am full of grief—
Grief born of thee, young angel! fairest thief!
Who stolen hast away the wings wherewith
I was to top the heavens. Dear maid, sith   110
Thou art my executioner, and I feel
Loving and hatred, misery and weal,
Will in a few short hours be nothing to me,
And all my story that much passion slew me;
Do smile upon the evening of my days:
And, for my tortur'd brain begins to craze,
Be thou my nurse; and let me understand
How dying I shall kiss that lily hand.—
Dost weep for me? Then should I be content.
Scowl on, ye fates! until the firmament   120
Outblackens Erebus, and the full-cavern'd earth
Crumbles into itself. By the cloud girth
Of Jove, those tears have given me a thirst
To meet oblivion.'—As her heart would burst
The maiden sobb'd awhile, and then replied:
'Why must such desolation betide
As that thou speakest of? Are not these green nooks
Empty of all misfortune? Do the brooks
Utter a gorgon voice? Does yonder thrush,
Schooling itself half-fledg'd little ones to brush   130
About the dewy forest, whisper tales?—

Speak not of grief, young stranger, or cold snails
Will slime the rose to night. Though if thou wilt,
Methinks 'twould be a guilt—a very guilt—
Not to companion thee, and sigh away
The light—the dusk—the dark—till break of day!'
'Dear lady,' said Endymion, ''tis past:
I love thee! and my days can never last.
That I may pass in patience still speak:
Let me have music dying, and I seek   140
No more delight—I bid adieu to all.
Didst thou not after other climates call,
And murmur about Indian streams?'—Then she,
Sitting beneath the midmost forest tree,
For pity sang this roundelay—

    'O Sorrow,
    Why dost borrow
The natural hue of health, from vermeil lips?—
    To give maiden blushes
    To the white rose bushes?   150
Or is't thy dewy hand the daisy tips?

    'O Sorrow,
    Why dost borrow
The lustrous passion from a falcon-eye?—
    To give the glow-worm light?
    Or, on a moonless light,
To tinge, on syren shores, the salt sea-spry?

    'O Sorrow,
    Why dost borrow
The mellow ditties from a mourning tongue?—   160
    To give at evening pale
    Unto the nightingale,
That thou mayst listen the cold dews among?

    'O Sorrow,
    Why dost borrow
Heart's lightness from the merriment of May?—
    A lover would not tread
    A cowslip on the head,

Though he should dance from eve till peep of day—
     Nor any drooping flower 170
     Held sacred for thy bower,
Wherever he may sport himself and play.

     'To Sorrow,
     I bade good-morrow,
And thought to leave her far away behind;
     But cheerly, cheerly,
     She loves me dearly;
She is so constant to me, and so kind:
     I would deceive her
     And so leave her, 180
But ah! she is so constant and so kind.

'Beneath my palm trees, by the river side,
I sat a weeping: in the whole world wide
There was no one to ask me why I wept,—
     And so I kept
Brimming the water-lily cups with tears
     Cold as my fears.

'Beneath my palm trees, by the river side,
I sat a weeping: what enamour'd bride,
Cheated by shadowy wooer from the clouds, 190
     But hides and shrouds
Beneath dark palm trees by a river side?

'And as I sat, over the light blue hills
There came a noise of revellers: the rills
Into the wide stream came of purple hue—
     'Twas Bacchus and his crew!
The earnest trumpet spake, and silver thrills
From kissing cymbals made a merry din—
     'Twas Bacchus and his kin!
Like to a moving vintage down they came, 200
Crown'd with green leaves, and faces all on flame;
All madly dancing through the pleasant valley,
     To scare thee, Melancholy!
O then, O then, thou wast a simple name!
And I forgot thee, as the berried holly

By shepherds is forgotten, when, in June,
Tall chestnuts keep away the sun and moon:—
      I rush'd into the folly!

'Within his car, aloft, young Bacchus stood,
Trifling his ivy-dart, in dancing mood,   210
      With sidelong laughing;
And little rills of crimson wine imbrued
His plump white arms, and shoulders, enough white
      For Venus' pearly bite:
And near him rode Silenus on his ass,
Pelted with flowers as he on did pass
      Tipsily quaffing.

'Whence came ye, merry Damsels! whence came ye!
So many, and so many, and such glee?
Why have ye left your bowers desolate,   220
      Your lutes, and gentler fate?—
"We follow Bacchus! Bacchus on the wing,
      A conquering!
Bacchus, young Bacchus! good or ill betide,
We dance before him thorough kingdoms wide:—
Come hither, lady fair, and joined be
      To our wild minstrelsy!"

'Whence came ye, jolly Satyrs! whence came ye!
So many, and so many, and such glee?
Why have ye left your forest haunts, why left   230
      Your nuts in oak-tree cleft?—
"For wine, for wine we left our kernel tree;
For wine we left our heath, and yellow brooms,
      And cold mushrooms;
For wine we follow Bacchus through the earth;
Great God of breathless cups and chirping mirth!—
Come hither, lady fair, and joined be
      To our mad minstrelsy!"

'Over wide streams and mountains great we went,
And, save when Bacchus kept his ivy tent,   240
Onward the tiger and the leopard pants,
      With Asian elephants:

Onward these myriads—with song and dance,
With zebras striped, and sleek Arabians' prance,
Web-footed alligators, crocodiles,
Bearing upon their scaly backs, in files,
Plump infant laughers mimicking the coil
Of seamen, and stout galley-rowers' toil:
With toying oars and silken sails they glide,
      Nor care for wind and tide.   250

'Mounted on panthers' fur and lions' manes,
From rear to van they scour about the plains;
A three days' journey in a moment done:
And always, at the rising of the sun,
About the wilds they hunt with spear and horn,
      On spleenful unicorn.

'I saw Osirian Egypt kneel adown
      Before the vine-wreath crown!
I saw parch'd Abyssinia rouse and sing
      To the silver cymbals' ring!   260
I saw the whelming vintage hotly pierce
      Old Tartary the fierce!
The kings of Inde their jewel-sceptres vail,
And from their treasures scatter pearled hail;
Great Brahma from his mystic heaven groans,
      And all his priesthood moans;
Before young Bacchus' eye-wink turning pale.—
Into these regions came I following him,
Sick hearted, weary—so I took a whim
To stray away into these forests drear   270
      Alone, without a peer:
And I have told thee all thou mayest hear.

      'Young stranger!
      I've been a ranger
In search of pleasure throughout every clime:
      Alas, 'tis not for me!
      Bewitch'd I sure must be,
To lose in grieving all my maiden prime.

      'Come then, Sorrow!
      Sweetest Sorrow!   280

Like an own babe I nurse thee on my breast:
I thought to leave thee
And deceive thee,
But now of all the world I love thee best.

'There is not one,
No, no, not one
But thee to comfort a poor lonely maid;
Thou art her mother,
And her brother,
Her playmate, and her wooer in the shade.'   290

.   .   .   .

On Oxford

1

The Gothic looks solemn,
The plain Doric column
Supports an old Bishop and Crosier;
The mouldering arch,
Shaded o'er by a larch
Stands next door to Wilson the Hosier.

2

Vice—that is, by turns,—
O'er pale faces mourns
The black tassell'd trencher and common hat;
The Chantry boy sings,   10
The Steeple-bell rings,
And as for the Chancellor—*dominat.*

3

There are plenty of trees,
And plenty of ease,
And plenty of fat deer for Parsons;
And when it is venison,
Short is the benison,—
Then each on a leg or thigh fastens.

'In drear nighted December'

In drear nighted December
   Too happy, happy tree
Thy branches ne'er remember
   Their green felicity—
The north cannot undo them
With a sleety whistle through them
Nor frozen thawings glew them
   From budding at the prime—

In drear nighted December
   Too happy happy Brook   10
Thy bubblings ne'er remember
   Apollo's Summer look
But with a sweet forgetting
They stay their crystal fretting
Never never petting
   About the frozen time—

Ah! would 'twere so with many
   A gentle girl and boy—
But were there ever any
   Writh'd not of passed joy: 20
The feel of not to feel it
When there is none to heal it
Nor numbed sense to steel it
   Was never said in rhyme—

'Before he went to live with owls and bats'

Before he went to live with owls and bats,
   Nebuchadnezzar had an ugly dream,
   Worse than a Housewife's, when she thinks her cream
Made a Naumachia for mice and rats:
So scared, he sent for that 'good king of cats,'
   Young Daniel, who did straightway pluck the beam
   From out his eye, and said—'I do not deem

Your sceptre worth a straw, your cushions old door mats.'
A horrid Nightmare, similar somewhat,
 Of late has haunted a most valiant crew   10
  Of Loggerheads and Chapmen;—we are told
That any Daniel, though he be a sot,
 Can make their lying lips turn pale of hue,
  By drawling out—'Ye are that head of gold!'

To Mrs Reynoldse's Cat

Cat! who hast past thy Grand Climacteric,
 How many mice and Rats hast in thy days
 Destroyed?—how many tit bits stolen? Gaze
With those bright languid segments green and prick
Those velvet ears—but prythee do not stick
 Thy latent talons in me—and upraise
 Thy gentle mew—and tell me all thy frays
Of Fish and Mice and Rats and tender chick.
Nay look not down, nor lick thy dainty wrists—
 For all the weezy Asthma—and for all   10
Thy tail's tip is nicked off—and though the fists
 Of many a Maid have given thee many a mawl
Still is that fur as soft as when the lists
 In youth thou enterd'st on glass bottled wall—

Lines on seeing a Lock of Milton's hair

  Chief of organic Numbers!
   Old Scholar of the Spheres!
  Thy Spirit never slumbers,
   But rolls about our ears
  For ever, and for ever:
  O, what a mad endeavour
   Worketh he,
 Who, to thy sacred and ennobled hearse,
 Would offer a burnt sacrifice of verse
   And Melody.   10

How heavenward thou soundedst,
 Live Temple of sweet noise;
And discord unconfoundedst,—
 Giving delight new joys,
And pleasure nobler pinions—
O, where are thy dominions?
 Lend thine ear,
To a young delian oath,—aye, by the soul,
By all that from thy mortal Lips did roll;
And by the Kernel of thine earthly Love,   20
Beauty, in things on earth and things above;
 When every childish fashion
  Has vanish'd from my rhyme
 Will I, grey-gone in passion,
  Leave to an after time
  Hymning and Harmony
Of thee, and of thy works, and of thy Life;
But vain is now the burning, and the strife,
Pangs are in vain—until I grow high-rife
  With old Philosophy;   30
And mad with glimpses of futurity!

For many years my offerings must be hush'd.
 When I do speak, I'll think upon this hour,
Because I feel my forehead hot and flush'd—
 Even at the simplest vassal of thy Power—
 A Lock of thy bright hair—sudden it came,
And I was startled, when I caught thy name
  Coupled so unaware—
Yet at the moment, temperate was my blood—
Methought I had beheld it from the flood— 40

On Sitting Down to Read King Lear Once Again

O Golden-tongued Romance, with serene Lute!
 Fair plumed Syren, Queen of far-away!
 Leave melodizing on this wintry day
Shut up thine olden Pages, and be mute.

Adieu! for, once again, the fierce dispute,
  Betwixt Damnation and impassion'd clay
  Must I burn through; once more humbly assay
The bitter-sweet of this Shaksperean fruit.
Chief Poet! and ye Clouds of Albion,
  Begetters of our deep eternal theme!   10
When through the old oak forest I am gone,
  Let me not wander in a barren dream:
But, when I am consumed in the fire,
Give me new Phœnix Wings to fly at my desire.

'When I have fears that I may cease to be'

When I have fears that I may cease to be
  Before my pen has glean'd my teeming brain,
Before high piled Books in charactery
  Hold like rich garners the full ripen'd grain—
When I behold upon the night's starr'd face
  Huge cloudy symbols of a high romance,
And feel that I may never live to trace
  Their shadows with the magic hand of Chance:
And when I feel, fair creature of an hour,
  That I shall never look upon thee more   10
Never have relish in the fairy power
  Of unreflecting Love: then on the Shore
Of the wide world I stand alone and think
Till Love and Fame to Nothingness do sink.—

'O blush not so, O blush not so'

I

O blush not so, O blush not so
  Or I shall think you knowing;
And if you smile, the blushing while
  Then Maidenheads are going.

2

There's a blush for want, and a blush for shan't
  And a blush for having done it,
There's a blush for thought, and a blush for naught,
  And a blush for just begun it.

3

O sigh not so, O sigh not so
  For it sounds of Eve's sweet Pipin;   10
By those loosen'd hips, you have tasted the pips
  And fought in an amorous nipping.

4

Will ye play once more, at nice cut-core
  For it only will last our youth out;
And we have the prime of the Kissing time
  We have not one sweet tooth out.

5

There's a sigh for yes, and a sigh for no,
  And a sigh for 'I can't bear it'—
O what can be done, shall we stay or run?
  O cut the sweet apple and share it—   20

Lines on the Mermaid Tavern

Souls of Poets dead and gone,
What Elysium have ye known,
Happy field or mossy cavern,
Choicer than the Mermaid Tavern?
Have ye tippled drink more fine
Than mine host's Canary wine?
Or are fruits of Paradise
Sweeter than those dainty pies
Of venison? O generous food!
Drest as though bold Robin Hood   10

Would, with his maid Marian,
Sup and bowse from horn and can.

I have heard that on a day
Mine host's sign-board flew away,
Nobody knew whither, till
An astrologer's old quill
To a sheepskin gave the story,
Said he saw you in your glory,
Underneath a new old sign
Sipping beverage divine,   20
And pledging with contented smack
The Mermaid in the Zodiac.

Souls of Poets dead and gone,
What Elysium have ye known,
Happy field or mossy cavern,
Choicer than the Mermaid Tavern?

Robin Hood

To a friend

No! those days are gone away,
And their hours are old and gray,
And their minutes buried all
Under the down-trodden pall
Of the leaves of many years:
Many times have winter's shears,
Frozen North, and chilling East,
Sounded tempests to the feast
Of the forest's whispering fleeces,
Since men knew nor rent nor leases.   10

No, the bugle sounds no more,
And the twanging bow no more;
Silent is the ivory shrill
Past the heath and up the hill;
There is no mid-forest laugh,

Where lone Echo gives the half
To some wight, amaz'd to hear
Jesting, deep in forest drear.

On the fairest time of June
You may go, with sun or moon,   20
Or the seven stars to light you,
Or the polar ray to right you;
But you never may behold
Little John, or Robin bold;
Never one, of all the clan,
Thrumming on an empty can
Some old hunting ditty, while
He doth his green way beguile
To fair hostess Merriment,
Down beside the pasture Trent;   30
For he left the merry tale
Messenger for spicy ale.

Gone, the merry morris din;
Gone, the song of Gamelyn;
Gone, the tough-belted outlaw
Idling in the 'grenè shawe';
All are gone away and past!
And if Robin should be cast
Sudden from his turfed grave,
And if Marian should have   40
Once again her forest days,
She would weep, and he would craze:
He would swear, for all his oaks,
Fall'n beneath the dockyard strokes,
Have rotted on the briny seas;
She would weep that her wild bees
Sang not to her—strange! that honey
Can't be got without hard money!

So it is: yet let us sing,
Honour to the old bow-string!   50
Honour to the bugle-horn!
Honour to the woods unshorn!
Honour to the Lincoln green!

Honour to the archer keen!
Honour to tight little John,
And the horse he rode upon!
Honour to bold Robin Hood,
Sleeping in the underwood!
Honour to maid Marian,
And to all the Sherwood-clan!   60
Though their days have hurried by
Let us two a burden try.

'O thou whose face hath felt the Winter's wind'

'O thou whose face hath felt the Winter's wind;
Whose eye has seen the Snow clouds hung in Mist
And the black-elm tops 'mong the freezing Stars
To thee the Spring will be a harvest-time—
O thou whose only book has been the light
Of supreme darkness which thou feddest on
Night after night, when Phœbus was away
To thee the Spring shall be a tripple morn—
O fret not after Knowledge—I have none
And yet my song comes native with the warmth   10
O fret not after Knowledge—I have none
And yet the Evening listens—He who saddens
At thought of Idleness cannot be idle,
And he's awake who thinks himself asleep.'

The Human Seasons

Four seasons fill the measure of the year;
    There are four seasons in the mind of man:
He has his lusty Spring, when fancy clear
    Takes in all beauty with an easy span:
He has his Summer, when luxuriously
    Spring's honied cud of youthful thought he loves
To ruminate, and by such dreaming nigh
    His nearest unto heaven: quiet coves

His soul has in its Autumn, when his wings
  He furleth close; contented so to look   10
On mists in idleness—to let fair things
  Pass by unheeded as a threshold brook.
    He has his Winter too of pale misfeature,
    Or else he would forget his mortal nature.

'For there's Bishop's Teign'

1

For there's Bishop's Teign
And King's Teign
And Coomb at the clear Teign head.
Where close by the Stream
You may have your cream
All spread upon barley bread—

2

There's Arch Brook
And there's Larch Brook,
Both turning many a Mill
And cooling the drouth   10
Of the salmon's mouth
And fattening his silver gill.

3

There is Wild Wood
A mild hood
To the sheep on the lea o' the down
Where the golden furze
With its green thin spurs
Doth catch at the Maiden's gown.

4

There is Newton Marsh
With its spear grass harsh—   20
A pleasant summer level

Where the Maidens sweet
Of the Market Street
Do meet in the dusk to revel.

5

There's the Barton rich
With dyke and ditch
And hedge for the thrush to live in
And the hollow tree
For the buzzing bee
And a bank for the Wasp to hive in—   30

6

And O, and O
The Daisies blow
And the Primroses are waken'd
And the violet white
Sits in silver plight
And the green bud's as long as the spike end.

7

Then who would go
Into dark Soho
And chatter with dack'd hair'd critics
Where he can stay   40
For the new mown hay
And startle the dappled Prickets?

'Where be ye going you Devon maid'

I

Where be ye going you Devon maid
   And what have ye there i' the Basket?
Ye tight little fairy—just fresh from the dairy
   Will ye give me some cream if I ask it—

2

I love your Meads and I love your flowers
And I love your junkets mainly
But 'hind the door, I love kissing more
O look not so disdainly!

3

I love your Hills and I love your dales
And I love your flocks a bleating—   10
But O on the hether to lie together
With both our hearts a beating—

4

I'll put your Basket all safe in a *nook*
And your shawl I hang up *on this willow*
And we will sigh in the daisy's eye
And kiss on a grass green pillow.

'Over the hill and over the dale'

Over the hill and over the dale,
And over the bourn to Dawlish—
Where Gingerbread Wives have a scanty sale
And gingerbread nuts are smallish—

Rantipole Betty she ran down a hill
And kick'd up her petticoats fairly
Says I I'll be Jack if you will be Gill—
So she sat on the Grass debonnairly—

Here's somebody coming, here's somebody coming!
Says I 'tis the Wind at a parley   10
So without any fuss any hawing and humming
She lay on the grass debonnairly—

Here's somebody here and here's somebody *there*!
Says I hold your tongue you young Gipsey.

So she held her tongue and lay plump and fair
  And dead as a venus tipsy—

O who wouldn't hie to Dawlish fair
  O who wouldn't stop in a Meadow
O who would not rumple the daisies there
  And make the wild fern for a bed do—   20

To J. H. Reynolds Esq.

Dear Reynolds, as last night I lay in bed,
There came before my eyes that wonted thread
Of shapes, and Shadows and Remembrances,
That every other minute vex and please:
Things all disjointed come from North and South,
Two witch's eyes above a cherub's mouth,
Voltaire with casque and shield and Habergeon,
And Alexander with his night-cap on—
Old Socrates a tying his cravat;
And Hazlitt playing with Miss Edgworth's cat;   10
And Junius Brutus pretty well so so,
Making the best of 's way towards Soho.

  Few are there who escape these visitings—
P'rhaps one or two, whose lives have patent wings;
And through whose curtains peeps no hellish nose,
No wild boar tushes, and no Mermaid's toes:
But flowers bursting out with lusty pride;
And young Æolian harps personified,
Some, Titian colours touch'd into real life.—
The sacrifice goes on; the pontif knife   20
Gloams in the sun, the milk-white heifer lows,
The pipes go shrilly, the libation flows:
A white sail shews above the green-head cliff
Moves round the point, and throws her anchor stiff.
The Mariners join hymn with those on land.—
You know the Enchanted Castle—it doth stand
Upon a Rock on the Border of a Lake
Nested in Trees, which all do seem to shake

From some old Magic like Urganda's sword.
O Phœbus that I had thy sacred word   30
To shew this Castle in fair dreaming wise
Unto my friend, while sick and ill he lies.

   You know it well enough, where it doth seem
A mossy place, a Merlin's Hall, a dream.
You know the clear lake, and the little Isles,
The Mountains blue, and cold near neighbour rills—
All which elsewhere are but half animate
Here do they look alive to love and hate;
To smiles and frowns; they seem a lifted mound
Above some giant, pulsing underground.   40

   Part of the building was a chosen See
Built by a banish'd santon of Chaldee:
The other part two thousand years from him
Was built by Cuthbert de Saint Aldebrim;
Then there's a little wing, far from the sun,
Built by a Lapland Witch turn'd maudlin nun—
And many other juts of aged stone
Founded with many a mason-devil's groan.

   The doors all look as if they oped themselves,
The windows as if latch'd by fays and elves—   50
And from them comes a silver flash of light
As from the Westward of a summer's night;
Or like a beauteous woman's large blue eyes
Gone mad through olden songs and Poesies—

   See what is coming from the distance dim!
A golden galley all in silken trim!
Three rows of oars are lightening moment-whiles
Into the verdurous bosoms of those Isles.
Towards the shade under the Castle Wall
It comes in silence—now 'tis hidden all.   60
The clarion sounds; and from a postern grate
An echo of sweet music doth create
A fear in the poor herdsman who doth bring
His beasts to trouble the enchanted spring:
He tells of the sweet music and the spot
To all his friends, and they believe him not.

O that our dreamings all of sleep or wake
Would all their colours from the sunset take:
From something of material sublime,
Rather than shadow our own Soul's daytime   70
In the dark void of Night. For in the world
We jostle—but my flag is not unfurl'd
On the Admiral staff—and to philosophize
I dare not yet!—Oh never will the prize,
High reason, and the lore of good and ill
Be my award. Things cannot to the will
Be settled, but they tease us out of thought.
Or is it that Imagination brought
Beyond its proper bound, yet still confined,—
Lost in a sort of Purgatory blind,   80
Cannot refer to any standard law
Of either earth or heaven?—It is a flaw
In happiness to see beyond our bourn—
It forces us in Summer skies to mourn:
It spoils the singing of the Nightingale.

Dear Reynolds. I have a mysterious tale
And cannot speak it. The first page I read
Upon a Lampit Rock of green sea weed
Among the breakers—'Twas a quiet Eve;
The rocks were silent—the wide sea did weave   90
An untumultuous fringe of silver foam
Along the flat brown sand. I was at home,
And should have been most happy—but I saw
Too far into the sea; where every maw
The greater on the less feeds evermore:—
But I saw too distinct into the core
Of an eternal fierce destruction,
And so from Happiness I far was gone.
Still am I sick of it: and though to-day
I've gathered young spring-leaves, and flowers gay   100
Of Periwinkle and wild strawberry,
Still do I that most fierce destruction see,
The shark at savage prey—the hawk at pounce,
The gentle Robin, like a pard or ounce,
Ravening a worm—Away ye horrid moods,

Moods of one's mind! You know I hate them well,
You know I'd sooner be a clapping bell
To some Kamschatkan missionary church,
Than with these horrid moods be left in lurch—
Do you get health—and Tom the same—I'll dance,   110
And from detested moods in new Romance
Take refuge—Of bad lines a Centaine dose
Is sure enough—and so 'here follows prose.'—

Isabella;
or,
The Pot of Basil

A story from Boccaccio

I

Fair Isabel, poor simple Isabel!
   Lorenzo, a young palmer in Love's eye!
They could not in the self-same mansion dwell
   Without some stir of heart, some malady;
They could not sit at meals but feel how well
   It soothed each to be the other by;
They could not, sure, beneath the same roof sleep
But to each other dream, and nightly weep.

2

With every morn their love grew tenderer,
   With every eve deeper and tenderer still;   10
He might not in house, field, or garden stir,
   But her full shape would all his seeing fill;
And his continual voice was pleasanter
   To her, than noise of trees or hidden rill;
Her lute-string gave an echo of his name,
She spoilt her half-done broidery with the same.

3

He knew whose gentle hand was at the latch,
  Before the door had given her to his eyes;
And from her chamber-window he would catch
  Her beauty farther than the falcon spies;   20
And constant as her vespers would he watch,
  Because her face was turn'd to the same skies;
And with sick longing all the night outwear,
To hear her morning-step upon the stair.

4

A whole long month of May in this sad plight
  Made their cheeks paler by the break of June:
'To-morrow will I bow to my delight,
  To-morrow will I ask my lady's boon.'—
'O may I never see another night,
  Lorenzo, if thy lips breathe not love's tune.'—   30
So spake they to their pillows; but alas,
Honeyless days and days did he let pass;

5

Until sweet Isabella's untouch'd cheek
  Fell sick within the rose's just domain,
Fell thin as a young mother's, who doth seek
  By every lull to cool her infant's pain:
'How ill she is,' said he, 'I may not speak,
  And yet I will, and tell my love all plain:
If looks speak love-laws, I will drink her tears,
And at the least 'twill startle off her cares.'   40

6

So said he one fair morning, and all day
  His heart beat awfully against his side;
And to his heart he inwardly did pray
  For power to speak; but still the ruddy tide
Stifled his voice, and puls'd resolve away—
  Fever'd his high conceit of such a bride,
Yet brought him to the meekness of a child:
Alas! when passion is both meek and wild!

7

So once more he had wak'd and anguished
 A dreary night of love and misery,   50
If Isabel's quick eye had not been wed
 To every symbol on his forehead high;
She saw it waxing very pale and dead,
 And straight all flush'd; so, lisped tenderly,
'Lorenzo!'—here she ceas'd her timid quest,
But in her tone and look he read the rest.

8

'O Isabella, I can half perceive
 That I may speak my grief into thine ear;
If thou didst ever any thing believe,
 Believe how I love thee, believe how near   60
My soul is to its doom: I would not grieve
 Thy hand by unwelcome pressing, would not fear
Thine eyes by gazing; but I cannot live
Another night, and not my passion shrive.

9

'Love! thou art leading me from wintry cold,
 Lady! thou leadest me to summer clime,
And I must taste the blossoms that unfold
 In its ripe warmth this gracious morning time.'
So said, his erewhile timid lips grew bold,
 And poesied with hers in dewy rhyme: 70
Great bliss was with them, and great happiness
Grew, like a lusty flower in June's caress.

10

Parting they seem'd to tread upon the air,
 Twin roses by the zephyr blown apart
Only to meet again more close, and share
 The inward fragrance of each other's heart.
She, to her chamber gone, a ditty fair
 Sang, of delicious love and honey'd dart;
He with light steps went up a western hill,
And bade the sun farewell, and joy'd his fill.   80

11

All close they met again, before the dusk
   Had taken from the stars its pleasant veil,
All close they met, all eves, before the dusk
   Had taken from the stars its pleasant veil,
Close in a bower of hyacinth and musk,
   Unknown of any, free from whispering tale.
Ah! better had it been for ever so,
Than idle ears should pleasure in their woe.

12

Were they unhappy then?—It cannot be—
   Too many tears for lovers have been shed,   90
Too many sighs give we to them in fee,
   Too much of pity after they are dead,
Too many doleful stories do we see,
   Whose matter in bright gold were best be read;
Except in such a page where Theseus' spouse
Over the pathless waves towards him bows.

13

But, for the general award of love,
   The little sweet doth kill much bitterness;
Though Dido silent is in under-grove,
   And Isabella's was a great distress,   100
Though young Lorenzo in warm Indian clove
   Was not embalm'd, this truth is not the less—
Even bees, the little almsmen of spring-bowers,
Know there is richest juice in poison-flowers.

14

With her two brothers this fair lady dwelt,
   Enriched from ancestral merchandize,
And for them many a weary hand did swelt
   In torched mines and noisy factories,
And many once proud-quiver'd loins did melt
   In blood from stinging whip; with hollow eyes   110
Many all day in dazzling river stood,
To take the rich-ored driftings of the flood.

15

For them the Ceylon diver held his breath,
  And went all naked to the hungry shark;
For them his ears gush'd blood; for them in death
  The seal on the cold ice with piteous bark
Lay full of darts; for them alone did seethe
  A thousand men in troubles wide and dark:
Half-ignorant, they turn'd an easy wheel,
That set sharp racks at work, to pinch and peel. 120

16

Why were they proud? Because their marble founts
  Gush'd with more pride than do a wretch's tears?—
Why were they proud? Because fair orange-mounts
  Were of more soft ascent than lazar stairs?—
Why were they proud? Because red-lin'd accounts
  Were richer than the songs of Grecian years?—
Why were they proud? again we ask aloud,
Why in the name of Glory were they proud?

17

Yet were these Florentines as self-retired
  In hungry pride and gainful cowardice, 130
As two close Hebrews in that land inspired,
  Paled in and vineyarded from beggar-spies;
The hawks of ship-mast forests—the untired
  And pannier'd mules for ducats and old lies—
Quick cat's-paws on the generous stray-away,—
Great wits in Spanish, Tuscan, and Malay.

18

How was it these same ledger-men could spy
  Fair Isabella in her downy nest?
How could they find out in Lorenzo's eye
  A straying from his toil? Hot Egypt's pest 140
Into their vision covetous and sly!
  How could these money-bags see east and west?—
Yet so they did—and every dealer fair
Must see behind, as doth the hunted hare.

19

O eloquent and famed Boccaccio!
   Of thee we now should ask forgiving boon,
And of thy spicy myrtles as they blow,
   And of thy roses amorous of the moon,
And of thy lilies, that do paler grow
   Now they can no more hear thy ghittern's tune,   150
For venturing syllables that ill beseem
The quiet glooms of such a piteous theme.

20

Grant thou a pardon here, and then the tale
   Shall move on soberly, as it is meet;
There is no other crime, no mad assail
   To make old prose in modern rhyme more sweet:
But it is done—succeed the verse or fail—
   To honour thee, and thy gone spirit greet;
To stead thee as a verse in English tongue,
An echo of thee in the north-wind sung.   160

21

These brethren having found by many signs
   What love Lorenzo for their sister had,
And how she lov'd him too, each unconfines
   His bitter thoughts to other, well nigh mad
That he, the servant of their trade designs,
   Should in their sister's love be blithe and glad,
When 'twas their plan to coax her by degrees
To some high noble and his olive-trees.

22

And many a jealous conference had they,
   And many times they bit their lips alone,   170
Before they fix'd upon a surest way
   To make the youngster for his crime atone;
And at the last, these men of cruel clay
   Cut Mercy with a sharp knife to the bone;
For they resolved in some forest dim
To kill Lorenzo, and there bury him.

23

So on a pleasant morning, as he leant
  Into the sun-rise, o'er the balustrade
Of the garden-terrace, towards him they bent
  Their footing through the dews; and to him said,   180
'You seem there in the quiet of content,
  Lorenzo, and we are most loth to invade
Calm speculation; but if you are wise,
Bestride your steed while cold is in the skies.

24

'To-day we purpose, ay, this hour we mount
  To spur three leagues towards the Apennine;
Come down, we pray thee, ere the hot sun count
  His dewy rosary on the eglantine.'
Lorenzo, courteously as he was wont,
  Bow'd a fair greeting to these serpents' whine;   190
And went in haste, to get in readiness,
With belt, and spur, and bracing huntsman's dress.

25

And as he to the court-yard pass'd along,
  Each third step did he pause, and listen'd oft
If he could hear his lady's matin-song,
  Or the light whisper of her footstep soft;
And as he thus over his passion hung,
  He heard a laugh full musical aloft;
When, looking up, he saw her features bright
Smile through an in-door lattice, all delight.   200

26

'Love, Isabel!' said he, 'I was in pain
  Lest I should miss to bid thee a good morrow:
Ah! what if I should lose thee, when so fain
  I am to stifle all the heavy sorrow
Of a poor three hours' absence? but we'll gain
  Out of the amorous dark what day doth borrow.
Good bye! I'll soon be back.'—'Good bye!' said she:—
And as he went she chanted merrily.

27

So the two brothers and their murder'd man
  Rode past fair Florence, to where Arno's stream   210
Gurgles through straiten'd banks, and still doth fan
  Itself with dancing bulrush, and the bream
Keeps head against the freshets. Sick and wan
  The brothers' faces in the ford did seem,
Lorenzo's flush with love.—They pass'd the water
Into a forest quiet for the slaughter.

28

There was Lorenzo slain and buried in,
  There in that forest did his great love cease;
Ah! when a soul doth thus its freedom win,
  It aches in loneliness—is ill at peace   220
As the break-covert blood-hounds of such sin:
  They dipp'd their swords in the water, and did tease
Their horses homeward, with convulsed spur,
Each richer by his being a murderer.

29

They told their sister how, with sudden speed,
  Lorenzo had ta'en ship for foreign lands,
Because of some great urgency and need
  In their affairs, requiring trusty hands.
Poor Girl! put on thy stifling widow's weed,
  And 'scape at once from Hope's accursed bands;   230
To-day thou wilt not see him, nor to-morrow,
And the next day will be a day of sorrow.

30

She weeps alone for pleasures not to be;
  Sorely she wept until the night came on,
And then, instead of love, O misery!
  She brooded o'er the luxury alone:
His image in the dusk she seem'd to see,
  And to the silence made a gentle moan,
Spreading her perfect arms upon the air,
And on her couch low murmuring 'Where? O where?'   240

3 1

But Selfishness, Love's cousin, held not long
   Its fiery vigil in her single breast;
She fretted for the golden hour, and hung
   Upon the time with feverish unrest—
Not long—for soon into her heart a throng
   Of higher occupants, a richer zest,
Came tragic; passion not to be subdued,
And sorrow for her love in travels rude.

3 2

In the mid days of autumn, on their eves
   The breath of Winter comes from far away,   250
And the sick west continually bereaves
   Of some gold tinge, and plays a roundelay
Of death among the bushes and the leaves,
   To make all bare before he dares to stray
From his north cavern. So sweet Isabel
By gradual decay from beauty fell,

3 3

Because Lorenzo came not. Oftentimes
   She ask'd her brothers, with an eye all pale,
Striving to be itself, what dungeon climes
   Could keep him off so long? They spake a tale   260
Time after time, to quiet her. Their crimes
   Came on them, like a smoke from Hinnom's vale;
And every night in dreams they groan'd aloud,
To see their sister in her snowy shroud.

3 4

And she had died in drowsy ignorance,
   But for a thing more deadly dark than all;
It came like a fierce potion, drunk by chance,
   Which saves a sick man from the feather'd pall
For some few gasping moments; like a lance,
   Waking an Indian from his cloudy hall   270
With cruel pierce, and bringing him again
Sense of the gnawing fire at heart and brain.

35

It was a vision.—In the drowsy gloom,
  The dull of midnight, at her couch's foot
Lorenzo stood, and wept: the forest tomb
  Had marr'd his glossy hair which once could shoot
Lustre into the sun, and put cold doom
  Upon his lips, and taken the soft lute
From his lorn voice, and past his loamed ears
Had made a miry channel for his tears.   280

36

Strange sound it was, when the pale shadow spake;
  For there was striving, in its piteous tongue,
To speak as when on earth it was awake,
  And Isabella on its music hung:
Languor there was in it, and tremulous shake,
  As in a palsied Druid's harp unstrung;
And through it moan'd a ghostly under-song,
Like hoarse night-gusts sepulchral briars among.

37

Its eyes, though wild, were still all dewy bright
  With love, and kept all phantom fear aloof   290
From the poor girl by magic of their light,
  The while it did unthread the horrid woof
Of the late darken'd time,—the murderous spite
  Of pride and avarice,—the dark pine roof
In the forest,—and the sodden turfed dell,
Where, without any word, from stabs he fell.

38

Saying moreover, 'Isabel, my sweet!
  Red whortle-berries droop above my head,
And a large flint-stone weighs upon my feet;
  Around me beeches and high chestnuts shed   300
Their leaves and prickly nuts; a sheep-fold bleat
  Comes from beyond the river to my bed:
Go, shed one tear upon my heather-bloom,
And it shall comfort me within the tomb.

39

'I am a shadow now, alas! alas!
  Upon the skirts of human-nature dwelling
Alone: I chant alone the holy mass,
  While little sounds of life are round me knelling,
And glossy bees at noon do fieldward pass,
  And many a chapel bell the hour is telling,   310
Paining me through: those sounds grow strange to me,
And thou art distant in Humanity.

40

'I know what was, I feel full well what is,
  And I should rage, if spirits could go mad;
Though I forget the taste of earthly bliss,
  That paleness warms my grave, as though I had
A Seraph chosen from the bright abyss
  To be my spouse: thy paleness makes me glad;
Thy beauty grows upon me, and I feel
A greater love through all my essence steal.'   320

41

The Spirit mourn'd 'Adieu!'—dissolv'd, and left
  The atom darkness in a slow turmoil;
As when of healthful midnight sleep bereft,
  Thinking on rugged hours and fruitless toil,
We put our eyes into a pillowy cleft,
  And see the spangly gloom froth up and boil:
It made sad Isabella's eyelids ache,
And in the dawn she started up awake;

42

'Ha! ha!' said she, 'I knew not this hard life,
  I thought the worst was simply misery;   330
I thought some Fate with pleasure or with strife
  Portion'd us—happy days, or else to die;
But there is crime—a brother's bloody knife!
  Sweet Spirit, thou hast school'd my infancy:
I'll visit thee for this, and kiss thine eyes,
And greet thee morn and even in the skies.'

43

When the full morning came, she had devised
  How she might secret to the forest hie;
How she might find the clay, so dearly prized,
  And sing to it one latest lullaby;   340
How her short absence might be unsurmised,
  While she the inmost of the dream would try.
Resolv'd, she took with her an aged nurse,
And went into that dismal forest-hearse.

44

See, as they creep along the river side,
  How she doth whisper to that aged Dame,
And, after looking round the champaign wide,
  Shows her a knife.—'What feverous hectic flame
Burns in thee, child?—What good can thee betide,
  That thou should'st smile again?'—The evening came,   350
And they had found Lorenzo's earthy bed;
The flint was there, the berries at his head.

45

Who hath not loiter'd in a green church-yard,
  And let his spirit, like a demon-mole,
Work through the clayey soil and gravel hard,
  To see scull, coffin'd bones, and funeral stole;
Pitying each form that hungry Death hath marr'd
  And filling it once more with human soul?
Ah! this is holiday to what was felt
When Isabella by Lorenzo knelt.   360

46

She gaz'd into the fresh-thrown mould, as though
  One glance did fully all its secrets tell;
Clearly she saw, as other eyes would know
  Pale limbs at bottom of a crystal well;
Upon the murderous spot she seem'd to grow,
  Like a native lily of the dell:
Then with her knife, all sudden, she began
To dig more fervently than misers can.

47

Soon she turn'd up a soiled glove, whereon
   Her silk had play'd in purple phantasies,   370
She kiss'd it with a lip more chill than stone,
   And put it in her bosom, where it dries
And freezes utterly unto the bone
   Those dainties made to still an infant's cries:
Then 'gan she work again; nor stay'd her care,
But to throw back at times her veiling hair.

48

That old nurse stood beside her wondering,
   Until her heart felt pity to the core
At sight of such a dismal labouring,
   And so she kneeled, with her locks all hoar,   380
And put her lean hands to the horrid thing:
   Three hours they labour'd at this travail sore;
At last they felt the kernel of the grave,
And Isabella did not stamp and rave.

49

Ah! wherefore all this wormy circumstance?
   Why linger at the yawning tomb so long?
O for the gentleness of old Romance,
   The simple plaining of a minstrel's song!
Fair reader, at the old tale take a glance,
   For here, in truth, it doth not well belong   390
To speak:—O turn thee to the very tale,
And taste the music of that vision pale.

50

With duller steel than the Perséan sword
   They cut away no formless monster's head,
But one, whose gentleness did well accord
   With death, as life. The ancient harps have said,
Love never dies, but lives, immortal Lord:
   If love impersonate was ever dead,
Pale Isabella kiss'd it, and low moan'd.
'Twas love; cold,—dead indeed, but not dethroned.   400

51

In anxious secrecy they took it home,
  And then the prize was all for Isabel:
She calm'd its wild hair with a golden comb,
  And all around each eye's sepulchral cell
Pointed each fringed lash; the smeared loam
  With tears, as chilly as a dripping well,
She drench'd away:—and still she comb'd, and kept
Sighing all day—and still she kiss'd, and wept.

52

Then in a silken scarf,—sweet with the dews
  Of precious flowers pluck'd in Araby,   410
And divine liquids come with odorous ooze
  Through the cold serpent-pipe refreshfully,—
She wrapp'd it up; and for its tomb did choose
  A garden-pot, wherein she laid it by,
And cover'd it with mould, and o'er it set
Sweet Basil, which her tears kept ever wet.

53

And she forgot the stars, the moon, and sun,
  And she forgot the blue above the trees,
And she forgot the dells where waters run,
  And she forgot the chilly autumn breeze;   420
She had no knowledge when the day was done,
  And the new morn she saw not: but in peace
Hung over her sweet Basil evermore,
And moisten'd it with tears unto the core.

54

And so she ever fed it with thin tears,
  Whence thick, and green, and beautiful it grew,
So that it smelt more balmy than its peers
  Of Basil-tufts in Florence; for it drew
Nurture besides, and life, from human fears,
  From the fast mouldering head there shut from view: 430
So that the jewel, safely casketed,
Came forth, and in perfumed leafits spread.

55

O Melancholy, linger here awhile!
　O Music, Music, breathe despondingly!
O Echo, Echo, from some sombre isle,
　Unknown, Lethean, sigh to us—O sigh!
Spirits in grief, lift up your heads, and smile;
　Lift up your heads, sweet Spirits, heavily,
And make a pale light in your cypress glooms,
Tinting with silver wan your marble tombs. 440

56

Moan hither, all ye syllables of woe,
　From the deep throat of sad Melpomene!
Through bronzed lyre in tragic order go,
　And touch the strings into a mystery;
Sound mournfully upon the winds and low;
　For simple Isabel is soon to be
Among the dead: She withers, like a palm
Cut by an Indian for its juicy balm.

57

O leave the palm to wither by itself;
　Let not quick Winter chill its dying hour!— 450
It may not be—those Baälites of pelf,
　Her brethren, noted the continual shower
From her dead eyes; and many a curious elf,
　Among her kindred, wonder'd that such dower
Of youth and beauty should be thrown aside
By one mark'd out to be a Noble's bride.

58

And, furthermore, her brethren wonder'd much
　Why she sat drooping by the Basil green,
And why it flourish'd, as by magic touch;
　Greatly they wonder'd what the things might mean: 460
They could not surely give belief, that such
　A very nothing would have power to wean
Her from her own fair youth, and pleasures gay,
And even remembrance of her love's delay.

59

Therefore they watch'd a time when they might sift
   This hidden whim; and long they watch'd in vain;
For seldom did she go to chapel-shrift,
   And seldom felt she any hunger-pain;
And when she left, she hurried back, as swift
   As bird on wing to breast its eggs again;   470
And, patient as a hen-bird, sat her there
Beside her Basil, weeping through her hair.

60

Yet they contriv'd to steal the Basil-pot,
   And to examine it in secret place:
The thing was vile with green and livid spot,
   And yet they knew it was Lorenzo's face:
The guerdon of their murder they had got,
   And so left Florence in a moment's space,
Never to turn again.—Away they went,
With blood upon their heads, to banishment.   480

61

O Melancholy, turn thine eyes away!
   O Music, Music, breathe despondingly!
O Echo, Echo, on some other day,
   From isles Lethean, sigh to us—O sigh!
Spirits of grief, sing not your 'Well-a-way!'
   For Isabel, sweet Isabel, will die;
Will die a death too lone and incomplete,
Now they have ta'en away her Basil sweet.

62

Piteous she look'd on dead and senseless things,
   Asking for her lost Basil amorously;   490
And with melodious chuckle in the strings
   Of her lorn voice, she oftentimes would cry
After the Pilgrim in his wanderings,
   To ask him where her Basil was; and why
T'was hid from her: 'For cruel 'tis,' said she,
'To steal my Basil-pot away from me.'

63

And so she pined, and so she died forlorn,
   Imploring for her Basil to the last.
No heart was there in Florence but did mourn
   In pity of her love, so overcast.   500
And a sad ditty of this story born
   From mouth to mouth through all the country pass'd:
Still is the burthen sung—'O cruelty,
To steal my Basil-pot away from me!'

'Old Meg she was a Gipsey'

Old Meg she was a Gipsey
   And liv'd upon the Moors;
Her bed it was the brown heath turf,
   And her house was out of doors—
Her apples were swart blackberries,
   Her currants pods o' Broom,
Her wine was dew o' the wild white rose,
   Her book a churchyard tomb—
Her brothers were the craggy hills,
   Her sisters larchen trees—   10
Alone with her great family
   She liv'd as she did please.
No Breakfast had she many a morn,
   No dinner many a noon;
And 'stead of supper she would stare
   Full hard against the Moon—
But every Morn, of wood bine fresh
   She made her garlanding;
And every night the dark glen Yew
   She wove and she would sing—   20
And with her fingers old and brown
   She plaited Mats o' Rushes
And gave them to the Cottagers
   She met among the Bushes—
Old Meg was brave as Margaret Queen
   And tall as Amazon:

An old red blanket cloak she wore
A chip hat had she on—
God rest her aged bones somewhere
She died full long agone!   30

'There was a naughty Boy'

There was a naughty Boy
A naughty boy was he
He would not stop at home
He could not quiet be—
He took
In his Knapsack
A Book
Full of vowels
And a shirt
With some towels—   10
A slight cap
For night cap—
A hair brush
Comb ditto
New Stockings
For old ones
Would split O!
This Knapsack
Tight at 's back
He revetted close   20
And follow'd his Nose
To the North
To the North
And follow'd his nose
To the North—

There was a naughty boy
And a naughty boy was he
For nothing would he do
But scribble poetry—
He took   30
An inkstand

In his hand
And a Pen
Big as ten
In the other
And away
In a Pother
He ran
To the mountains
And fountains   40
And ghostes
And Postes
And witches
And ditches
And wrote
In his coat
When the weather
Was cool
Fear of gout
And without   50
When the weather
Was warm—
Och the charm
When we choose
To follow one's nose
To the north
To the north
To follow one's nose to the north!

There was a naughty boy
And a naughty boy was he   60
He kept little fishes
In washing tubs three
In spite
Of the might
Of the Maid
Nor affraid
Of his Granny-good—
He often would
Hurly burly
Get up early   70
And go

By hook or crook
To the brook
And bring home
Miller's thumb
Tittle bat
Not over fat
Minnows small
As the stall
Of a glove   80
Not above
The size
Of a nice
Little Baby's
Little finger—
O he made
'T was his trade
Of Fish a pretty kettle
A kettle—A kettle
Of Fish a pretty kettle   90
A kettle!

There was a naughty Boy
    And a naughty Boy was he
He ran away to Scotland
    The people for to see—
        There he found
        That the ground
        Was as hard
        That a yard
        Was as long,   100
        That a song,
        Was as merry,
        That a cherry
        Was as red—
        That lead
        Was as weighty
        That fourscore
        Was as eighty
        That a door
        Was as wooden   110
        As in england—

So he stood in
His shoes
And he wonderd
He wonderd
He stood in his
Shoes and he wonder'd—

Sonnet to Ailsa Rock

Hearken, thou craggy ocean pyramid!
  Give answer from thy voice, the sea fowls' screams!
  When were thy shoulders mantled in huge streams?
When, from the sun, was thy broad forehead hid?
How long is't since the mighty powers bid
  Thee heave to airy sleep from fathom dreams?
  Sleep in the lap of thunder or sunbeams,
  Or when grey clouds are thy cold coverlid.

Thou answer'st not, for thou art dead asleep;
  Thy life is but two dead eternities—   10
The last in air, the former in the deep;
  First with the whales, last with the eagle-skies—
Drown'd wast thou till an earthquake made thee steep,
  Another cannot wake thy giant size.

'There is a joy in footing slow across a silent plain'

There is a joy in footing slow across a silent plain
Where Patriot Battle has been fought when Glory had the gain;
There is a pleasure on the heath where Druids old have been,
Where Mantles grey have rustled by and swept the nettles
    green:
There is a joy in every spot, made known by times of old,
New to the feet, although the tale a hundred times be told:
There is a deeper joy than all, more solemn in the heart,
More parching to the tongue than all, of more divine a smart,
When weary feet forget themselves upon a pleasant turf,

Upon hot sand, or flinty road, or Sea shore iron scurf,   10
Toward the Castle or the Cot where long ago was born
One who was great through mortal days and died of fame
    unshorn.
Light Hether-bells may tremble then, but they are far away;
Woodlark may sing from sandy fern,—the Sun may hear his Lay;
Runnels may kiss the grass on shelves and shallows clear
But their low voices are not heard though come on travels
    drear;
Bloodred the sun may set behind black mountain peaks;
Blue tides may sluice and drench their time in Caves and
    weedy creeks;
Eagles may seem to sleep wing wide upon the Air;
Ring doves may fly convuls'd across to some high cedar'd lair;   20
But the forgotten eye is still fast wedded to the ground—
As Palmer's that with weariness mid desert shrine hath found.
At such a time the Soul's a Child, in Childhood is the brain
Forgotten is the worldly heart—alone, it beats in vain—
Aye if a Madman could have leave to pass a healthful day,
To tell his forehead's swoon and faint when first began decay,
He might make tremble many a Man whose Spirit had gone
    forth
To find a Bard's low Cradle place about the silent north.
Scanty the hour and few the steps beyond the Bourn of Care,
Beyond the sweet and bitter world—beyond it unaware;   30
Scanty the hour and few the steps because a longer stay
Would bar return and make a Man forget his mortal way.
O horrible! to lose the sight of well remember'd face,
Of Brother's eyes, of Sister's Brow, constant to every place;
Filling the Air as on we move with Portraiture intense
More warm than those heroic tints that fill a Painter's sense,
When Shapes of old come striding by and visages of old,
Locks shining black, hair scanty grey and passions manifold.
No, no that horror cannot be—for at the Cable's length
Man feels the gentle Anchor pull and gladdens in its   40
    strength—
One hour half idiot he stands by mossy waterfall,
But in the very next he reads his Soul's memorial:
He reads it on the Mountain's height where chance he may
    sit down
Upon rough marble diadem, that Hill's eternal crown.

Yet be the Anchor e'er so fast, room is there for a prayer
That Man may never loose his Mind on Mountains bleak and
bare;
That he may stray league after League some great Birthplace to
find,
And keep his vision clear from speck, his inward sight
unblind—

'Not Aladin magian'

Not Aladin magian
Ever such a work began,
Not the Wizard of the Dee
Ever such a dream could see;
Not St John in Patmos' isle
In the passion of his toil
When he saw the churches seven
Golden aisled built up in heaven
Gazed at such a rugged wonder.
As I stood its roofing under   10
Lo! I saw one sleeping there
On the marble cold and bare
While the surges washed his feet
And his garments white did beat
Drench'd about the sombre rocks,
On his neck his well-grown locks
Lifted dry above the Main
Were upon the curl again—
'What is this and what art thou?'
Whisper'd I and touch'd his brow.   20
'What art thou and what is this?'
Whisper'd I and strove to kiss
The Spirit's hand to wake his eyes.
Up he started in a thrice.
'I am Lycidas,' said he,
'Fam'd in funeral Minstrelsy—
This was architected thus
By the great Oceanus,
Here his mighty waters play

Hollow Organs all the day,   30
Here by turns his dolphins all
Finny palmers great and small
Come to pay devotion due—
Each a mouth of pearls must strew;
Many a Mortal of these days
Dares to pass our sacred ways,
Dares to touch audaciously
This Cathedral of the Sea—
I have been the Pontif priest
Where the Waters never rest,   40
Where a fledgy sea bird choir
Soars for ever—holy fire
I have hid from Mortal Man.
Proteus is my Sacristan.
But the stupid eye of Mortal
Hath pass'd beyond the Rocky portal
So for ever will I leave
Such a taint and soon unweave
All the magic of the place—
'Tis now free to stupid face,   50
To cutters and to fashion boats,
To cravats and to Petticoats.
The great Sea shall war it down
For its fame shall not be blown
At every farthing quadrille dance.'
So saying with a Spirit's glance
He dived—

'Upon my Life Sir Nevis I am piqued'

Mrs C——

Upon my Life Sir Nevis I am piqued
That I have so far panted tugg'd and reek'd
To do an honor to your old bald pate
And now am sitting on you just to bate,
Without your paying me one compliment.
Alas 'tis so with all, when our intent

Is plain, and in the eye of all Mankind
We fair ones show a preference, too blind!
You Gentlemen immediately turn tail.
O let me then my hapless fate bewail!   10
Ungrateful Baldpate have I not disdain'd
The pleasant Valleys—have I not mad brain'd
Deserted all my Pickles and preserves
My China closet too—with wretched Nerves
To boot—say wretched ingrate have I not
Left my soft cushion chair and caudle pot.
'Tis true I had no corns—no! thank the fates
My Shoemaker was always Mr. Bates.
And if not Mr. Bates why I'm not old!
Still dumb ungrateful Nevis—still so cold!   20

{ Here the lady took some more whiskey and }
{ was putting even more to her lips when she }
{ dashed it to the Ground for the Mountain }
{ began to grumble which continued for a few }
Minutes before he thus began,

                     Ben Nevis

What whining bit of tongue and Mouth thus dares
Disturb my Slumber of a thousand years—
Even so long my sleep has been secure
And to be so awaked I'll not endure.
Oh pain—for since the Eagle's earliest scream
I've had a damned confounded ugly dream
A Nightmare sure—What Madam was it you?
It cannot be! My old eyes are not true!
A domestic Red-Crag, my Spectacles! Now let me see!
of Ben's   Good Heavens Lady how the gemini   30
Did you get here? O I shall split my Sides!
I shall earthquake—

                     Mrs C——

Sweet Nevis do not quake, for though I love
Your honest Countenance all things above
Truly I should not like to be convey'd

So far into your Bosom—gentle Maid
Loves not too rough a treatment, gentle sir
Pray thee be calm and do not quake nor stir—
No not a Stone or I shall go in fits—

Ben Nevis

I must—I shall—I meet not such tit bits   40
I meet not such sweet creatures every day
By my old night cap night cap night and day
I must have one sweet Buss—I must and shall!
Red-Crag!—What Madam can you then repent
Of all the toil and vigour you have spent
To see Ben Nevis and to touch his nose?
Red—Crag I say! O I must have you close!
Red-Crag, there lies beneath my farthest toe
A vein of Sulphur—go dear Red-Crag go—
And rub your flinty back against it—budge!   50
Dear Madam I must kiss you, faith I must!
I must embrace you with my dearest gust!

another   Block-head*, d'ye hear—Block-head, I'll make her feel
domestic of There lies beneath my east leg's northern heel
Ben's   A cave of young earth dragons—well my boy
Go thither quick and so complete my joy—
Take you a bundle of the largest pines
And where the sun on fiercest Phosphor shines
Fire them and ram them in the Dragon's nest
Then will the dragons fry and fizz their best   60
Until ten thousand, now no bigger than
Poor Aligators poor things of one span,
Will each one swell to twice ten times the size
Of northern whale—then for the tender prize—
The moment then—for then will Red-Crag rub
His flinty back and I shall kiss and snub
And press my dainty morsel to my breast
Block-head make haste!

                        O Muses weep the rest—
The Lady fainted and he thought her dead
So pulled the clouds again about his head   70
And went to sleep again—soon she was rous'd

By her affrighted Servants—next day hous'd
Safe on the lowly ground she bless'd her fate
That fainting fit was not delayed too late—

Nature withheld Cassandra in the Skies

Nature withheld Cassandra in the Skies
 For meet adornment a full thousand years;
She took their cream of Beauty, fairest dies
 And shaped and tinted her above all peers;
Love meanwhile held her dearly with his wings
 And underneath their shadow charm'd her eyes
To such a richness, that the cloudy Kings
 Of high Olympus utter'd slavish sighs—
When I beheld her on the Earth descend
 My heart began to burn—and only pains 10
They were my pleasures—they my sad Life's end—
 Love pour'd her Beauty into my warm veins—

"Tis "the witching time of night"'

 'Tis 'the witching time of night'
 Orbed is the Moon and bright
 And the Stars they glisten, glisten
 Seeming with bright eyes to listen—
 For what listen they?
 For a song and for a charm
 See they glisten in alarm
 And the Moon is waxing warm
 To hear what I shall say.
 Moon keep wide thy golden ears 10
 Hearken Stars, and hearken Spheres
 Hearken thou eternal Sky
 I sing an infant's lullaby,
 A pretty Lullaby!
 Listen, Listen, listen, listen
 Glisten, glisten, glisten, glisten

And hear my lullaby!
Though the Rushes that will make
Its cradle still are in the lake:
Though the linnen that will be   20
Its swathe is on the cotton tree;
Though the wollen that will keep
It warm, is on the silly sheep;
Listen Stars' light, listen, listen
Glisten, Glisten, glisten, glisten
And hear my lullaby!
Child! I see thee! Child I've found thee
Midst of the quiet all around thee!
Child I see thee! Child I spy thee
And thy mother sweet is nigh thee!   30
Child I know thee! Child no more
But a Poet *ever*more.
See, See the Lyre, the Lyre
In a flame of fire
Upon the little cradle's top
Flaring, flaring, flaring.
Past the eyesight's bearing—
Awake it from its sleep
And see if it can keep
Its eyes upon the blaze.   40
Amaze, Amaze!
It stares, it stares, it stares
It dares what no one dares
It lifts its little hand into the flame
Unharm'd, and on the strings
Paddles a little tune and sings
With dumb endeavour sweetly!
Bard art thou completely!
Little Child
O' the western wild   50
Bard art thou completely!—
Sweetly, with dumb endeavour,—
A Poet now or never!
Little Child
O' the western wild
A Poet now or never!

'And what is Love?—It is a doll dress'd up'

And what is Love?—It is a doll dress'd up
For idleness to cosset, nurse, and dangle;
A thing of soft misnomers, so divine
That silly youth doth think to make itself
Divine by loving, and so goes on
Yawning and doating a whole summer long,
Till Miss's comb is made a pearl tiara,
And common Wellingtons turn Romeo boots;
Till Cleopatra lives at Number Seven,
And Anthony resides in Brunswick Square.   10
Fools! if some passions high have warm'd the world,
If Queens and Soldiers have play'd high for hearts,
It is no reason why such agonies
Should be more common than the growth of weeds.
Fools! make me whole again that weighty pearl
The Queen of Œgypt melted, and I'll say
That ye may love in spite of beaver hats.

Fragment: 'Welcome joy, and welcome sorrow'

> Under the flag
> Of each his faction, they to battle bring
> Their embryo atoms.
>
> MILTON

Welcome joy, and welcome sorrow,
  Lethe's weed, and Hermes' feather,
Come to-day, and come to-morrow,
  I do love you both together!
  I love to mark sad faces in fair weather,
And hear a merry laugh amid the thunder;
  Fair and foul I love together;
Meadows sweet where flames burn under;
And a giggle at a wonder;
Visage sage at Pantomime;   10
Funeral and steeple-chime;
Infant playing with a skull;

Morning fair and storm-wreck'd hull;
Night-shade with the woodbine kissing;
Serpents in red roses hissing;
Cleopatra, regal drest,
With the aspics at her breast;
Dancing Music, Music sad,
Both together, sane and mad;
Muses bright and Muses pale;   20
Sombre Saturn, Momus hale,
Laugh and sigh, and laugh again,
Oh! the sweetness of the pain!
Muses bright and Muses pale,
Bare your faces of the veil,
Let me see, and let me write
Of the day, and of the night,
Both together,—let me slake
All my thirst for sweet heart-ache!
Let my bower be of Yew,   30
Interwreath'd with Myrtles new,
Pines, and Lime-trees full in bloom,
And my couch a low grass tomb.

Fragment: 'Where's the Poet? Show him! show him!'

Where's the Poet? Show him! show him!
Muses nine, that I may know him!
'Tis the man, who with a man
  Is an equal, be he King,
Or poorest of the beggar-clan,
  Or any other wondrous thing
A man may be 'twixt ape and Plato;
  'Tis the man who with a bird,
Wren or eagle, finds his way to
  All its instincts;—he hath heard   10
The Lion's roaring, and can tell
  What his horny throat expresseth;
And to him the Tiger's yell
  Comes articulate, and presseth
On his ear like mother-tongue;

To Homer

Standing aloof in giant ignorance,
　Of thee I hear and of the Cyclades,
As one who sits ashore and longs perchance
　To visit dolphin-coral in deep seas,
So wast thou blind;—but then the veil was rent,
　For Jove uncurtain'd Heaven to let thee live,
And Neptune made for thee a spumy tent,
　And Pan made sing for thee his forest-hive;
Aye on the shores of darkness there is light,
　And precipices show untrodden green,　　　　10
There is a budding morrow in midnight,
　There is a triple sight in blindness keen;
Such seeing hadst thou, as it once befel
To Dian, Queen of Earth, and Heaven, and Hell.

Hyperion: A Fragment

Book I

Deep in the shady sadness of a vale
Far sunken from the healthy breath of morn,
Far from the fiery noon, and eve's one star,
Sat gray-hair'd Saturn, quiet as a stone,
Still as the silence round about his lair;
Forest on forest hung above his head
Like cloud on cloud. No stir of air was there,
Not so much life as on a summer's day
Robs not one light seed from the feather'd grass,
But where the dead leaf fell, there did it rest.　　　　10
A stream went voiceless by, still deadened more
By reason of his fallen divinity
Spreading a shade: the Naiad 'mid her reeds
Press'd her cold finger closer to her lips.

　Along the margin-sand large foot-marks went,
No further than to where his feet had stray'd,

And slept there since. Upon the sodden ground
His old right hand lay nerveless, listless, dead,
Unsceptred; and his realmless eyes were closed;
While his bow'd head seem'd list'ning to the Earth,   20
His ancient mother, for some comfort yet.

　　It seem'd no force could wake him from his place;
But there came one, who with a kindred hand
Touch'd his wide shoulders, after bending low
With reverence, though to one who knew it not.
She was a Goddess of the infant world;
By her in stature the tall Amazon
Had stood a pigmy's height: she would have ta'en
Achilles by the hair and bent his neck;
Or with a finger stay'd Ixion's wheel.   30
Her face was large as that of Memphian sphinx,
Pedestal'd haply in a palace court,
When sages look'd to Egypt for their lore.
But oh! how unlike marble was that face:
How beautiful, if sorrow had not made
Sorrow more beautiful than Beauty's self.
There was a listening fear in her regard,
As if calamity had but begun;
As if the vanward clouds of evil days
Had spent their malice, and the sullen rear   40
Was with its stored thunder labouring up.
One hand she press'd upon that aching spot
Where beats the human heart, as if just there,
Though an immortal, she felt cruel pain:
The other upon Saturn's bended neck
She laid, and to the level of his ear
Leaning with parted lips, some words she spake
In solemn tenour and deep organ tone;
Some mourning words, which in our feeble tongue
Would come in these like accents; O how frail   50
To that large utterance of the early Gods!
'Saturn, look up!—though wherefore, poor old King?
I have no comfort for thee, no not one:
I cannot say, "O wherefore sleepest thou?"
For heaven is parted from thee, and the earth
Knows thee not, thus afflicted, for a God;

And ocean too, with all its solemn noise,
Has from thy sceptre pass'd; and all the air
Is emptied of thine hoary majesty.
Thy thunder, conscious of the new command,   60
Rumbles reluctant o'er our fallen house;
And thy sharp lightning in unpractised hands
Scorches and burns our once serene domain.
O aching time! O moments big as years!
All as ye pass swell out the monstrous truth,
And press it so upon our weary griefs
That unbelief has not a space to breathe.
Saturn, sleep on:—O thoughtless, why did I
Thus violate thy slumbrous solitude?
Why should I ope thy melancholy eyes?   70
Saturn, sleep on! while at thy feet I weep.'

    As when, upon a tranced summer-night,
Those green-rob'd senators of mighty woods,
Tall oaks, branch-charmed by the earnest stars,
Dream, and so dream all night without a stir,
Save from one gradual solitary gust
Which comes upon the silence, and dies off,
As if the ebbing air had but one wave;
So came these words and went; the while in tears
She touch'd her fair large forehead to the ground, 80
Just where her falling hair might be outspread
A soft and silken mat for Saturn's feet.
One moon, with alteration slow, had shed
Her silver seasons four upon the night,
And still these two were postured motionless,
Like natural sculpture in cathedral cavern;
The frozen God still couchant on the earth,
And the sad Goddess weeping at his feet:
Until at length old Saturn lifted up
His faded eyes, and saw his Kingdom gone,   90
And all the gloom and sorrow of the place,
And that fair kneeling Goddess; and then spake,
As with a palsied tongue, and while his beard
Shook horrid with such aspen-malady:
'O tender spouse of gold Hyperion,
Thea, I feel thee ere I see thy face;

Look up, and let me see our doom in it;
Look up, and tell me if this feeble shape
Is Saturn's; tell me, if thou hear'st the voice
Of Saturn; tell me, if this wrinkling brow,   100
Naked and bare of its great diadem,
Peers like the front of Saturn. Who had power
To make me desolate? whence came the strength?
How was it nurtur'd to such bursting forth,
While Fate seem'd strangled in my nervous grasp?
But it is so; and I am smother'd up,
And buried from all godlike exercise
Of influence benign on planets pale,
Of admonitions to the winds and seas,
Of peaceful sway above man's harvesting,   110
And all those acts which Deity supreme
Doth ease its heart of love in.—I am gone
Away from my own bosom: I have left
My strong identity, my real self,
Somewhere between the throne, and where I sit
Here on this spot of earth. Search, Thea, search!
Open thine eyes eterne, and sphere them round
Upon all space: space starr'd, and lorn of light;
Space region'd with life-air; and barren void;
Spaces of fire, and all the yawn of hell.—   120
Search, Thea, search! and tell me, if thou seest
A certain shape or shadow, making way
With wings or chariot fierce to repossess
A heaven he lost erewhile: it must—it must
Be of ripe progress—Saturn must be King.
Yes, there must be a golden victory;
There must be Gods thrown down, and trumpets blown
Of triumph calm, and hymns of festival
Upon the gold clouds metropolitan,
Voices of soft proclaim, and silver stir   130
Of strings in hollow shells; and there shall be
Beautiful things made new, for the surprise
Of the sky-children; I will give command:
Thea! Thea! Thea! where is Saturn?'

This passion lifted him upon his feet,
And made his hands to struggle in the air,

His Druid locks to shake and ooze with sweat,
His eyes to fever out, his voice to cease.
He stood, and heard not Thea's sobbing deep;
A little time, and then again he snatch'd   140
Utterance thus.—'But cannot I create?
Cannot I form? Cannot I fashion forth
Another world, another universe,
To overbear and crumble this to nought?
Where is another Chaos? Where?'—That word
Found way unto Olympus, and made quake
The rebel three.—Thea was startled up,
And in her bearing was a sort of hope,
As thus she quick-voic'd spake, yet full of awe.

'This cheers our fallen house: come to our friends,   150
O Saturn! come away, and give them heart;
I know the covert, for thence came I hither.'
Thus brief; then with beseeching eyes she went
With backward footing through the shade a space:
He follow'd, and she turn'd to lead the way
Through aged boughs, that yielded like the mist
Which eagles cleave upmounting from their nest.

Meanwhile in other realms big tears were shed,
More sorrow like to this, and such like woe,
Too huge for mortal tongue or pen of scribe: 160
The Titans fierce, self-hid, or prison-bound,
Groan'd for the old allegiance once more,
And listen'd in sharp pain for Saturn's voice.
But one of the whole mammoth-brood still kept
His sov'reignty, and rule, and majesty;—
Blazing Hyperion on his orbed fire
Still sat, still snuff'd the incense, teeming up
From man to the sun's God; yet unsecure:
For as among us mortals omens drear
Fright and perplex, so also shuddered he—   170
Not at dog's howl, or gloom-bird's hated screech,
Or the familiar visiting of one
Upon the first toll of his passing-bell,
Or prophesyings of the midnight lamp;
But horrors, portion'd to a giant nerve,

Oft made Hyperion ache. His palace bright
Bastion'd with pyramids of glowing gold,
And touch'd with shade of bronzed obelisks,
Glar'd a blood-red through all its thousand courts,
Arches, and domes, and fiery galleries;   180
And all its curtains of Aurorian clouds
Flush'd angerly: while sometimes eagle's wings,
Unseen before by Gods or wondering men,
Darken'd the place; and neighing steeds were heard,
Not heard before by Gods or wondering men.
Also, when he would taste the spicy wreaths
Of incense, breath'd aloft from sacred hills,
Instead of sweets, his ample palate took
Savour of poisonous brass and metal sick:
And so, when harbour'd in the sleepy west,   190
After the full completion of fair day,—
For rest divine upon exalted couch
And slumber in the arms of melody,
He pac'd away the pleasant hours of ease
With stride colossal, on from hall to hall;
While far within each aisle and deep recess,
His winged minions in close clusters stood,
Amaz'd and full of fear; like anxious men
Who on wide plains gather in panting troops,
When earthquakes jar their battlements and towers.   200
Even now, while Saturn, rous'd from icy trance,
Went step for step with Thea through the woods,
Hyperion, leaving twilight in the rear,
Came slope upon the threshold of the west;
Then, as was wont, his palace-door flew ope
In smoothest silence, save what solemn tubes,
Blown by the serious Zephyrs, gave of sweet
And wandering sounds, slow-breathed melodies;
And like a rose in vermeil tint and shape,
In fragrance soft, and coolness to the eye,   210
That inlet to severe magnificence
Stood full blown, for the God to enter in.

He enter'd, but he enter'd full of wrath;
His flaming robes stream'd out beyond his heels,
And gave a roar, as if of earthy fire,

That scar'd away the meek ethereal Hours
And made their dove-wings tremble. On he flared,
From stately nave to nave, from vault to vault,
Through bowers of fragrant and enwreathed light,
And diamond-paved lustrous long arcades,   220
Until he reach'd the great main cupola;
There standing fierce beneath, he stampt his foot,
And from the basements deep to the high towers
Jarr'd his own golden region; and before
The quavering thunder thereupon had ceas'd,
His voice leapt out, despite of godlike curb,
To this result: 'O dreams of day and night!
O monstrous forms! O effigies of pain!
O spectres busy in a cold, cold gloom!
O lank-eared Phantoms of black-weeded pools!   230
Why do I know ye? why have I seen ye? why
Is my eternal essence thus distraught
To see and to behold these horrors new?
Saturn is fallen, am I too to fall?
Am I to leave this haven of my rest,
This cradle of my glory, this soft clime,
This calm luxuriance of blissful light,
These crystalline pavilions, and pure fanes,
Of all my lucent empire? It is left
Deserted, void, nor any haunt of mine.   240
The blaze, the splendor, and the symmetry,
I cannot see—but darkness, death and darkness.
Even here, into my centre of repose,
The shady visions come to domineer,
Insult, and blind, and stifle up my pomp.—
Fall!—No, by Tellus and her briny robes!
Over the fiery frontier of my realms
I will advance a terrible right arm
Shall scare that infant thunderer, rebel Jove,
And bid old Saturn take his throne again.'—   250
He spake, and ceas'd, the while a heavier threat
Held struggle with his throat but came not forth;
For as in theatres of crowded men
Hubbub increases more they call out 'Hush!'
So at Hyperion's words the Phantoms pale
Bestirr'd themselves, thrice horrible and cold;

And from the mirror'd level where he stood
A mist arose, as from a scummy marsh.
At this, through all his bulk an agony
Crept gradual, from the feet unto the crown,   260
Like a lithe serpent vast and muscular
Making slow way, with head and neck convuls'd
From over-strained might. Releas'd, he fled
To the eastern gates, and full six dewy hours
Before the dawn in season due should blush,
He breath'd fierce breath against the sleepy portals,
Clear'd them of heavy vapours, burst them wide
Suddenly on the ocean's chilly streams.
The planet orb of fire, whereon he rode
Each day from east to west the heavens through,   270
Spun round in sable curtaining of clouds;
Not therefore veiled quite, blindfold, and hid,
But ever and anon the glancing spheres,
Circles, and arcs, and broad-belting colure,
Glow'd through, and wrought upon the muffling dark
Sweet-shaped lightnings from the nadir deep
Up to the zenith,—hieroglyphics old,
Which sages and keen-eyed astrologers
Then living on the earth, with labouring thought
Won from the gaze of many centuries: 280
Now lost, save what we find on remnants huge
Of stone, or marble swart; their import gone,
Their wisdom long since fled.—Two wings this orb
Possess'd for glory, two fair argent wings,
Ever exalted at the God's approach:
And now, from forth the gloom their plumes immense
Rose, one by one, till all outspreaded were;
While still the dazzling globe maintain'd eclipse,
Awaiting for Hyperion's command.
Fain would he have commanded, fain took throne   290
And bid the day begin, if but for change.
He might not:—No, though a primeval God:
The sacred seasons might not be disturb'd.
Therefore the operations of the dawn
Stay'd in their birth, even as here 'tis told.
Those silver wings expanded sisterly,
Eager to sail their orb; the porches wide

Open'd upon the dusk demesnes of night;
And the bright Titan, phrenzied with new woes,
Unus'd to bend, by hard compulsion bent   300
His spirit to the sorrow of the time;
And all along a dismal rack of clouds,
Upon the boundaries of day and night,
He stretch'd himself in grief and radiance faint.
There as he lay, the Heaven with its stars
Look'd down on him with pity, and the voice
Of Cœlus, from the universal space,
Thus whisper'd low and solemn in his ear.
'O brightest of my children dear, earth-born
And sky-engendered, Son of Mysteries   310
All unrevealed even to the powers
Which met at thy creating; at whose joys
And palpitations sweet, and pleasures soft,
I, Cœlus, wonder, how they came and whence;
And at the fruits thereof what shapes they be,
Distinct, and visible; symbols divine,
Manifestations of that beauteous life
Diffus'd unseen throughout eternal space:
Of these new-form'd art thou, oh brightest child!
Of these, thy brethren and the Goddesses!   320
There is sad feud among ye, and rebellion
Of son against his sire. I saw him fall,
I saw my first-born tumbled from his throne!
To me his arms were spread, to me his voice
Found way from forth the thunders round his head!
Pale wox I, and in vapours hid my face.
Art thou, too, near such doom? vague fear there is:
For I have seen my sons most unlike Gods.
Divine ye were created, and divine
In sad demeanour, solemn, undisturb'd,   330
Unruffled, like high Gods, ye liv'd and ruled:
Now I behold in you fear, hope, and wrath;
Actions of rage and passion; even as
I see them, on the mortal world beneath,
In men who die.—This is the grief, O Son!
Sad sign of ruin, sudden dismay, and fall!
Yet do thou strive; as thou art capable,
As thou canst move about, an evident God;

And canst oppose to each malignant hour
Ethereal presence:—I am but a voice;   340
My life is but the life of winds and tides,
No more than winds and tides can I avail:—
But thou canst.—Be thou therefore in the van
Of circumstance; yea, seize the arrow's barb
Before the tense string murmur.—To the earth!
For there thou wilt find Saturn, and his woes.
Meantime I will keep watch on thy bright sun,
And of thy seasons be a careful nurse.'—
Ere half this region-whisper had come down,
Hyperion arose, and on the stars   350
Lifted his curved lids, and kept them wide
Until it ceas'd; and still he kept them wide:
And still they were the same bright, patient stars.
Then with a slow incline of his broad breast,
Like to a diver in the pearly seas,
Forward he stoop'd over the airy shore,
And plung'd all noiseless into the deep night.

Book II

Just at the self-same beat of Time's wide wings
Hyperion slid into the rustled air,
And Saturn gain'd with Thea that sad place
Where Cybele and the bruised Titans mourn'd.
It was a den where no insulting light
Could glimmer on their tears; where their own groans
They felt, but heard not, for the solid roar
Of thunderous waterfalls and torrents hoarse,
Pouring a constant bulk, uncertain where.
Crag jutting forth to crag, and rocks that seem'd   10
Ever as if just rising from a sleep,
Forehead to forehead held their monstrous horns;
And thus in thousand hugest phantasies
Made a fit roofing to this nest of woe.
Instead of thrones, hard flint they sat upon,
Couches a rugged stone, and slaty ridge
Stubborn'd with iron. All were not assembled:
Some chain'd in torture, and some wandering.
Cœus, and Gyges, and Briareüs,

Typhon, and Dolor, and Porphyrion,   20
With many more, the brawniest in assault,
Were pent in regions of laborious breath;
Dungeon'd in opaque element, to keep
Their clenched teeth still clench'd, and all their limbs
Lock'd up like veins of metal, crampt and screw'd;
Without a motion, save of their big hearts
Heaving in pain, and horribly convuls'd
With sanguine feverous boiling gurge of pulse.
Mnemosyne was straying in the world;
Far from her moon had Phœbe wandered;   30
And many else were free to roam abroad,
But for the main, here found they covert drear.
Scarce images of life, one here, one there,
Lay vast and edgeways; like a dismal cirque
Of Druid stones, upon a forlorn moor,
When the chill rain begins at shut of eve,
In dull November, and their chancel vault,
The Heaven itself, is blinded throughout night.
Each one kept shroud, nor to his neighbour gave.
Or word, or look, or action of despair.   40
Creüs was one; his ponderous iron mace
Lay by him, and a shatter'd rib of rock
Told of his rage, ere he thus sank and pined.
Iäpetus another; in his grasp,
A serpent's plashy neck; its barbed tongue
Squeez'd from the gorge, and all its uncurl'd length
Dead; and because the creature could not spit
Its poison in the eyes of conquering Jove.
Next Cottus: prone he lay, chin uppermost,
As though in pain; for still upon the flint   50
He ground severe his skull, with open mouth
And eyes at horrid working. Nearest him
Asia, born of most enormous Caf,
Who cost her mother Tellus keener pangs,
Though feminine, than any of her sons:
More thought than woe was in her dusky face,
For she was prophesying of her glory;
And in her wide imagination stood
Palm-shaded temples, and high rival fanes,
By Oxus or in Ganges' sacred isles.   60

Even as Hope upon her anchor leans,
So leant she, not so fair, upon a tusk
Shed from the broadest of her elephants.
Above her, on a crag's uneasy shelve,
Upon his elbow rais'd, all prostrate else,
Shadow'd Enceladus; once tame and mild
As grazing ox unworried in the meads;
Now tiger-passion'd, lion-thoughted, wroth,
He meditated, plotted, and even now
Was hurling mountains in that second war,   70
Not long delay'd, that scar'd the younger Gods
To hide themselves in forms of beast and bird.
Not far hence Atlas; and beside him prone
Phorcus, the sire of Gorgons. Neighbour'd close
Oceanus, and Tethys, in whose lap
Sobb'd Clymene among her tangled hair.
In midst of all lay Themis, at the feet
Of Ops the queen all clouded round from sight;
No shape distinguishable, more than when
Thick night confounds the pine-tops with the clouds: 80
And many else whose names may not be told.
For when the Muse's wings are air-ward spread,
Who shall delay her flight? And she must chaunt
Of Saturn, and his guide, who now had climb'd
With damp and slippery footing from a depth
More horrid still. Above a sombre cliff
Their heads appear'd, and up their stature grew
Till on the level height their steps found ease:
Then Thea spread abroad her trembling arms
Upon the precincts of this nest of pain,   90
And sidelong fix'd her eye on Saturn's face:
There saw she direst strife; the supreme God
At war with all the frailty of grief,
Of rage, of fear, anxiety, revenge,
Remorse, spleen, hope, but most of all despair.
Against these plagues he strove in vain; for Fate
Had pour'd a mortal oil upon his head,
A disanointing poison: so that Thea,
Affrighted, kept her still, and let him pass
First onwards in, among the fallen tribe.   100

As with us mortal men, the laden heart
Is persecuted more, and fever'd more,
When it is nighing to the mournful house
Where other hearts are sick of the same bruise;
So Saturn, as he walk'd into the midst,
Felt faint, and would have sunk among the rest,
But that he met Enceladus's eye,
Whose mightiness, and awe of him, at once
Came like an inspiration; and he shouted,
'Titans, behold your God!' at which some groan'd;   110
Some started on their feet; some also shouted;
Some wept, some wail'd, all bow'd with reverence;
And Ops, uplifting her black folded veil,
Show'd her pale cheeks, and all her forehead wan,
Her eye-brows thin and jet, and hollow eyes.
There is a roaring in the bleak-grown pines
When Winter lifts his voice; there is a noise
Among immortals when a God gives sign,
With hushing finger, how he means to load
His tongue with the full weight of utterless thought,   120
With thunder, and with music, and with pomp:
Such noise is like the roar of bleak-grown pines;
Which, when it ceases in this mountain'd world,
No other sound succeeds; but ceasing here,
Among these fallen, Saturn's voice therefrom
Grew up like organ, that begins anew
Its strain, when other harmonies, stopt short,
Leave the dinn'd air vibrating silverly.
Thus grew it up—'Not in my own sad breast,
Which is its own great judge and searcher out,   130
Can I find reason why ye should be thus:
Not in the legends of the first of days,
Studied from that old spirit-leaved book
Which starry Uranus with finger bright
Sav'd from the shores of darkness, when the waves
Low-ebb'd still hid it up in shallow gloom;—
And the which book ye know I ever kept
For my firm-based footstool:—Ah, infirm!
Not there, nor in sign, symbol, or portent

Of element, earth, water, air, and fire,—   140
At war, at peace, or inter-quarreling
One against one, or two, or three, or all
Each several one against the other three,
As fire with air loud warring when rain-floods
Drown both, and press them both against earth's face,
Where, finding sulphur, a quadruple wrath
Unhinges the poor world;—not in that strife,
Wherefrom I take strange lore, and read it deep,
Can I find reason why ye should be thus:
No, no-where can unriddle, though I search,   150
And pore on Nature's universal scroll
Even to swooning, why ye, Divinities,
The first-born of all shap'd and palpable Gods,
Should cower beneath what, in comparison,
Is untremendous might. Yet ye are here,
O'erwhelm'd, and spurn'd, and batter'd, ye are here!
O Titans, shall I say 'Arise!'—Ye groan:
Shall I say 'Crouch!'—Ye groan. What can I then?
O Heaven wide! O unseen parent dear!
What can I? Tell me, all ye brethren Gods,   160
How we can war, how engine our great wrath!
O speak your counsel now, for Saturn's ear
Is all a-hunger'd. Thou, Oceanus,
Ponderest high and deep; and in thy face
I see, astonied, that severe content
Which comes of thought and musing: give us help!'

    So ended Saturn; and the God of the Sea,
Sophist and sage, from no Athenian grove,
But cogitation in his watery shades,
Arose, with locks not oozy, and began,   170
In murmurs, which his first-endeavouring tongue
Caught infant-like from the far-foamed sands.
'O ye, whom wrath consumes! who, passion-stung,
Writhe at defeat, and nurse your agonies!
Shut up your senses, stifle up your ears,
My voice is not a bellows unto ire.
Yet listen, ye who will, whilst I bring proof
How ye, perforce, must be content to stoop:
And in the proof much comfort will I give,

If ye will take that comfort in its truth.   180
We fall by course of Nature's law, not force
Of thunder, or of Jove. Great Saturn, thou
Hast sifted well the atom-universe;
But for this reason, that thou art the King,
And only blind from sheer supremacy,
One avenue was shaded from thine eyes,
Through which I wandered to eternal truth.
And first, as thou wast not the first of powers,
So art thou not the last; it cannot be:
Thou art not the beginning nor the end.   190
From Chaos and parental Darkness came
Light, the first fruits of that intestine broil,
That sullen ferment, which for wondrous ends
Was ripening in itself. The ripe hour came,
And with it Light, and Light, engendering
Upon its own producer, forthwith touch'd
The whole enormous matter into life.
Upon that very hour, our parentage,
The Heavens and the Earth, were manifest:
Then thou first-born, and we the giant-race,   200
Found ourselves ruling new and beauteous realms.
Now comes the pain of truth, to whom 'tis pain;
O folly! for to bear all naked truths,
And to envisage circumstance, all calm,
That is the top of sovereignty. Mark well!
As Heaven and Earth are fairer, fairer far
Than Chaos and blank Darkness, though once chiefs;
And as we show beyond that Heaven and Earth
In form and shape compact and beautiful,
In will, in action free, companionship,   210
And thousand other signs of purer life;
So on our heels a fresh perfection treads,
A power more strong in beauty, born of us
And fated to excel us, as we pass
In glory that old Darkness: nor are we
Thereby more conquer'd, than by us the rule
Of shapeless Chaos. Say, doth the dull soil
Quarrel with the proud forests it hath fed,
And feedeth still, more comely than itself?
Can it deny the chiefdom of green groves?   220

Or shall the tree be envious of the dove
Because it cooeth, and hath snowy wings
To wander wherewithal and find its joys?
We are such forest-trees, and our fair boughs
Have bred forth, not pale solitary doves,
But eagles, golden-feather'd, who do tower
Above us in their beauty, and must reign
In right thereof; for 'tis the eternal law
That first in beauty should be first in might:
Yea, by that law, another race may drive   230
Our conquerors to mourn as we do now.
Have ye beheld the young God of the Seas,
My dispossessor? Have ye seen his face?
Have ye beheld his chariot, foam'd along
By noble winged creatures he hath made?
I saw him on the calmed waters scud,
With such a glow of beauty in his eyes,
That it enforc'd me to bid sad farewell
To all my empire: farewell sad I took,
And hither came, to see how dolorous fate   240
Had wrought upon ye; and how I might best
Give consolation in this woe extreme.
Receive the truth, and let it be your balm.'

    Whether through poz'd conviction, or disdain,
They guarded silence, when Oceanus
Left murmuring, what deepest thought can tell?
But so it was, none answer'd for a space,
Save one whom none regarded, Clymene;
And yet she answer'd not, only complain'd,
With hectic lips, and eyes up-looking mild,   250
Thus wording timidly among the fierce:
'O Father, I am here the simplest voice,
And all my knowledge is that joy is gone,
And this thing woe crept in among our hearts,
There to remain for ever, as I fear:
I would not bode of evil, if I thought
So weak a creature could turn off the help
Which by just right should come of mighty Gods;
Yet let me tell my sorrow, let me tell

Of what I heard, and how it made me weep,   260
And know that we had parted from all hope.
I stood upon a shore, a pleasant shore,
Where a sweet clime was breathed from a land
Of fragrance, quietness, and trees, and flowers.
Full of calm joy it was, as I of grief;
Too full of joy and soft delicious warmth;
So that I felt a movement in my heart
To chide, and to reproach that solitude
With songs of misery, music of our woes;
And sat me down, and took a mouthed shell   270
And murmur'd into it, and made melody—
O melody no more! for while I sang,
And with poor skill let pass into the breeze
The dull shell's echo, from a bowery strand
Just opposite, an island of the sea,
There came enchantment with the shifting wind,
That did both drown and keep alive my ears.
I threw my shell away upon the sand,
And a wave fill'd it, as my sense was fill'd
With that new blissful golden melody.   280
A living death was in each gush of sounds,
Each family of rapturous hurried notes,
That fell, one after one, yet all at once,
Like pearl beads dropping sudden from their string:
And then another, then another strain,
Each like a dove leaving its olive perch,
With music wing'd instead of silent plumes,
To hover round my head, and make me sick
Of joy and grief at once. Grief overcame,
And I was stopping up my frantic ears,   290
When, past all hindrance of my trembling hands,
A voice came sweeter, sweeter than all tune,
And still it cried, 'Apollo! young Apollo!
The morning-bright Apollo! young Apollo!'
I fled, it follow'd me, and cried 'Apollo!'
O Father, and O Brethren, had ye felt
Those pains of mine; O Saturn, hadst thou felt,
Ye would not call this too indulged tongue
Presumptuous, in thus venturing to be heard.'

So far her voice flow'd on, like timorous brook   300
That, lingering along a pebbled coast,
Doth fear to meet the sea: but sea it met,
And shudder'd; for the overwhelming voice
Of huge Enceladus swallow'd it in wrath:
The ponderous syllables, like sullen waves
In the half-glutted hollows of reef-rocks,
Came booming thus, while still upon his arm
He lean'd; not rising, from supreme contempt.
'Or shall we listen to the over-wise,
Or to the over-foolish, Giant-Gods?   310
Not thunderbolt on thunderbolt, till all
That rebel Jove's whole armoury were spent,
Not world on world upon these shoulders piled,
Could agonize me more than baby-words
In midst of this dethronement horrible.
Speak! roar! shout! yell! ye sleepy Titans all.
Do ye forget the blows, the buffets vile?
Are ye not smitten by a youngling arm?
Dost thou forget, sham Monarch of the Waves,
Thy scalding in the seas? What, have I rous'd   320
Your spleens with so few simple words as these?
O joy! for now I see ye are not lost:
O joy! for now I see a thousand eyes
Wide glaring for revenge!'—As this he said,
He lifted up his stature vast, and stood,
Still without intermission speaking thus:
'Now ye are flames, I'll tell you how to burn,
And purge the ether of our enemies;
How to feed fierce the crooked stings of fire,
And singe away the swollen clouds of Jove,   330
Stifling that puny essence in its tent.
O let him feel the evil he hath done;
For though I scorn Oceanus's lore,
Much pain have I for more than loss of realms:
The days of peace and slumberous calm are fled;
Those days, all innocent of scathing war,
When all the fair Existences of heaven
Came open-eyed to guess what we would speak:—
That was before our brows were taught to frown,
Before our lips knew else but solemn sounds;   340

That was before we knew the winged thing,
Victory, might be lost, or might be won.
And be ye mindful that Hyperion,
Our brightest brother, still is undisgraced—
Hyperion, lo! his radiance is here!'

    All eyes were on Enceladus's face,
And they beheld, while still Hyperion's name
Flew from his lips up to the vaulted rocks,
A pallid gleam across his features stern:
Not savage, for he saw full many a God   350
Wroth as himself. He look'd upon them all,
And in each face he saw a gleam of light,
But splendider in Saturn's, whose hoar locks
Shone like the bubbling foam about a keel
When the prow sweeps into a midnight cove.
In pale and silver silence they remain'd,
Till suddenly a splendour, like the morn,
Pervaded all the beetling gloomy steeps,
All the sad spaces of oblivion,
And every gulf, and every chasm old,   360
And every height, and every sullen depth,
Voiceless, or hoarse with loud tormented streams:
And all the everlasting cataracts,
And all the headlong torrents far and near,
Mantled before in darkness and huge shade,
Now saw the light and made it terrible.
It was Hyperion:—a granite peak
His bright feet touch'd, and there he stay'd to view
The misery his brilliance had betray'd
To the most hateful seeing of itself.   370
Golden his hair of short Numidian curl,
Regal his shape majestic, a vast shade
In midst of his own brightness, like the bulk
Of Memnon's image at the set of sun
To one who travels from the dusking East:
Sighs, too, as mournful as that Memnon's harp
He utter'd, while his hands contemplative
He press'd together, and in silence stood.
Despondence seiz'd again the fallen Gods
At sight of the dejected King of Day,   380

And many hid their faces from the light:
But fierce Enceladus sent forth his eyes
Among the brotherhood; and, at their glare,
Uprose Iäpetus, and Creüs too,
And Phorcus, sea-born, and together strode
To where he towered on his eminence.
There those four shouted forth old Saturn's name;
Hyperion from the peak loud answered, 'Saturn!'
Saturn sat near the Mother of the Gods,
In whose face was no joy, though all the Gods   390
Gave from their hollow throats the name of 'Saturn!'

Book III

Thus in alternate uproar and sad peace,
Amazed were those Titans utterly.
O leave them, Muse! O leave them to their woes;
For thou art weak to sing such tumults dire:
A solitary sorrow best befits
Thy lips, and antheming a lonely grief.
Leave them, O Muse! for thou anon wilt find
Many a fallen old Divinity
Wandering in vain about bewildered shores.
Meantime touch piously the Delphic harp,   10
And not a wind of heaven but will breathe
In aid soft warble from the Dorian flute;
For lo! 'tis for the Father of all verse.
Flush every thing that hath a vermeil hue,
Let the rose glow intense and warm the air,
And let the clouds of even and of morn
Float in voluptuous fleeces o'er the hills;
Let the red wine within the goblet boil,
Cold as a bubbling well; let faint-lipp'd shells,
On sands, or in great deeps, vermilion turn   20
Through all their labyrinths; and let the maid
Blush keenly, as with some warm kiss surpris'd.
Chief isle of the embowered Cyclades,
Rejoice, O Delos, with thine olives green,
And poplars, and lawn-shading palms, and beech,
In which the Zephyr breathes the loudest song,

And hazels thick, dark-stemm'd beneath the shade:
Apollo is once more the golden theme!
Where was he, when the Giant of the Sun
Stood bright, amid the sorrow of his peers?   30
Together had he left his mother fair
And his twin-sister sleeping in their bower,
And in the morning twilight wandered forth
Beside the osiers of a rivulet,
Full ankle-deep in lilies of the vale.
The nightingale had ceas'd, and a few stars
Were lingering in the heavens, while the thrush
Began calm-throated. Throughout all the isle
There was no covert, no retired cave
Unhaunted by the murmurous noise of waves,   40
Though scarcely heard in many a green recess.
He listen'd, and he wept, and his bright tears
Went trickling down the golden bow he held.
Thus with half-shut suffused eyes he stood,
While from beneath some cumbrous boughs hard by
With solemn step an awful Goddess came,
And there was purport in her looks for him,
Which he with eager guess began to read
Perplex'd, the while melodiously he said:
'How cam'st thou over the unfooted sea?   50
Or hath that unique mien and robed form
Mov'd in these vales invisible till now?
Sure I have heard those vestments sweeping o'er
The fallen leaves, when I have sat alone
In cool mid-forest. Surely I have traced
The rustle of those ample skirts about
These grassy solitudes, and seen the flowers
Lift up their heads, as still the whisper pass'd.
Goddess! I have beheld those eyes before,
And their eternal calm, and all that face,   60
Or I have dream'd.'—'Yes,' said the supreme shape,
'Thou hast dream'd of me; and awaking up
Didst find a lyre all golden by thy side,
Whose strings touch'd by thy fingers, all the vast
Unwearied ear of the whole universe
Listen'd in pain and pleasure at the birth
Of such new tuneful wonder. Is't not strange

That thou shouldst weep, so gifted? Tell me, youth,
What sorrow thou canst feel; for I am sad
When thou dost shed a tear: explain thy griefs   70
To one who in this lonely isle hath been
The watcher of thy sleep and hours of life,
From the young day when first thy infant hand
Pluck'd witless the weak flowers, till thine arm
Could bend that bow heroic to all times.
Show thy heart's secret to an ancient Power
Who hath forsaken old and sacred thrones
For prophecies of thee, and for the sake
Of loveliness new born.'—Apollo then,
With sudden scrutiny and gloomless eyes,   80
Thus answer'd, while his white melodious throat
Throbb'd with the syllables.—'Mnemosyne!
Thy name is on my tongue, I know not how;
Why should I tell thee what thou so well seest?
Why should I strive to show what from thy lips
Would come no mystery? For me, dark, dark,
And painful vile oblivion seals my eyes:
I strive to search wherefore I am so sad,
Until a melancholy numbs my limbs;
And then upon the grass I sit, and moan,   90
Like one who once had wings.—O why should I
Feel curs'd and thwarted, when the liegeless air
Yields to my step aspirant? why should I
Spurn the green turf as hateful to my feet?
Goddess benign, point forth some unknown thing:
Are there not other regions than this isle?
What are the stars? There is the sun, the sun!
And the most patient brilliance of the moon!
And stars by thousands! Point me out the way
To any one particular beauteous star,   100
And I will flit into it with my lyre,
And make its silvery splendour pant with bliss.
I have heard the cloudy thunder: Where is power?
Whose hand, whose essence, what divinity
Makes this alarum in the elements,
While I here idle listen on the shores
In fearless yet in aching ignorance?
O tell me, lonely Goddess, by thy harp,

That waileth every morn and eventide,
Tell me why thus I rave, about these groves! 110
Mute thou remainest—Mute! yet I can read
A wondrous lesson in thy silent face:
Knowledge enormous makes a God of me.
Names, deeds, gray legends, dire events, rebellions,
Majesties, sovran voices, agonies,
Creations and destroyings, all at once
Pour into the wide hollows of my brain,
And deify me, as if some blithe wine
Or bright elixir peerless I had drunk,
And so become immortal.'—Thus the God, 120
While his enkindled eyes, with level glance
Beneath his white soft temples, stedfast kept
Trembling with light upon Mnemosyne.
Soon wild commotions shook him, and made flush
All the immortal fairness of his limbs;
Most like the struggle at the gate of death;
Or liker still to one who should take leave
Of pale immortal death, and with a pang
As hot as death's is chill, with fierce convulse
Die into life: so young Apollo anguish'd: 130
His very hair, his golden tresses famed
Kept undulation round his eager neck.
During the pain Mnemosyne upheld
Her arms as one who prophesied.—At length
Apollo shriek'd;—and lo! from all his limbs
Celestial

Fancy

Ever let the Fancy roam,
Pleasure never is at home:
At a touch sweet Pleasure melteth,
Like to bubbles when rain pelteth;
Then let winged Fancy wander
Through the thought still spread beyond her:
Open wide the mind's cage-door,
She'll dart forth, and cloudward soar.
O sweet Fancy! let her loose;
Summer's joys are spoilt by use, 10

And the enjoying of the Spring
Fades as does its blossoming;
Autumn's red-lipp'd fruitage too,
Blushing through the mist and dew,
Cloys with tasting: What do then?
Sit thee by the ingle, when
The sear faggot blazes bright,
Spirit of a winter's night;
When the soundless earth is muffled,
And the caked snow is shuffled   20
From the ploughboy's heavy shoon;
When the Night doth meet the Noon
In a dark conspiracy
To banish Even from her sky.
Sit thee there, and send abroad,
With a mind self-overaw'd,
Fancy, high-commission'd:—send her!
She has vassels to attend her:
She will bring, in spite of frost,
Beauties that the earth hath lost;   30
She will bring thee, all together,
All delights of summer weather;
All the buds and bells of May,
From dewy sward or thorny spray;
All the heaped Autumn's wealth,
With a still, mysterious stealth:
She will mix these pleasures up
Like three fit wines in a cup,
And thou shalt quaff it:—thou shalt hear
Distant harvest-carols clear;   40
Rustle of the reaped corn;
Sweet birds antheming the morn:
And, in the same moment—hark!
'Tis the early April lark,
Or the rooks, with busy caw,
Foraging for sticks and straw.
Thou shalt, at one glance, behold
The daisy and the marigold;
White-plum'd lilies, and the first
Hedge-grown primrose that hath burst;   50
Shaded hyacinth, alway

Sapphire queen of the mid-May;
And every leaf, and every flower
Pearled with the self-same shower.
Thou shalt see the field-mouse peep
Meagre from its celled sleep;
And the snake all winter-thin
Cast on sunny bank its skin;
Freckled nest-eggs thou shalt see
Hatching in the hawthorn-tree,   60
When the hen-bird's wing doth rest
Quiet on her mossy nest;
Then the hurry and alarm
When the bee-hive casts its swarm;
Acorns ripe down-pattering,
While the autumn breezes sing.

Oh sweet Fancy! let her loose;
Every thing is spoilt by use:
Where's the cheek that doth not fade,
Too much gaz'd at? Where's the maid   70
Whose lip mature is ever new?
Where's the eye, however blue,
Doth not weary? Where's the face
One would meet in every place?
Where's the voice, however soft,
One would hear so very oft?
At a touch sweet Pleasure melteth
Like to bubbles when rain pelteth.
Let, then, winged Fancy find
Thee a mistress to thy mind: 80
Dulcet-eyed as Ceres' daughter,
Ere the God of Torment taught her
How to frown and how to chide;
With a waist and with a side
White as Hebe's, when her zone
Slipt its golden clasp, and down
Fell her kirtle to her feet,
While she held the goblet sweet,
And Jove grew languid.—Break the mesh
Of the Fancy's silken leash;   90
Quickly break her prison-string

And such joys as these she'll bring.—
Let the winged Fancy roam,
Pleasure never is at home.

Ode: 'Bards of Passion and of Mirth'

Bards of Passion and of Mirth,
Ye have left your souls on earth!
Have ye souls in heaven too,
Doubled-lived in regions new?
Yes, and those of heaven commune
With the spheres of sun and moon;
With the noise of fountains wond'rous,
And the parle of voices thund'rous;
With the whisper of heaven's trees
And one another, in soft ease   10
Seated on Elysian lawns
Brows'd by none but Dian's fawns;
Underneath large blue-bells tented,
Where the daisies are rose-scented,
And the rose herself has got
Perfume which on earth is not;
Where the nightingale doth sing
Not a senseless, tranced thing,
But divine melodious truth;
Philosophic numbers smooth;   20
Tales and golden histories
Of heaven and its mysteries.

    Thus ye live on high, and then
On the earth ye live again;
And the souls ye left behind you
Teach us, here, the way to find you,
Where your other souls are joying,
Never slumber'd, never cloying.
Here, your earth-born souls still speak
To mortals, of their little week;   30
Of their sorrows and delights;
Of their passions and their spites;

Of their glory and their shame;
What doth strengthen and what maim.
Thus ye teach us, every day,
Wisdom, though fled far away.

Bards of Passion and of Mirth,
Ye have left your souls on earth!
Ye have souls in heaven too,
Double-lived in regions new!   40

'I had a dove and the sweet dove died'

I had a dove and the sweet dove died,
  And I have thought it died of grieving:
O what could it mourn for? it was tied
  With a silken thread of my own hand's weaving.
Sweet little red-feet why did you die?
Why would you leave me—sweet dove why?
You lived alone on the forest tree—
Why pretty thing could you not live with me?
I kiss'd you oft, and I gave you white peas—
Why not live sweetly as in the green trees?   10

Song: 'Hush, hush, tread softly, hush, hush my dear'

I

Hush, hush, tread softly, hush, hush my dear,
  All the house is asleep, but we know very well
That the jealous, the jealous old Baldpate may hear,
  Though you've padded his night-cap, O sweet Isabel.
    Though your feet are more light than a fairy's feet,
    Who dances on bubbles where brooklets meet.
Hush hush, tread softly, hush hush, my dear,
For less than a nothing the jealous can hear:

2

No leaf doth tremble, no ripple is there
  On the river—All's still, and the night's sleepy eye   10
Closes up, and forgets all its Lethean care
  Charmed to death by the drone of the humming may fly.
    And the moon, whether prudish or complaisant,
    Hath fled to her bower, well knowing I want
No light in the darkness, no torch in the gloom;
But my Isabel's eyes and her lips pulped with bloom.

3

Lift the latch, ah gently! ah tenderly, sweet
  We are dead, if that latchet gives one little chink:
Well done, now those lips and a flowery seat—
  The old man may dream and the planets may wink;   20
    The shut rose shall dream of our loves and awake
    Full blown and such warmth for the morning take;
The stockdove shall hatch her soft brace and shall coo,
While I kiss to the melody aching all through.

The Eve of St. Agnes

I

St. Agnes' Eve—Ah, bitter chill it was!
The owl, for all his feathers, was a-cold;
The hare limp'd trembling through the frozen grass,
And silent was the flock in woolly fold:
Numb were the Beadsman's fingers, while he told
His rosary, and while his frosted breath,
Like pious incense, from a censer old,
Seem'd taking flight for heaven, without a death,
Past the sweet Virgin's picture, while his prayer he saith.

2

His prayer he saith, this patient, holy man;   10
Then takes his lamp, and riseth from his knees,
And back returneth, meagre, barefoot, wan,

Along the chapel aisle by slow degrees:
The sculptur'd dead, on each side, seem to freeze,
Emprison'd in black, purgatorial rails:
Knights, ladies, praying in dumb orat'ries,
He passeth by; and his weak spirit fails
To think how they may ache in icy hoods and mails.

3

Northward he turneth through a little door,
And scarce three steps, ere Music's golden tongue   20
Flatter'd to tears this aged man and poor;
But no—already had his deathbell rung;
The joys of all his life were said and sung:
His was harsh penance on St. Agnes' Eve:
Another way he went, and soon among
Rough ashes sat he for his soul's reprieve,
And all night kept awake, for sinners' sake to grieve.

4

That ancient Beadsman heard the prelude soft;
And so it chanc'd, for many a door was wide,
From hurry to and fro. Soon, up aloft,   30
The silver, snarling trumpets 'gan to chide:
The level chambers, ready with their pride,
Were glowing to receive a thousand guests:
The carved angels, ever eager-eyed,
Star'd, where upon their heads the cornice rests,
With hair blown back, and wings put cross-wise on their
     breasts.

5

At length burst in the argent revelry,
With plume, tiara, and all rich array,
Numerous as shadows haunting fairily
The brain, new stuff'd, in youth, with triumphs gay   40
Of old romance. These let us wish away,
And turn, sole-thoughted, to one lady there,
Whose heart had brooded, all that wintry day,
On love, and wing'd St. Agnes' saintly care,
As she had heard old dames full many times declare.

6

They told her how, upon St. Agnes' Eve,
Young virgins might have visions of delight,
And soft adorings from their loves receive
Upon the honey'd middle of the night,
If ceremonies due they did aright;   50
As, supperless to bed they must retire,
And couch supine their beauties, lily white;
Nor look behind, nor sideways, but require
Of Heaven with upward eyes for all that they desire.

7

Full of this whim was thoughtful Madeline:
The music, yearning like a God in pain,
She scarcely heard: her maiden eyes divine,
Fix'd on the floor, saw many a sweeping train
Pass by—she heeded not at all: in vain
Came many a tiptoe, amorous cavalier,   60
And back retir'd, not cool'd by high disain;
But she saw not: her heart was otherwhere:
She sigh'd for Agnes' dreams, the sweetest of the year.

8

She danc'd along with vague, regardless eyes,
Anxious her lips, her breathing quick and short:
The hallow'd hour was near at hand: she sighs
Amid the timbrels, and the throng'd resort
Of whisperers in anger, or in sport;
'Mid looks of love, defiance, hate, and scorn,
Hoodwink'd with faery fancy; all amort,   70
Save to St. Agnes and her lambs unshorn,
And all the bliss to be before to-morrow morn.

9

So, purposing each moment to retire,
She linger'd still. Meantime, across the moors,
Had come young Porphyro, with heart on fire
For Madeline. Beside the portal doors,
Buttress'd from moonlight, stands he, and implores

All saints to give him sight of Madeline,
But for one moment in the tedious hours,
That he might gaze and worship all unseen;   80
Perchance speak, kneel, touch, kiss—in sooth such things have
    been.

                              10

He ventures in: let no buzz'd whisper tell:
All eyes be muffled, or a hundred swords
Will storm his heart, Love's fev'rous citadel:
For him, those chambers held barbarian hordes,
Hyena foemen, and hot-blooded lords,
Whose very dogs would execrations howl
Against his lineage: not one breast affords
Him any mercy, in that mansion foul,
Save one old beldame, weak in body and in soul.   90

                              11

Ah, happy chance! the aged creature came,
Shuffling along with ivory-headed wand,
To where he stood, hid from the torch's flame,
Behind a broad hall-pillar, far beyond
The sound of merriment and chorus bland:
He startled her; but soon she knew his face,
And grasp'd his fingers in her palsied hand,
Saying, 'Mercy, Porphyro! hie thee from this place;
They are all here to-night, the whole blood-thirsty race!

                              12

'Get hence! get hence! there's dwarfish Hildebrand;   100
He had a fever late, and in the fit
He cursed thee and thine, both house and land:
Then there's that old Lord Maurice, not a whit
More tame for his gray hairs—Alas me! flit!
Flit like a ghost away.'—'Ah, Gossip dear,
We're safe enough; here in this arm-charm sit,
And tell me how'—'Good Saints! not here, not here;
Follow me, child, or else these stones will be thy bier.'

13

He follow'd through a lowly arched way,
Brushing the cobwebs with his lofty plume,   110
And as she mutter'd 'Well-a—well-a-day!'
He found him in a little moonlight room,
Pale, lattic'd, chill, and silent as a tomb.
'Now tell me where is Madeline,' said he,
'O tell me, Angela, by the holy loom
Which none but secret sisterhood may see,
When they St. Agnes' wool are weaving piously.'

14

'St Agnes! Ah! it is St. Agnes' Eve—
Yet men will murder upon holy days:
Thou must hold water in a witch's sieve,   120
And be liege-lord of all the Elves and Fays,
To venture so: it fills me with amaze
To see thee, Porphyro!—St. Agnes' Eve!
God's help! my lady fair the conjuror plays
This very night: good angels her deceive!
But let me laugh awhile, I've mickle time to grieve.'

15

Feebly she laugheth in the languid moon,
While Porphyro upon her face doth look,
Like puzzled urchin on an aged crone
Who keepeth clos'd a wond'rous riddle-book,   130
As spectacled she sits in chimney nook.
But soon his eyes grew brilliant, when she told
His lady's purpose; and he scarce could brook
Tears, at the thought of those enchantments cold,
And Madeline asleep in lap of legends old.

16

Sudden a thought came like a full-blown rose,
Flushing his brow, and in his pained heart
Made purple riot: then doth he propose
A stratagem, that makes the beldame start:
'A cruel man and impious thou art: 140

Sweet lady, let her pray, and sleep, and dream
Alone with her good angels, far apart
From wicked men like thee. Go, go!—I deem
Thou canst not surely be the same that thou didst seem.'

17

'I will not harm her, by all saints I swear,'
Quoth Porphyro: 'O may I ne'er find grace
When my weak voice shall whisper its last prayer,
If one of her soft ringlets I displace,
Or look with ruffian passion in her face:
Good Angela, believe me by these tears;   150
Or I will, even in a moment's space,
Awake, with horrid shout, my foemen's ears,
And beard them, though they be more fang'd than wolves and
    bears.'

18

'Ah! why wilt thou affright a feeble soul?
A poor, weak, palsy-stricken, churchyard thing,
Whose passing-bell may ere the midnight toll;
Whose prayers for thee, each morn and evening,
Were never miss'd'—Thus plaining, doth she bring
A gentler speech from burning Porphyro;
So woful, and of such deep sorrowing,   160
That Angela gives promise she will do
Whatever he shall wish, betide her weal or woe.

19

Which was, to lead him, in close secrecy,
Even to Madeline's chamber, and there hide
Him in a closet, of such privacy
That he might see her beauty unespied,
And win perhaps that night a peerless bride,
While legion'd fairies pac'd the coverlet,
And pale enchantment held her sleepy-eyed.
Never on such a night have lovers met,   170
Since Merlin paid his Demon all the monstrous debt.

20

'It shall be as thou wishest,' said the Dame:
'All cates and dainties shall be stored there
Quickly on this feast-night: by the tambour frame
Her own lute thou wilt see: no time to spare,
For I am slow and feeble, and scarce dare
On such a catering trust my dizzy head.
Wait here, my child, with patience; kneel in prayer
The while: Ah! thou must needs the lady wed,
Or may I never leave my grave among the dead.'   180

21

So saying, she hobbled off with busy fear.
The lover's endless minutes slowly pass'd;
The dame return'd, and whisper'd in his ear
To follow her; with aged eyes aghast
From fright of dim espial. Safe at last,
Through many a dusky gallery, they gain
The maiden's chamber, silken, hush'd, and chaste;
Where Porphyro took covert, pleas'd amain.
His poor guide hurried back with agues in her brain.

22

Her falt'ring hand upon the balustrade,   190
Old Angela was feeling for the stair,
When Madeline, St. Agnes' charmed maid,
Rose, like a mission'd spirit, unaware:
With silver taper's light, and pious care,
She turn'd, and down the aged gossip led
To a safe level matting. Now prepare,
Young Porphyro, for gazing on that bed;
She comes, she comes again, like ring-dove fray'd and fled.

23

Out went the taper as she hurried in;
Its little smoke, in pallid moonshine, died: 200
She clos'd the door, she panted, all akin
To spirits of the air, and visions wide:
No uttered syllable, or, woe betide!

But to her heart, her heart was voluble,
Paining with eloquence her balmy side;
As though a tongueless nightingale should swell
Her throat in vain, and die, heart-stifled, in her dell.

24

A casement high and triple-arch'd there was,
All garlanded with carven imag'ries
Of fruits, and flowers, and bunches of knot-grass,   210
And diamonded with panes of quaint device,
Innumerable of stains and splendid dyes,
As are the tiger-moth's deep-damask'd wings;
And in the midst, 'mong thousand heraldries,
And twilight saints, and dim emblazonings,
A shielded scutcheon blush'd with blood of queens and kings.

25

Full on this casement shone the wintry moon,
And threw warm gules on Madeline's fair breast,
As down she knelt for heaven's grace and boon;
Rose-bloom fell on her hands, together prest,   220
And on her silver cross soft amethyst,
And on her hair a glory, like a saint:
She seem'd a splendid angel, newly drest,
Save wings, for heaven:—Porphyro grew faint:
She knelt, so pure a thing, so free from mortal taint.

26

Anon his heart revives: her vespers done,
Of all its wreathed pearls her hair she frees;
Unclasps her warmed jewels one by one;
Loosens her fragrant boddice; by degrees
Her rich attire creeps rustling to her knees: 230
Half-hidden, like a mermaid in sea-weed,
Pensive awhile she dreams awake, and sees,
In fancy, fair St. Agnes in her bed,
But dares not look behind, or all the charm is fled.

27

Soon, trembling in her soft and chilly nest,
In sort of wakeful swoon, perplex'd she lay,
Until the poppied warmth of sleep oppress'd
Her soothed limbs, and soul fatigued away;
Flown, like a thought, until the morrow-day;
Blissfully haven'd both from joy and pain;   240
Clasp'd like a missal where swart Paynims pray;
Blinded alike from sunshine and from rain,
As though a rose should shut, and be a bud again.

28

Stol'n to this paradise, and so entranced,
Porphyro gazed upon her empty dress,
And listen'd to her breathing, if it chanced
To wake into a slumberous tenderness;
Which when he heard, that minute did he bless,
And breath'd himself: then from the closet crept,
Noiseless as fear in a wide wilderness,   250
And over the hush'd carpet, silent, stept,
And 'tween the curtains peep'd, where, lo!—how fast she slept.

29

Then by the bed-side, where the faded moon
Made a dim, silver twilight, soft he set
A table, and, half anguish'd, threw thereon
A cloth of woven crimson, gold, and jet:—
O for some drowsy Morphean amulet!
The boisterous, midnight, festive clarion,
The kettle-drum, and far-heard clarionet,
Affray his ears, though but in dying tone:—   260
The hall door shuts again, and all the noise is gone.

30

And still she slept an azure-lidded sleep,
In blanched linen, smooth, and lavender'd,
While he from forth the closet brought a heap
Of candied apple, quince, and plum, and gourd;
With jellies soother than the creamy curd,

And lucent syrops, tinct with cinnamon;
Manna and dates, in argosy transferr'd
From Fez; and spiced dainties, every one,
From silken Samarcand to cedar'd Lebanon.   270

31

These delicates he heap'd with glowing hand
On golden dishes and in baskets bright
Of wreathed silver: sumptuous they stand
In the retired quiet of the night,
Filling the chilly room with perfume light.—
'And now, my love, my seraph fair, awake!
Thou art my heaven, and I thine eremite:
Open thine eyes, for meek St. Agnes' sake,
Or I shall drowse beside thee, so my soul doth ache.'

32

Thus whispering, his warm, unnerved arm   280
Sank in her pillow. Shaded was her dream
By the dusk curtains:—'twas a midnight charm
Impossible to melt as iced stream:
The lustrous salvers in the moonlight gleam;
Broad golden fringe upon the carpet lies:
It seem'd he never, never could redeem
From such a stedfast spell his lady's eyes;
So mus'd awhile, entoil'd in woofed phantasies.

33

Awakening up, he took her hollow lute,—
Tumultuous,—and, in chords that tenderest be,   290
He play'd an ancient ditty, long since mute,
In Provence call'd, 'La belle dame sans mercy':
Close to her ear touching the melody;—
Wherewith disturb'd, she utter'd a soft moan:
He ceased—she panted quick—and suddenly
Her blue affrayed eyes wide open shone:
Upon his knees he sank, pale as smooth-sculptured stone.

34

Her eyes were open, but she still beheld,
Now wide awake, the vision of her sleep:
There was a painful change, that nigh expell'd   300
The blisses of her dream so pure and deep
At which fair Madeline began to weep,
And moan forth witless words with many a sigh;
While still her gaze on Porphyro would keep;
Who knelt, with joined hands and piteous eye,
Fearing to move or speak, she look'd so dreamingly.

35

'Ah Porphyro!' said she, 'but even now
Thy voice was at sweet tremble in mine ear,
Made tuneable with every sweetest vow;
And those sad eyes were spiritual and clear: 310
How chang'd thou art! how pallid, chill, and drear!
Give me that voice again, my Porphyro,
Those looks immortal, those complainings dear!
Oh leave me not in this eternal woe,
For if thou diest, my Love, I know not where to go.'

36

Beyond a mortal man impassion'd far
At these voluptuous accents, he arose,
Ethereal, flush'd, and like a throbbing star
Seen mid the sapphire heaven's deep repose;
Into her dream he melted, as the rose   320
Blendeth its odour with the violet,—
Solution sweet: meantime the frost-wind blows
Like Love's alarum pattering the sharp sleet
Against the window-panes; St. Agnes' moon hath set.

37

'Tis dark: quick pattereth the flaw-blown sleet:
'This is no dream, my bride, my Madeline!'
'Tis dark: the iced gusts still rave and beat:
'No dream, alas! alas! and woe is mine!
Porphyro will leave me here to fade and pine.—

Cruel! what traitor could thee hither bring?   330
I curse not, for my heart is lost in thine,
Though thou forsakest a deceived thing;—
A dove forlorn and lost with sick unpruned wing.'

38

'My Madeline! sweet dreamer! lovely bride!
Say, may I be for aye thy vassal blest?
Thy beauty's shield, heart-shap'd and vermeil dyed?
Ah, silver shrine, here will I take my rest
After so many hours of toil and quest,
A famish'd pilgrim,—saved by miracle.
Though I have found, I will not rob thy nest   340
Saving of thy sweet self; if thou think'st well
To trust, fair Madeline, to no rude infidel.

39

'Hark! 'tis an elfin-storm from faery land,
Of haggard seeming, but a boon indeed:
Arise—arise! the morning is at hand;—
The bloated wassaillers will never heed:—
Let us away, my love, with happy speed;
There are no ears to hear, or eyes to see,—
Drown'd all in Rhenish and the sleepy mead:
Awake! arise! my love, and fearless be,   350
For o'er the southern moors I have a home for thee.'

40

She hurried at his words, beset with fears,
For there were sleeping dragons all around,
At glaring watch, perhaps, with ready spears—
Down the wide stairs a darkling way they found.—
In all the house was heard no human sound.
A chain-droop'd lamp was flickering by each door;
The arras, rich with horseman, hawk, and hound,
Flutter'd in the besieging wind's uproar;
And the long carpets rose along the gusty floor.   360

41

They glide, like phantoms, into the wide hall;
Like phantoms, to the iron porch, they glide;
Where lay the Porter, in uneasy sprawl,
With a huge empty flaggon by his side:
The wakeful bloodhound rose, and shook his hide,
But his sagacious eye an inmate owns:
By one, and one, the bolts full easy slide:—
The chains lie silent on the footworn stones;—
The key turns, and the door upon its hinges groans.

42

And they are gone: ay, ages long ago   370
These lovers fled away into the storm.
That night the Baron dreamt of many a woe,
And all his warrior-guests, with shade and form
Of witch, and demon, and large coffin-worm,
Were long be-nightmar'd. Angela the old
Died palsy-twitch'd, with meagre face deform;
The Beadsman, after thousand aves told,
For aye unsought for slept among his ashes cold.

The Eve of St. Mark

Upon a sabbath day it fell,
Twice holy was the sabbath bell,
That call'd the folk to evening prayer—
The City streets were clean and fair
From wholesome drench of April rains
And on the western window panes
The chilly sunset faintly told
Of unmatur'd green vallies cold,
Of the green thorny bloomless hedge,
Of rivers new with springtide sedge,   10
Of Primroses by shelter'd rills
And daisies on the aguish hills—
Twice holy was the sabbath bell:
The silent Streets were crowded well

With staid and pious companies
Warm from their fireside orat'ries
And moving with demurest air
To even song and vesper prayer.
Each arched porch and entry low
Was fill'd with patient folk and slow,   20
With whispers hush and shuffling feet
While play'd the organs loud and sweet—

The Bells had ceas'd, the prayers begun
And Bertha had not yet half done:
A curious volume patch'd and torn
That all day long from earliest morn
Had taken captive her two eyes
Among its golden broideries—
Perplex'd her with a thousand things—
The Stars of heaven and angels' wings,   30
Martyrs in a fiery blaze—
Azure saints mid silver rays,
Aaron's breastplate, and the seven
Candlesticks John saw in heaven—
The winged Lion of St. Mark
And the covenantal Ark
With its many mysteries,
Cherubim and golden Mice.

Bertha was a maiden fair
Dwelling in the old Minster Square;   40
From her fireside she could see
Sidelong its rich antiquity—
Far as the Bishop's garden wall
Where Sycamores and elm trees tall
Full leav'd the forest had outstript—
By no sharp north wind ever nipt
So shelter'd by the mighty pile—
Bertha arose and read awhile
With forehead 'gainst the window pane—
Again she tried and then again   50
Until the dusk eve left her dark
Upon the Legend of St. Mark.
From pleated lawn-frill fine and thin

She lifted up her soft warm chin,
With aching neck and swimming eyes
And dazed with saintly imageries.

All was gloom, and silent all
Save now and then the still footfall
Of one returning townwards late—
Past the echoing minster gate—   60
The clamorous daws that all the day
Above tree tops and towers play
Pair by pair had gone to rest,
Each in its ancient belfry nest
Where asleep they fall betimes
To musick of the drowsy chimes.
All was silent—all was gloom
Abroad and in the homely room—
Down she sat poor cheated soul
And struck a Lamp from the dismal coal,   70
Leaned forward, with bright drooping hair
And slant book full against the glare.
Her shadow in uneasy guize
Hover'd about a giant size
On ceiling beam and old oak chair,
The Parrot's cage and pannel square
And the warm angled winter screen
On which were many monsters seen
Call'd Doves of Siam, Lima Mice
And legless birds of Paradise,   80
Macaw and tender av'davat
And silken furr'd angora cat—
Untir'd she read; her shadow still
Glower'd about as it would fill
The Room with wildest forms and shades
As though some ghostly Queens of spades
Had come to mock behind her back—
And dance, and ruffle their garments black.
Untir'd she read the Legend page
Of holy Mark from youth to age;   90
On Land, on Seas, in pagan-chains,
Rejoicing for his many pains—
Sometimes the learned Eremite

With golden star, or dagger bright
Referr'd to pious poesies
Written in smallest crowquill size
Beneath the text; and thus the rhyme
Was parcel'd out from time to time:
—'Als writith he of swevenis
Men han beforne they wake in bliss,   100
Whanne thate hir friendes thinke hem bound
In crimpid shroude farre under grounde;
And how a litling child mote be
A sainte er its nativitie;
Gif that the modre (god her blesse)
Kepen in solitarinesse,
And kissen devoute the holy croce.
Of Goddis love and Sathan's force
He writith; and thinges many mo:
Of swiche thinges I may not shew;   110
Bot I must tellen verilie
Somdel of Sainte Cicilie;
And chieflie whate he auctorethe
Of Sainte Markis life and dethe.'

At length her constant eyelids come
Upon the fervent Martyrdom;
Then lastly to his holy shrine
Exalt amid the tapers' shine
At Venice—

'Gif ye wol stonden hardie wight'

Gif ye wol stonden hardie wight—
Amiddes of the blacke night—
Righte in the churche porch, pardie
Ye wol behold a companie
Approuchen thee full dolorouse
For sooth to sain from everich house
Be it in City or village
Wol come the Phantom and image
Of ilka gent and ilka carle

Whome coldè Deathè hath in parle   10
And wol some day that very year
Touchen with foulè venime spear
And sadly do them all to die—
Hem all shalt thou see verilie
And everichon shall by the pass
All who must die that year Alas—

'Why did I laugh tonight? No voice will tell'

Why did I laugh tonight? No voice will tell:
  No God, no Demon of severe response
Deigns to reply from heaven or from Hell.—
  Then to my human heart I turn at once—
Heart! thou and I are here sad and alone;
  Say, wherefore did I laugh? O mortal pain!
O Darkness! Darkness! ever must I moan
  To question Heaven and Hell and Heart in vain!
Why did I laugh? I know this being's lease
  My fancy to its utmost blisses spreads: 10
Yet could I on this very midnight cease,
  And the world's gaudy ensigns see in shreds.
Verse, fame and Beauty are intense indeed
But Death intenser—Death is Life's high meed.

'He is to weet a melancholy Carle'

He is to weet a melancholy Carle
Thin in the waist, with bushy head of hair
As hath the seeded thistle when in parle
It holds the Zephyr ere it sendeth fair
Its light balloons into the summer air;
Thereto his beard had not begun to bloom
No brush had touch'd his chin or razor sheer
No care had touch'd his cheek with mortal doom
But new he was and bright as scarf from Persian loom—

Ne cared he for wine, or half and half   10
Ne cared he for fish or flesh or fowl
And sauces held he worthless as the chaff;
He 'sdeign'd the swine-herd at the wassail bowl
Ne with lewd ribbalds sat he by cheek by jowl,
Ne with sly Lemans in the scorner's chair
But after water brooks this Pilgrim's soul
Panted, and all his food was woodland air
Though he would ofttimes feast on gilliflowers rare—

The slang of cities in no wise he knew—
Tipping the wink to him was heathen Greek—   20
He sipp'd no olden Tom or ruin blue
Or nantz, or cheery brandy drank full meek
By many a Damsel hoarse and rouge of cheek
Nor did he know each aged Watchman's beat—
Nor in obscured purlieus would he seek
For curled Jewesses with ankles neat
Who as they walk abroad make tinkling with their feet—

A dream, after reading Dante's Episode of Paolo and Francesca

As Hermes once took to his feathers light,
   When lulled Argus, baffled, swoon'd and slept,
So on a Delphic reed my idle spright
   So play'd, so charm'd, so conquer'd, so bereft
The dragon-world of all its hundred eyes;
   And, seeing it asleep, so fled away—
Not unto Ida with its snow-cold skies,
   Nor unto Tempe, where Jove griev'd a day;
But to that second circle of sad hell,
   Where 'mid the gust, the world-wind, and the flaw   10
Of rain and hailstones, lovers need not tell
   Their sorrows. Pale were the sweet lips I saw,
Pale were the lips I kiss'd, and fair the form
I floated with about that melancholy storm.

La belle dame sans merci

O what can ail thee knight at arms
   Alone and palely loitering?
The sedge has withered from the Lake
   And no birds sing!

O what can ail thee knight at arms
   So haggard and so woe begone?
The squirrel's granary is full
   And the harvest's done.

I see a lilly on thy brow
   With anguish moist and fever dew,   10
And on thy cheeks a fading rose
   Fast withereth too—

I met a Lady in the Meads
   Full beautiful, a faery's child
Her hair was long, her foot was light
   And her eyes were wild—

I made a Garland for her head,
   And bracelets too, and fragrant Zone:
She look'd at me as she did love
   And made sweet moan—   20

I set her on my pacing steed
   And nothing else saw all day long
For sidelong would she bend and sing
   A faery's song—

She found me roots of relish sweet
   And honey wild and manna dew
And sure in language strange she said
   'I love thee true'—

She took me to her elfin grot
   And there she wept and sigh'd full sore   30
And there I shut her wild wild eyes
   With kisses four.

And there she lulled me asleep
  And there I dream'd—Ah Woe betide!
The latest dream I ever dreamt
  On the cold hill side.

I saw pale kings and Princes too
  Pale warriors, death pale were they all;
They cried 'La belle dame sans merci
  Thee hath in thrall.'   40

I saw their starv'd lips in the gloam
  With horrid warning gaped wide
And I awoke and found me here
  On the cold hill's side

And this is why I sojourn here
  Alone and palely loitering;
Though the sedge is wither'd from the Lake
  And no birds sing—

Sonnet to Sleep

O soft embalmer of the still midnight,
  Shutting with careful fingers and benign
Our gloom-pleas'd eyes, embower'd from the light,
  Enshaded in forgetfulness divine:
O soothest sleep! if so it please thee, close,
  In midst of this thine hymn my willing eyes,
Or wait the Amen ere thy poppy throws
  Around my bed its lulling charities.
Then save me or the passed day will shine
  Upon my pillow breeding many woes: 10
Save me from curious conscience that still hoards
  Its strength for darkness, burrowing like the mole;
Turn the Key deftly in the oiled wards
  And seal the hushed Casket of my soul—

Ode to Psyche

O Goddess! hear these tuneless numbers, wrung
    By sweet enforcement and remembrance dear,
And pardon that thy secrets should be sung
    Even into thine own soft-conched ear:
Surely I dreamt to-day, or did I see
    The winged Psyche with awaken'd eyes?
I wander'd in a forest thoughtlessly,
    And, on the sudden, fainting with surprise,
Saw two fair creatures, couched side by side
    In deepest grass, beneath the whisp'ring roof   10
    Of leaves and trembled blossoms, where there ran
       A brooklet, scarce espied:
'Mid hush'd, cool-rooted flowers, fragrant-eyed,
    Blue, silver-white, and budded Tyrian,
They lay calm-breathing on the bedded grass;
    Their arms embraced, and their pinions too;
    Their lips touch'd not, but had not bade adieu
As if disjoined by soft-handed slumber,
And ready still past kisses to outnumber
    At tender eye-dawn of aurorean love: 20
       The winged boy I knew;
    But who wast thou, O happy, happy dove?
       His Psyche true!

O latest born and loveliest vision far
    Of all Olympus' faded hierarchy!
Fairer than Phœbe's sapphire-region'd star
    Or Vesper, amorous glow-worm of the sky;
Fairer than these, though temple thou hast none,
       Nor altar heap'd with flowers;
Nor virgin-choir to make delicious moan   30
       Upon the midnight hours;
No voice, no lute, no pipe, no incense sweet
    From chain-swung censer teeming;
No shrine, no grove, no oracle, no heat
    Of pale-mouth'd prophet dreaming.

O brightest! though too late for antique vows,
    Too, too late for the fond believing lyre,

When holy were the haunted forest boughs,
   Holy the air, the water, and the fire;
Yet even in these days so far retir'd 40
   From happy pieties, thy lucent fans,
   Fluttering among the faint Olympians,
I see, and sing, by my own eyes inspired.
So let me be thy choir, and make a moan
      Upon the midnight hours;
Thy voice, thy lute, thy pipe, thy incense sweet
   From swinged censer teeming;
Thy shrine, thy grove, thy oracle, thy heat
   Of pale-mouth'd prophet dreaming.

Yes, I will be thy priest, and build a fane 50
   In some untrodden region of my mind,
Where branched thoughts, new grown with pleasant pain,
   Instead of pines shall murmur in the wind:
Far, far around shall those dark-cluster'd trees
   Fledge the wild-ridged mountains steep by steep;
And there by zephyrs, streams, and birds, and bees,
   The moss-lain Dryads shall be lull'd to sleep;
And in the midst of this wide quietness
A rosy sanctuary will I dress
With the wreath'd trellis of a working brain, 60
   With buds, and bells, and stars without a name,
With all the gardener Fancy e'er could feign,
   Who breeding flowers, will never breed the same:
And there shall be for thee all soft delight
   That shadowy thought can win,
A bright torch, and a casement ope at night,
   To let the warm Love in!

On Fame

Fame like a wayward girl will still be coy
   To those who woo her with too slavish knees
   But makes surrender to some thoughtless boy
And dotes the more upon a heart at ease—
She is a Gipsey will not speak to those
   Who have not learnt to be content without her,

A Jilt whose ear was never whisper'd close
   Who think they scandal her who talk about her—
A very Gipsey is she Nilus born,
Sister in law to jealous Potiphar.—   10
Ye lovesick Bards, repay her scorn for scorn.
Ye lovelorn Artists madmen that ye are,
Make your best bow to her and bid adieu
Then if she likes it she will follow you—

On Fame

You cannot eat your cake and have it too.—PROVERB

How fever'd is that Man who cannot look
   Upon his mortal days with temperate blood,
Who vexes all the leaves of his Life's book
   And robs his fair name of its maidenhood;
It is as if the rose should pluck herself
   Or the ripe plum finger its misty bloom;
As if a clear Lake meddling with itself
   Should cloud its pureness with a muddy gloom.
But the rose leaves herself upon the Briar
For winds to kiss and grateful Bees to feed   10
And the ripe plum still wears its dim attire—
   The undisturbed Lake has crystal space—
   Why then should Man teasing the world for grace
Spoil his salvation by a fierce miscreed?

'If by dull rhymes our English must be chain'd'

If by dull rhymes our English must be chain'd,
   And, like Andromeda, the Sonnet sweet
      Fetter'd, in spite of pained loveliness;
Let us find out, if we must be constrain'd,
   Sandals more interwoven and complete
To fit the naked foot of Poesy;
      Let us inspect the Lyre, and weigh the stress
Of every chord, and see what may be gain'd

By ear industrious, and attention meet;
 Misers of sound and syllable, no less   10
Than Midas of his coinage, let us be
 Jealous of dead leaves in the bay wreath crown,
So, if we may not let the Muse be free,
 She will be bound with garlands of her own.

Two or three Posies

Two or three Posies
With two or three simples
Two or three Noses
With two or three pimples,
Two or three wise men
And two or three ninnys
Two or three purses
And two or three guineas
Two or three raps
At two or three doors   10
Two or three naps
Of two or three hours—
Two or three Cats
And two or three mice
Two or three sprats
At a very great price—
Two or three sandies
And two or three tabbies
Two or three dandies—
And Two Mrs.— mum! 20
Two or three Smiles
And two or three frowns
Two or three Miles
To two or three towns
Two or three pegs
For two or three bonnets
Two or three dove's eggs
To hatch into sonnets—

Ode on Indolence

They toil not, neither do they spin.

1

One morn before me were three figures seen,
  With bowed necks, and joined hands, side-faced;
And one behind the other stepp'd serene,
  In placid sandals, and in white robes graced:
They pass'd, like figures on a marble Urn,
  When shifted round to see the other side;
    They came again; as when the Urn once more
Is shifted round, the first seen Shades return;
  And they were strange to me, as may betide
    With Vases, to one deep in Phidian lore.   10

2

How is it, Shadows, that I knew ye not?
  How came ye muffled in so hush a Masque?
Was it a silent deep-disguised plot
  To steal away, and leave without a task
My idle days? Ripe was the drowsy hour;
  The blissful cloud of summer-indolence
    Benumb'd my eyes; my pulse grew less and less;
Pain had no sting, and pleasure's wreath no flower.
  O, why did ye not melt, and leave my sense
    Unhaunted quite of all but—nothingness?   20

3

A third time pass'd they by, and, passing, turn'd
  Each one the face a moment whiles to me;
Then faded, and to follow them I burn'd
  And ached for wings, because I knew the three:
The first was a fair Maid, and Love her name;
  The second was Ambition, pale of cheek,
    And ever watchful with fatigued eye;
The last, whom I love more, the more of blame
  Is heap'd upon her. Maiden most unmeek,—
    I knew to be my demon Poesy.   30

4

They faded, and, forsooth! I wanted wings:
  O folly! What is love? and where is it?
And for that poor Ambition—it springs
  From a man's little heart's short fever-fit;
For Poesy!—no,—she has not a joy,—
    At least for me,—so sweet as drowsy noons,
      And evenings steep'd in honied indolence;
O, for an age so shelter'd from annoy,
    That I may never know how change the moons,
      Or hear the voice of busy common-sense!   40

5

A third time came they by;—alas! wherefore?
  My sleep had been embroider'd with dim dreams;
My soul had been a lawn besprinkled o'er
  With flowers, and stirring shades, and baffled beams:
The morn was clouded, but no shower fell,
    Though in her lids hung the sweet tears of May;
      The open casement press'd a new-leaved vine,
    Let in the budding warmth and throstle's lay;
O Shadows! 'twas a time to bid farewell!
      Upon your skirts had fallen no tears of mine.   50

6

So, ye three Ghosts, adieu! Ye cannot raise
  My head cool-bedded in the flowery grass;
For I would not be dieted with praise,
  A pet-lamb in a sentimental Farce!
Fade softly from my eyes, and be once more
    In masque-like figures on the dreamy Urn;
      Farewell! I yet have visions for the night,
And for the day faint visions there is store;
      Vanish, ye Phantoms, from my idle spright,
Into the clouds, and never more return!   60

'Shed no tear—O shed no tear'

Shed no tear—O shed no tear
The Flower will bloom another year—
Weep no more—O weep no more—
Young buds sleep in the root's white core—
Dry your eyes—O dry your eyes
For I was taught in Paradise
To ease my breast of Melodies—
                    Shed no tear—

Over head—look over head
'Mong the blossoms white and red—   10
Look up, look up—I flutter now
On this flush pomgranate bow—
See me 'tis this silvery bill
Ever cures the good man's ill—
Shed no tear—O shed no tear
The flower will bloom another year
Adieu—Adieu—I fly adieu
I vanish in the heaven's blue—
                    Adieu Adieu—

Ode to a Nightingale

I

My heart aches, and a drowsy numbness pains
    My sense, as though of hemlock I had drunk,
Or emptied some dull opiate to the drains
    One minute past, and Lethe-wards had sunk:
'Tis not through envy of thy happy lot,
    But being too happy in thine happiness,—
        That thou, light-winged Dryad of the trees,
            In some melodious plot
Of beechen green, and shadows and numberless,
    Singest of summer in full-throated ease.   10

2

O, for a draught of vintage! that hath been
 Cool'd a long age in the deep-delved earth,
Tasting of Flora and the country green,
 Dance, and Provençal song, and sunburnt mirth!
O for a beaker full of the warm South,
 Full of the true, the blushful Hippocrene,
  With beaded bubbles winking at the brim,
   And purple-stained mouth;
 That I might drink, and leave the world unseen,
 And with thee fade away into the forest dim: 20

3

Fade far away, dissolve, and quite forget
 What thou among the leaves hast never known,
The weariness, the fever, and the fret
 Here, where men sit and hear each other groan;
Where palsy shakes a few, sad, last gray hairs,
Where youth grows pale, and spectre-thin, and dies;
 Where but to think is to be full of sorrow
  And leaden-eyed despairs,
Where Beauty cannot keep her lustrous eyes,
 Or new Love pine at them beyond tomorrow.   30

4

Away! away! for I will fly to thee,
 Not charioted by Bacchus and his pards,
But on the viewless wings of Poesy,
 Though the dull brain perplexes and retards:
Already with thee! tender is the night,
 And haply the Queen-Moon is on her throne,
  Cluster'd around by all her starry Fays;
   But here there is no light,
 Save what from heaven is with the breezes blown
  Through vendurous glooms and winding mossy ways.   40

5

I cannot see what flowers are at my feet,
 Nor what soft incense hangs upon the boughs,

But, in embalmed darkness, guess each sweet
   Wherewith the seasonable month endows
The grass, the thicket, and the fruit-tree wild;
   White hawthorn, and the pastoral eglantine;
     Fast fading violets cover'd up in leaves;
      And mid-May's eldest child,
The coming musk-rose, full of dewy wine,
     The murmurous haunt of flies on summer eves.   50

6

Darkling I listen; and, for many a time
   I have been half in love with easeful Death,
Call'd him soft names in many a mused rhyme,
   To take into the air my quiet breath;
     Now more than ever seems it rich to die,
To cease upon the midnight with no pain,
    While thou art pouring forth thy soul abroad
      In such an ecstasy!
Still wouldst thou sing, and I have ears in vain—
   To thy high requiem become a sod.   60

7

Thou wast not born for death, immortal Bird!
   No hungry generations tread thee down;
The voice I hear this passing night was heard
   In ancient days by emperor and clown:
Perhaps the self-same song that found a path
    Through the sad heart of Ruth, when, sick for home,
     She stood in tears amid the alien corn;
      The same that oft-times hath
Charm'd magic casements, opening on the foam
   Of perilous seas, in faery lands forlorn.   70

8

Forlorn! the very word is like a bell
   To toll me back from thee to my sole self!
Adieu! the fancy cannot cheat so well
   As she is fam'd to do, deceiving elf.
Adieu! adieu! thy plaintive anthem fades

Past the near meadows, over the still stream,
Up the hill-side; and now 'tis buried deep
In the next valley-glades:
Was it a vision, or a waking dream?
Fled is that music:—Do I wake or sleep? 80

Ode on a Grecian Urn

1

Thou still unravish'd bride of quietness,
Thou foster-child of silence and slow time,
Sylvan historian, who canst thus express
A flowery tale more sweetly than our rhyme:
What leaf-fring'd legend haunts about thy shape
Of deities or mortals, or of both,
In Tempe or the dales of Arcady?
What men or gods are these? What maidens loth?
What mad pursuit? What struggle to escape?
What pipes and timbrels? What wild ecstasy? 10

2

Heard melodies are sweet, but those unheard
Are sweeter; therefore, ye soft pipes, play on;
Not to the sensual ear, but, more endear'd,
Pipe to the spirit ditties of no tone:
Fair youth, beneath the trees, thou canst not leave
Thy song, nor ever can those trees be bare;
Bold Lover, never, never canst thou kiss,
Though winning near the goal—yet, do not grieve;
She cannot fade, though thou hast not thy bliss,
For ever wilt thou love, and she be fair! 20

3

Ah, happy, happy boughs! that cannot shed
Your leaves, nor ever bid the Spring adieu;
And, happy melodist, unwearied,
For ever piping songs for ever new;

More happy love! more happy, happy love!
  For ever warm and still to be enjoy'd,
    For ever panting, and for ever young;
All breathing human passion far above,
  That leaves a heart high-sorrowful and cloy'd,
    A burning forehead, and a parching tongue.   30

4

Who are these coming to the sacrifice?
  To what green altar, O mysterious priest,
Lead'st thou that heifer lowing at the skies,
  And all her silken flanks with garlands drest?
What little town by river or sea shore,
  Or mountain-built with peaceful citadel,
    Is emptied of this folk, this pious morn?
And, little town, thy streets for evermore
  Will silent be; and not a soul to tell
    Why thou art desolate, can e'er return.   40

5

O Attic shape! Fair attitude! with brede
  Of marble men and maidens overwrought,
With forest branches and the trodden weed;
  Thou, silent form, dost tease us out of thought
As doth eternity: Cold Pastoral!
  When old age shall this generation waste,
    Thou shalt remain, in midst of other woe
Than ours, a friend to man, to whom thou say'st,
  'Beauty is truth, truth beauty,'—that is all
    Ye know on earth, and all ye need to know.   50

Ode on Melancholy

1

No, no, go not to Lethe, neither twist
  Wolf's-bane, tight-rooted, for its poisonous wine;
Nor suffer thy pale forehead to be kiss'd
  By nightshade, ruby grape of Proserpine;
Make not your rosary of yew-berries,

Nor let the beetle, nor the death-moth be
  Your mournful Psyche, nor the downy owl
A partner in your sorrow's mysteries;
  For shade to shade will come too drowsily,
    And drown the wakeful anguish of the soul.   10

                          2

But when the melancholy fit shall fall
  Sudden from heaven like a weeping cloud,
That fosters the droop-headed flowers all,
  And hides the green hill in an April shroud;
Then glut thy sorrow on a morning rose,
  Or on the rainbow of the salt sand-wave,
    Or on the wealth of globed peonies;
Or if thy mistress some rich anger shows,
  Emprison her soft hand, and let her rave,
    And feed deep, deep upon her peerless eyes.   20

                          3

She dwells with Beauty—Beauty that must die;
  And Joy, whose hand is ever at his lips
Bidding adieu; and aching Pleasure nigh,
  Turning to poison while the bee-mouth sips:
Ay, in the very temple of Delight
  Veil'd Melancholy has her sovran shrine,
    Though seen of none save him whose strenuous tongue
Can burst Joy's grape against his palate fine;
  His soul shall taste the sadness of her might,
    And be among her cloudy trophies hung.   30

              The Fall of Hyperion:
                    A Dream

                      Canto I

    Fanatics have their dreams, wherewith they weave
    A paradise for a sect; the savage too
    From forth the loftiest fashion of his sleep
    Guesses at Heaven: pity these have not

Trac'd upon vellum or wild Indian leaf
The shadows of melodious utterance.
But bare of laurel they live, dream and die;
For Poesy alone can tell her dreams,
With the fine spell of words alone can save
Imagination from the sable charm   10
And dumb enchantment. Who alive can say
'Thou art no Poet; may'st not tell thy dreams'?
Since every man whose soul is not a clod
Hath visions, and would speak, if he had lov'd
And been well nurtured in his mother tongue.
Whether the dream now purposed to rehearse
Be poet's or Fanatic's will be known
When this warm scribe my hand is in the grave.

Methought I stood where trees of every clime,
Palm, Myrtle, oak, and sycamore, and beech,   20
With plantane, and spice blossoms, made a screen;
In neighbourhood of fountains, by the noise
Soft showering in mine ears; and, by the touch
Of scent, not far from roses. Turning round,
I saw an arbour with a drooping roof
Of trellis vines, and bells, and larger blooms,
Like floral-censers swinging light in air;
Before its wreathed doorway, on a mound
Of moss, was spread a feast of summer fruits,
Which nearer seen, seem'd refuse of a meal   30
By Angel tasted, or our Mother Eve;
For empty shells were scattered on the grass,
And grape stalks but half bare, and remnants more,
Sweet smelling, whose pure kinds I could not know.
Still was more plenty than the fabled horn
Thrice emptied could pour forth, at banqueting
For Proserpine return'd to her own fields,
Where the white heifers low. And appetite
More yearning than on earth I ever felt
Growing within, I ate deliciously;   40
And, after not long, thirsted, for thereby
Stood a cool vessel of transparent juice,
Sipp'd by the wander'd bee, the which I took,
And, pledging all the Mortals of the World,

And all the dead whose names are in our lips,
Drank. That full draught is parent of my theme.
No Asian poppy, nor Elixir fine
Of the soon fading jealous Caliphat;
No poison gender'd in close Monkish cell
To thin the scarlet conclave of old Men,   50
Could so have rapt unwilling life away.
Among the fragrant husks and berries crush'd,
Upon the grass I struggled hard against
The domineering potion; but in vain:
The cloudy swoon came on, and down I sunk
Like a Silenus on an antique vase.
How long I slumber'd 'tis a chance to guess.
When sense of life return'd, I started up
As if with wings; but the fair trees were gone,
The mossy mound and arbour were no more;   60
I look'd around upon the carved sides
Of an old sanctuary with roof august,
Builded so high, it seem'd that filmed clouds
Might spread beneath, as o'er the stars of heaven;
So old the place was, I remembered none
The like upon the earth; what I had seen
Of grey Cathedrals, buttress'd walls, rent towers,
The superannuations of sunk realms,
Or Nature's Rocks toil'd hard in waves and winds,
Seem'd but the faulture of decrepit things   70
To that eternal domed Monument.
Upon the marble at my feet there lay
Store of strange vessels, and large draperies,
Which needs had been of dyed asbestus wove,
Or in that place the moth could not corrupt,
So white the linen; so, in some, distinct
Ran imageries from a sombre loom.
All in a mingled heap confus'd there lay
Robes, golden tongs, censer, and chafing dish.
Girdles, and chains, and holy jewelries—   80

   Turning from these with awe, once more I rais'd
My eyes to fathom the space every way;
The embossed roof, the silent massy range
Of columns north and South, ending in mist

Of nothing, then to Eastward, where black gates
Were shut against the sunrise evermore.
Then to the West I look'd, and saw far off
An Image, huge of feature as a cloud,
At level of whose feet an altar slept,
To be approach'd on either side by steps,   90
And marble balustrade, and patient travail
To count with toil the innumerable degrees.
Towards the altar sober-pac'd I went,
Repressing haste, as too unholy there;
And, coming nearer, saw beside the shrine
One minist'ring; and there arose a flame.
When in mid-May the sickening East Wind
Shifts sudden to the South, the small warm rain
Melts out the frozen incense from all flowers,
And fills the air with so much pleasant health   100
That even the dying man forgets his shroud;
Even so that lofty sacrificial fire,
Sending forth Maian incense, spread around
Forgetfulness of every thing but bliss,
And clouded all the altar with soft smoke,
From whose white fragrant curtains thus I heard
Language pronounc'd. 'If thou canst not ascend
These steps, die on that marble where thou art.
Thy flesh, near cousin to the common dust,
Will parch for lack of nutriment—thy bones   110
Will wither in few years, and vanish so
That not the quickest eye could find a grain
Of what thou now art on that pavement cold.
The sands of thy short life are spent this hour,
And no hand in the Universe can turn
Thy hour glass, if these gummed leaves be burnt
Ere thou canst mount up these immortal steps.'
I heard, I look'd: two senses both at once
So fine, so subtle, felt the tyranny
Of that fierce threat, and the hard task proposed.   120
Prodigious seem'd the toil, the leaves were yet
Burning,—when suddenly a palsied chill
Struck from the paved level up my limbs,
And was ascending quick to put cold grasp
Upon those streams that pulse beside the throat:

I shriek'd; and the sharp anguish of my shriek
Stung my own ears—I strove hard to escape
The numbness; strove to gain the lowest step.
Slow, heavy, deadly was my pace: the cold
Grew stifling, suffocating, at the heart;   130
And when I clasp'd my hands I felt them not.
One minute before death, my iced foot touch'd
The lowest stair; and as it touch'd, life seem'd
To pour in at the toes: I mounted up,
As once fair Angels on a ladder flew
From the green turf to heaven.—'Holy Power,'
Cried I, approaching near the horned shrine,
'What am I that should so be sav'd from death?
What am I, that another death come not
To choak my utterance sacrilegious here?'   140
Then said the veiled shadow—'Thou hast felt
What 'tis to die and live again before
Thy fated hour. That thou hadst power to do so
Is thy own safety; thou hast dated on
Thy doom.'—'High Prophetess,' said I, 'purge off
Benign, if so it please thee, my mind's film'—
'None can usurp this height,' return'd that shade,
'But those to whom the miseries of the world
Are misery, and will not let them rest.
All else who find a haven in the world,   150
Where they may thoughtless sleep away their days,
If by a chance into this fane they come,
Rot on the pavement where thou rotted'st half.'—
'Are there not thousands in the world,' said I,
Encourag'd by the sooth voice of the shade,
'Who love their fellows even to the death;
Who feel the giant agony of the world;
And more, like slaves to poor humanity,
Labour for mortal good? I sure should see
Other men here: but I am here alone.'   160
'They whom thou spak'st of are no vision'ries,'
Rejoin'd that voice—'They are no dreamers weak,
They seek no wonder but the human face;
No music but a happy-noted voice—
They come not here, they have no thought to come—
And thou art here, for thou art less than they—

What benefit canst thou do, or all thy tribe
To the great World? Thou art a dreaming thing;
A fever of thyself—think of the Earth;
What bliss even in hope is there for thee?   170
What haven? Every creature hath its home;
Every sole man hath days of joy and pain,
Whether his labours be sublime or low—
The pain alone; the joy alone; distinct:
Only the dreamer venoms all his days,
Bearing more woe than all his Sins deserve.
Therefore, that happiness be somewhat shar'd,
Such things as thou art are admitted oft
Into like gardens thou didst pass erewhile,
And suffer'd in these Temples; for that cause   180
Thou standest safe beneath this statue's knees.'
'That I am favored for unworthiness,
By such propitious parley medicin'd
In sickness not ignoble, I rejoice,
Aye, and could weep for love of such award.'
So answer'd I, continuing, 'If it please
Majestic shadow, tell me: sure not all
Those melodies sung into the world's ear
Are useless: sure a poet is a sage;
A humanist, Physician to all Men.   190
That I am none I feel, as Vultures feel
They are no birds when Eagles are abroad.
What am I then? Thou spakest of my tribe:
What tribe?'—The tall shade veil'd in drooping white
Then spake, so much more earnest, that the breath
Mov'd the thin linen folds that drooping hung
About a golden censer from the hand
Pendent.—'Art thou not of the dreamer tribe?
The poet and the dreamer are distinct,
Diverse, sheer opposite, antipodes.   200
The one pours out a balm upon the world,
The other vexes it.' Then shouted I
Spite of myself, and with a Pythia's spleen,
'Apollo! faded, far flown Apollo!
Where is thy misty pestilence to creep
Into the dwellings, through the door crannies,
Of all mock lyrists, large self worshipers,

And careless Hectorers in proud bad verse.
Though I breathe death with them it will be life
To see them sprawl before me into graves.   210
Majestic shadow, tell me where I am:
Whose altar this; for whom this incense curls:
What Image this, whose face I cannot see,
For the broad marble knees; and who thou art,
Of accent feminine, so courteous.'
Then the tall shade in drooping linens veil'd
Spake out, so much more earnest, that her breath
Stirr'd the thin folds of gauze that drooping hung
About a golden censer from her hand
Pendent; and by her voice I knew she shed   220
Long treasured tears. 'This temple sad and lone
Is all spar'd from the thunder of a war
Foughten long since by giant hierarchy
Against rebellion: this old image here,
Whose carved features wrinkled as he fell,
Is Saturn's; I, Moneta, left supreme
Sole Priestess of his desolation.'—
I had no words to answer; for my tongue,
Useless, could find about its roofed home
No syllable of a fit Majesty   230
To make rejoinder to Moneta's mourn.
There was a silence while the altar's blaze
Was fainting for sweet food: I look'd thereon
And on the paved floor, where nigh were pil'd
Faggots of cinnamon, and many heaps
Of other crisped spice-wood—then again
I look'd upon the altar and its horns
Whiten'd with ashes, and its lang'rous flame,
And then upon the offerings again;
And so by turns—till sad Moneta cried,   240
'The sacrifice is done, but not the less,
Will I be kind to thee for thy good will.
My power, which to me is still a curse,
Shall be to thee a wonder; for the scenes
Still swooning vivid through my globed brain
With an electral changing misery
Thou shalt with those dull mortal eyes behold,
Free from all pain, if wonder pain thee not.'

As near as an immortal's sphered words
Could to a Mother's soften, were these last: 250
But yet I had a terror of her robes,
And chiefly of the veils, that from her brow
Hung pale, and curtain'd her in mysteries
That made my heart too small to hold its blood.
This saw that Goddess, and with sacred hand
Parted the veils. Then saw I a wan face,
Not pin'd by human sorrows, but bright blanch'd
By an immortal sickness which kills not;
It works a constant change, which happy death
Can put no end to; deathwards progressing   260
To no death was that visage; it had pass'd
The lily and the snow; and beyond these
I must not think now, though I saw that face—
But for her eyes I should have fled away.
They held me back, with a benignant light,
Soft mitigated by divinest lids
Half closed, and visionless entire they seem'd
Of all external things—they saw me not,
But in blank splendor beam'd like the mild moon,
Who comforts those she sees not, who knows not   270
What eyes are upward cast. As I had found
A grain of gold upon a mountain's side,
And twing'd with avarice strain'd out my eyes
To search its sullen entrails rich with ore,
So at the view of sad Moneta's brow,
I ached to see what things the hollow brain
Behind enwombed: what high tragedy
In the dark secret Chambers of her skull
Was acting, that could give so dread a stress
To her cold lips, and fill with such a light   280
Her planetary eyes; and touch her voice
With such a sorrow—'Shade of Memory!'
Cried I, with act adorant at her feet,
'By all the gloom hung round thy fallen house,
By this last Temple, by the golden age,
By great Apollo, thy dear foster child,
And by thy self, forlorn divinity,
The pale Omega of a wither'd race,
Let me behold, according as thou said'st,

What in thy brain so ferments to and fro.'—   290
No sooner had this conjuration pass'd
My devout Lips, than side by side we stood.
(Like a stunt bramble by a solemn Pine)
Deep in the shady sadness of a vale,
Far sunken from the healthy breath of morn,
Far from the fiery noon, and Eve's one star.
Onward I look'd beneath the gloomy boughs,
And saw, what first I thought an Image huge.
Like to the Image pedestal'd so high
In Saturn's Temple. Then Moneta's voice   300
Came brief upon mine ear,—'So Saturn sat
When he had lost his realms'—Whereon there grew
A power within me of enormous ken,
To see as a God sees, and take the depth
Of things as nimbly as the outward eye
Can size and shape pervade. The lofty theme
At those few words hung vast before my mind,
With half unravel'd web. I set myself
Upon an Eagle's watch, that I might see,
And seeing ne'er forget. No stir of life   310
Was in this shrouded vale, not so much air
As in the zoning of a Summer's day
Robs not one light seed from the feather'd grass,
But where the dead leaf fell there did it rest:
A stream went voiceless by, still deaden'd more
By reason of the fallen Divinity
Spreading more shade: the Naiad mid her reeds
Press'd her cold finger closer to her lips.
Along the margin sand large footmarks went
No farther than to where old Saturn's feet   320
Had rested, and there slept, how long a sleep!
Degraded, cold, upon the sodden ground
His old right hand lay nerveless, listless, dead,
Unsceptred; and his realmless eyes were clos'd,
While his bow'd head seem'd listening to the Earth,
His antient mother, for some comfort yet.

It seemed no force could wake him from his place;
But there came one who with a kindred hand
Touch'd his wide shoulders, after bending low

With reverence, though to one who knew it not.   330
Then came the griev'd voice of Mnemosyne,
And griev'd I hearken'd. 'That divinity
Whom thou saw'st step from yon forlornest wood,
And with slow pace approach our fallen King,
Is Thea, softest-natur'd of our Brood.'
I mark'd the goddess in fair statuary
Surpassing wan Moneta by the head,
And in her sorrow nearer woman's tears.
There was a listening fear in her regard,
As if calamity had but begun;   340
As if the vanward clouds of evil days
Had spent their malice, and the sullen rear
Was with its stored thunder labouring up.
One hand she press'd upon that aching spot
Where beats the human heart; as if just there
Though an immortal, she felt cruel pain;
The other upon Saturn's bended neck
She laid, and to the level of his hollow ear
Leaning, with parted lips, some words she spake
In solemn tenor and deep organ tune;   350
Some mourning words, which in our feeble tongue
Would come in this-like accenting; how frail
To that large utterance of the early Gods!—
'Saturn! look up—and for what, poor lost King?
I have no comfort for thee, no—not one—
I cannot cry, *Wherefore thus sleepest thou?*
For heaven is parted from thee, and the earth
Knows thee not, so afflicted, for a God;
And Ocean too, with all its solemn noise,
Has from thy sceptre pass'd and all the air   360
Is emptied of thine hoary Majesty.
Thy thunder, captious at the new command,
Rumbles reluctant o'er our fallen house;
And thy sharp lightning in unpracticed hands
Scorches and burns our once serene domain.
With such remorseless speed still come new woes
That unbelief has not a space to breathe.
Saturn, sleep on:—Me thoughtless, why should I
Thus violate thy slumbrous solitude?

Why should I ope thy melancholy eyes?   370
Saturn, sleep on, while at thy feet I weep.—

As when, upon a tranced Summer Night,
Forests, branch-charmed by the earnest stars,
Dream, and so dream all night, without a noise,
Save from one gradual solitary gust,
Swelling upon the silence; dying off;
As if the ebbing air had but one wave;
So came these words, and went; the while in tears
She press'd her fair large forehead to the earth,
Just where her fallen hair might spread in curls,   380
A soft and silken mat for Saturn's feet.
Long, long, those two were postured motionless,
Like sculpture builded up upon the grave
Of their own power. A long awful time
I look'd upon them; still they were the same;
The frozen God still bending to the Earth,
And the sad Goddess weeping at his feet.
Moneta silent. Without stay or prop
But my own weak mortality, I bore
The load of this eternal quietude,   390
The unchanging gloom, and the three fixed shapes
Ponderous upon my senses a whole Moon.
For by my burning brain I measured sure
Her silver seasons shedded on the night
And every day by day methought I grew
More gaunt and ghostly—Oftentimes I pray'd
Intense, that Death would take me from the Vale
And all its burthens—Gasping with despair
Of change, hour after hour I curs'd myself:
Until old Saturn rais'd his faded eyes,   400
And look'd around, and saw his Kingdom gone,
And all the gloom and sorrow of the place,
And that fair kneeling Goddess at his feet.
As the moist scent of flowers, and grass, and leaves
Fills forest dells with a pervading air
Known to the woodland nostril, so the words
Of Saturn fill'd the mossy glooms around,
Even to the hollows of time-eaten oaks,

And to the windings in the foxes' hole,
With sad low tones, while thus he spake, and sent   410
Strange musings to the solitary Pan.

'Moan, brethren, moan; for we are swallow'd up
And buried from all godlike exercise
Of influence benign on planets pale,
And peaceful sway above man's harvesting,
And all those acts which Deity supreme
Doth ease its heart of love in. Moan and wail.
Moan, brethren, moan; for lo! the rebel spheres
Spin round, the stars their antient courses keep,
Clouds still with shadowy moisture haunt the earth,   420
Still suck their fill of light from Sun and Moon,
Still buds the tree, and still the sea-shores murmur.
There is no death in all the universe
No smell of Death—there shall be death—Moan, moan,
Moan, Cybele, moan, for thy pernicious babes
Have chang'd a God into a shaking Palsy.
Moan, brethren, moan; for I have no strength left,
Weak as the reed—weak—feeble as my voice—
O, O, the pain, the pain of feebleness.
Moan, moan; for still I thaw—or give me help: 430
Throw down those Imps and give me victory.
Let me hear other groans, and trumpets blown
Of triumph calm, and hymns of festival
From the gold peaks of Heaven's high piled clouds;
Voices of soft proclaim, and silver stir
Of strings in hollow shells; and let there be
Beautiful things made new for the surprize
Of the sky children'—So he feebly ceas'd,
With such a poor and sickly sounding pause,
Methought I heard some old Man of the earth   440
Bewailing earthly loss; nor could my eyes
And ears act with that pleasant unison of sense
Which marries sweet sound with the grace of form,
And dolourous accent from a tragic harp
With large limb'd visions—More I scrutinized:
Still fix'd he sat beneath the sable trees,
Whose arms spread straggling in wild serpent forms,
With leaves all hush'd: his awful presence there

(Now all was silent) gave a deadly lie
To what I erewhile heard: only his lips   450
Trembled amid the white curls of his beard.
They told the truth, though, round, the snowy locks
Hung nobly, as upon the face of heaven
A midday fleece of clouds. Thœa arose
And stretch'd her white arm through the hollow dark,
Pointing some whither: whereat he too rose
Like a vast giant seen by men at sea
To grow pale from the waves at dull midnight.
They melted from my sight into the woods:
Ere I could turn, Moneta cried—'These twain   460
Are speeding to the families of grief,
Where roof'd in by black rocks they waste in pain
And darkness for no hope.'—And she spake on,
As ye may read who can unwearied pass
Onward from the Antichamber of this dream,
Where even at the open doors awhile
I must delay, and glean my memory
Of her high phrase: perhaps no further dare.—

Canto II

'Mortal, that thou may'st understand aright,
I humanize my sayings to thine ear,
Making comparisons of earthly things;
Or thou might'st better listen to the wind,
Whose language is to thee a barren noise,
Though it blows legend-laden through the trees—
In melancholy realms big tears are shed,
More sorrow like to this, and such-like woe,
Too huge for mortal tongue, or pen of scribe.
The Titans fierce, self-hid, or prison-bound,   10
Groan for the old allegiance once more,
Listening in their doom for Saturn's voice.
But one of our whole eagle-brood still keeps
His sov'reignty, and Rule, and Majesty;
Blazing Hyperion on his orbed fire
Still sits, still snuffs the incense teeming up
From man to the Sun's God: yet unsecure,
For as upon the Earth dire prodigies

Fright and perplex, so also shudders he:
Nor at dog's howl, or gloom-bird's Even screech,   20
Or the familiar visitings of one
Upon the first toll of his passing bell:
But horrors portion'd to a giant nerve
Make great Hyperion ache. His palace bright,
Bastion'd with pyramids of glowing gold,
And touch'd with shade of bronzed obelisks,
Glares a blood red through all the thousand Courts,
Arches, and domes, and fiery galeries:
And all its curtains of Aurorian clouds
Flush angerly: when he would taste the wreaths   30
Of incense breath'd aloft from sacred hills,
Instead of sweets, his ample palate takes
Savour of poisonous brass and metals sick.
Wherefore when harbour'd in the sleepy West,
After the full completion of fair day,
For rest divine upon exalted couch
And slumber in the arms of melody,
He paces through the pleasant hours of ease,
With strides colossal, on from Hall to Hall;
While, far within each aisle and deep recess,   40
His winged minions in close clusters stand
Amaz'd, and full of fear; like anxious men
Who on a wide plain gather in sad troops,
When earthquakes jar their battlements and towers.
Even now, while Saturn, rous'd from icy trance
Goes, step for step, with Thea from yon woods,
Hyperion, leaving twilight in the rear,
Is sloping to the threshold of the west.—
Thither we tend.'—Now in clear light I stood,
Reliev'd from the dusk vale. Mnemosyne   50
Was sitting on a square edg'd polish'd stone,
That in its lucid depth reflected pure
Her priestess-garments. My quick eyes ran on
From stately nave to nave, from vault to vault,
Through bowers of fragrant and enwreathed light,
And diamond paved lustrous long arcades.
Anon rush'd by the bright Hyperion;
His flaming robes stream'd out beyond his heels,
And gave a roar, as if of earthly fire,

That scar'd away the meek ethereal hours   60
And made their dove-wings tremble: on he flared—

Lamia

Part I

Upon a time, before the faery broods
Drove Nymph and Satyr from the prosperous woods,
Before King Oberon's bright diadem,
Sceptre, and mantle, clasp'd with dewy gem,
Frighted away the Dryads and the Fauns
From rushes green, and brakes, and cowslip'd lawns,
The ever-smitten Hermes empty left
His golden throne, bent warm on amorous theft:
From high Olympus had he stolen light,
On this side of Jove's clouds, to escape the sight   10
Of his great summoner, and made retreat
Into a forest on the shores of Crete.
For somewhere in that sacred island dwelt
A nymph, to whom all hoofed Satyrs knelt;
At whose white feet the languid Tritons poured
Pearls, while on land they wither'd and adored.
Fast by the springs where she to bathe was wont,
And in those meads where sometime she might haunt,
Were strewn rich gifts, unknown to any Muse,
Though Fancy's casket were unlock'd to choose.   20
Ah, what a world of love was at her feet!
So Hermes thought, and a celestial heat
Burnt from his winged heels to either ear,
That from a whiteness, as the lily clear,
Blush'd into roses 'mid his golden hair,
Fallen in jealous curls about his shoulders bare.

From vale to vale, from wood to wood, he flew,
Breathing upon the flowers his passion new,
And wound with many a river to its head,
To find where this sweet nymph prepar'd her secret bed: 30
In vain; the sweet nymph might nowhere be found,

And so he rested, on the lonely ground,
Pensive, and full of painful jealousies
Of the Wood-Gods, and even the very trees.
There as he stood, he heard a mournful voice,
Such as once heard, in gentle heart, destroys
All pain but pity: thus the lone voice spake:
'When from this wreathed tomb shall I awake!
When move in a sweet body fit for life,
And love, and pleasure, and the ruddy strife   40
Of hearts and lips! Ah, miserable me!'
The God, dove-footed, glided silently
Round bush and tree, soft-brushing, in his speed,
The taller grasses and full-flowering weed,
Until he found a palpitating snake,
Bright, and cirque-couchant in a dusky brake.

She was a gordian shape of dazzling hue,
Vermilion-spotted, golden, green, and blue;
Striped like a zebra, freckled like a pard,
Eyed like a peacock, and all crimson barr'd;   50
And full of silver moons, that, as she breathed,
Dissolv'd, or brighter shone, or interwreathed
Their lustres with the gloomier tapestries—
So rainbow-sided, touch'd with miseries,
She seem'd, at once, some penanced lady elf,
Some demon's mistress, or the demon's self.
Upon her crest she wore a wannish fire
Sprinkled with stars, like Ariadne's tiar:
Her head was serpent, but ah, bitter-sweet!
She had a woman's mouth with all its pearls complete: 60
And for her eyes: what could such eyes do there
But weep, and weep, that they were born so fair?
As Proserpine still weeps for her Sicilian air.
Her throat was serpent, but the words she spake
Came, as through bubbling honey, for Love's sake,
And thus; while Hermes on his pinions lay,
Like a stoop'd falcon ere he takes his prey.

'Fair Hermes, crown'd with feathers, fluttering light,
I had a splendid dream of thee last night:
I saw thee sitting, on a throne of gold,   70

Among the Gods, upon Olympus old,
The only sad one; for thou didst not hear
The soft, lute-finger'd Muses chanting clear,
Nor even Apollo when he sang alone,
Deaf to his throbbing throat's long, long melodious moan.
I dreamt I saw thee, robed in purple flakes,
Break amorous through the clouds, as morning breaks,
And, swiftly as a bright Phœbean dart,
Strike for the Cretan isle; and here thou art!
Too gentle Hermes, hast thou found the maid?'   80
Whereat the star of Lethe not delay'd
His rosy eloquence, and thus inquired:
'Thou smooth-lipp'd serpent, surely high inspired!
Thou beauteous wreath, with melancholy eyes,
Possess whatever bliss thou canst devise,
Telling me only where my nymph is fled,—
Where she doth breathe!' 'Bright planet, thou hast said,'
Return'd the snake, 'but seal with oaths, fair God!'
'I swear,' said Hermes, 'by my serpent rod,
And by thine eyes, and by thy starry crown!'   90
Light flew his earnest words, among the blossoms blown.
Then thus again the brilliance feminine:
'Too frail of heart! for this lost nymph of thine,
Free as the air, invisibly, she strays
About these thornless wilds; her pleasant days
She tastes unseen; unseen her nimble feet
Leave traces in the grass and flowers sweet;
From weary tendrils, and bow'd branches green,
She plucks the fruit unseen, she bathes unseen:
And by my power is her beauty veil'd   100
To keep it unaffronted, unassail'd
By the love-glances of unlovely eyes,
Of Satyrs, Fauns, and blear'd Silenus' sighs.
Pale grew her immortality, for woe
Of all these lovers, and she grieved so
I took compassion on her, bade her steep
Her hair in weïrd syrops, that would keep
Her loveliness invisible, yet free
To wander as she loves, in liberty.
Thou shalt behold her, Hermes, thou alone,   110
If thou wilt, as thou swearest, grant my boon!'

Then, once again, the charmed God began
An oath, and through the serpent's ears it ran
Warm, tremulous, devout, psalterian.
Ravish'd, she lifted her Circean head,
Blush'd a live damask, and swift-lisping said,
'I was a woman, let me have once more
A woman's shape, and charming as before.
I love a youth of Corinth—O the bliss!
Give me my woman's form, and place me where he is.   120
Stoop, Hermes, let me breathe upon thy brow,
And thou shalt see thy sweet nymph even now.'
The God on half-shut feathers sank serene,
She breath'd upon his eyes, and swift was seen
Of both the guarded nymph near-smiling on the green.
It was no dream; or say a dream it was,
Real are the dreams of Gods, and smoothly pass
Their pleasures in a long immortal dream.
One warm, flush'd moment, hovering, it might seem
Dash'd by the wood-nymph's beauty, so he burn'd;   130
Then, lighting on the printless verdure, turn'd
To the swoon'd serpent, and with languid arm,
Delicate, put to proof the lythe Caducean charm.
So done, upon the nymph his eyes he bent
Full of adoring tears and blandishment,
And towards her stept: she, like a moon in wane,
Faded before him, cower'd, nor could restrain
Her fearful sobs, self-folding like a flower
That faints into itself at evening hour:
But the God fostering her chilled hand,   140
She felt the warmth, her eyelids open'd bland,
And, like new flowers at morning song of bees,
Bloom'd, and gave up her honey to the lees.
Into the green-recessed woods they flew;
Nor grew they pale, as mortal lovers do.

    Left to herself, the serpent now began
To change; her elfin blood in madness ran,
Her mouth foam'd, and the grass, therewith besprent,
Wither'd at dew so sweet and virulent;
Her eyes in torture fix'd, and anguish drear,   150
Hot, glaz'd, and wide, with lid-lashes all sear,

Flash'd phosphor and sharp sparks, without one cooling tear.
The colours all inflam'd throughout her train,
She writh'd about, convuls'd with scarlet pain:
A deep volcanian yellow took the place
Of all her milder-mooned body's grace;
And, as the lava ravishes the mead,
Spoilt all her silver mail, and golden brede;
Made gloom of all her frecklings, streaks and bars,
Eclips'd her crescents, and lick'd up her stars: 160
So that, in moments few, she was undrest
Of all her sapphires, greens, and amethyst,
And rubious-argent: of all these bereft,
Nothing but pain and ugliness were left.
Still shone her crown; that vanish'd, also she
Melted and disappear'd as suddenly;
And in the air, her new voice luting soft,
Cried, 'Lycius! gentle Lycius!'—Borne aloft
With the bright mists about the mountains hoar
These words dissolv'd: Crete's forests heard no more.   170

Whither fled Lamia, now a lady bright,
A full-born beauty new and exquisite?
She fled into that valley they pass o'er
Who go to Corinth from Cenchreas' shore;
And rested at the foot of those wild hills,
The rugged founts of the Peræan rills,
And of that other ridge whose barren back
Stretches, with all its mist and cloudy rack,
South-westward to Cleone. There she stood
About a young bird's flutter from a wood,   180
Fair, on a sloping green of mossy tread,
By a clear pool, wherein she passioned
To see herself escap'd from so sore ills,
While her robes flaunted with the daffodils.

Ah, happy Lycius!—for she was a maid
More beautiful than ever twisted braid,
Or sigh'd, or blush'd, or on spring-flowered lea
Spread a green kirtle to the minstrelsy:
A virgin purest lipp'd, yet in the lore
Of love deep learned to the red heart's core: 190

Not one hour old, yet of sciential brain
To unperplex bliss from its neighbour pain;
Define their pettish limits, and estrange
Their points of contact, and swift counterchange;
Intrigue with the specious chaos, and dispart
Its most ambiguous atoms with sure art;
As though in Cupid's college she had spent
Sweet days a lovely graduate, still unshent,
And kept his rosy terms in idle languishment.

Why this fair creature chose so fairily   200
By the wayside to linger, we shall see;
But first 'tis fit to tell how she could muse
And dream, when in the serpent prison-house,
Of all she list, strange or magnificent:
How, ever, where she will'd, her spirit went;
Whether to faint Elysium, or where
Down through tress-lifting waves the Nereids fair
Wind into Thetis' bower by many a pearly stair;
Or where in God Bacchus drains his cups divine,
Stretch'd out, at ease, beneath a glutinous pine;   210
Or where in Pluto's gardens palatine
Mulciber's columns gleam in far piazzian line.
And sometimes into cities she would send
Her dream, with feast and rioting to blend;
And once, while among mortals dreaming thus,
She saw the young Corinthian Lycius
Charioting foremost in the envious race,
Like a young Jove with calm uneager face,
And fell into a swooning love of him.
Now on the moth-time of that evening dim   220
He would return that way, as well she knew,
To Corinth from the shore; for freshly blew
The eastern soft wind, and his galley now
Grated the quaystones with her brazen prow
In port Cenchreas, from Egina isle
Fresh anchor'd; whither he had been awhile
To sacrifice to Jove, whose temple there
Waits with high marble doors for blood and incense rare.
Jove heard his vows, and better'd his desire;
For by some freakful chance he made retire   230

From his companions, and set forth to walk,
Perhaps grown wearied of their Corinth talk:
Over the solitary hills he fared,
Thoughtless at first, but ere eve's star appeared
His phantasy was lost, where reason fades,
In the calm'd twilight of Platonic shades.
Lamia beheld him coming, near, more near—
Close to her passing, in indifference drear,
His silent sandals swept the mossy green;
So neighbour'd to him, and yet so unseen   240
She stood: he pass'd, shut up in mysteries,
His mind wrapp'd like his mantle, while her eyes
Follow'd his steps, and her neck regal white
Turn'd—syllabling thus, 'Ah, Lycius bright,
And will you leave me on the hills alone?
Lycius, look back! and be some pity shown.'
He did; not with cold wonder fearingly,
But Orpheus-like at an Eurydice;
For so delicious were the words she sung,
It seem'd he had lov'd them a whole summer long: 250
And soon his eyes had drunk her beauty up,
Leaving no drop in the bewildering cup,
And still the cup was full,—while he, afraid
Lest she should vanish ere his lip had paid
Due adoration, thus began to adore;
Her soft look growing coy, she saw his chain so sure:
'Leave thee alone! Look back! Ah, Goddess, see
Whether my eyes can ever turn from thee!
For pity do not this sad heart belie—
Even as thou vanishest so I shall die.   260
Stay! though a Naiad of the rivers, stay!
To thy far wishes will thy streams obey:
Stay! though the greenest woods be thy domain,
Alone they can drink up the morning rain:
Though a descended Pleiad, will not one
Of thine harmonious sisters keep in tune
Thy spheres, and as thy silver proxy shine?
So sweetly to these ravish'd ears of mine
Came thy sweet greeting, that if thou shouldst fade
Thy memory will waste me to a shade:—   270
For pity do not melt!'—'If I should stay,'

Said Lamia, 'here, upon this floor of clay,
And pain my steps upon these flowers too rough,
What canst thou say or do of charm enough
To dull the nice remembrance of my home?
Thou canst not ask me with thee here to roam
Over these hills and vales, where no joy is,—
Empty of immortality and bliss!
Thou art a scholar, Lycius, and must know
That finer spirits cannot breathe below　　　　　　　　280
In human climes, and live: Alas! poor youth,
What taste of purer air hast thou to soothe
My essence? What serener palaces,
Where I may all my many senses please,
And by mysterious sleights a hundred thirsts appease?
It cannot be—Adieu!' So said, she rose
Tiptoe with white arms spread. He, sick to lose
The amorous promise of her lone complain,
Swoon'd, murmuring of love, and pale with pain.
The cruel lady, without any show　　　　　　　　　　290
Of sorrow for her tender favourite's woe,
But rather, if her eyes could brighter be,
With brighter eyes and slow amenity,
Put her new lips to his, and gave afresh
The life she had so tangled in her mesh:
And as he from one trance was wakening
Into another, she began to sing,
Happy in beauty, life, and love, and every thing,
A song of love, too sweet for earthly lyres,
While, like held breath, the stars drew in their panting fires.　　300
And then she whisper'd in such trembling tone,
As those who, safe together met alone
For the first time through many anguish'd days,
Use other speech than looks; bidding him raise
His drooping head, and clear his soul of doubt,
For that she was a woman, and without
Any more subtle fluid in her veins
Than throbbing blood, and that the self-same pains
Inhabited her frail-strung heart as his.
And next she wonder'd how his eyes could miss　　　310
Her face so long in Corinth, where, she said,
She dwelt but half retir'd, and there had led

Days happy as the gold coin could invent
Without the aid of love; yet in content
Till she saw him, as once she pass'd him by,
Where 'gainst a column he leant thoughtfully
At Venus' temple porch, 'mid baskets hcap'd
Of amorous herbs and flowers, newly reap'd
Late on that eve, as 'twas the night before
The Adonian feast; whereof she saw no more,   320
But wept alone those days, for why should she adore?
Lycius from death awoke into amaze,
To see her still, and singing so sweet lays;
Then from amaze into delight he fell
To hear her whisper woman's lore so well;
And every word she spake entic'd him on
To unperplex'd delight and pleasure known.
Let the mad poets say whate'er they please
Of the sweets of Fairies, Peris, Goddesses,
There is not such a treat among them all,   330
Haunters of cavern, lake, and waterfall,
As a real woman, lineal indeed
From Pyrrha's pebbles or old Adam's seed.
Thus gentle Lamia judg'd, and judg'd aright,
That Lycius could not love in half a fright,
So threw the goddess off, and won his heart
More pleasantly by playing woman's part,
With no more awe than what her beauty gave,
That, while it smote, still guaranteed to save.
Lycius to all made eloquent reply,   340
Marrying to every word a twinborn sigh;
And last, pointing to Corinth, ask'd her sweet,
If 'twas too far that night for her soft feet.
The way was short, for Lamia's eagerness
Made, by a spell, the triple league decrease
To a few paces; not at all surmised
By blinded Lycius, so in her comprized.
They pass'd the city gates, he knew not how,
So noiseless, and he never thought to know.

    As men talk in a dream, so Corinth all,   350
Throughout her palaces imperial,
And all her populous streets and temples lewd,

Mutter'd, like tempest in the distance brew'd,
To the wide-spreaded night above her towers.
Men, women, rich and poor, in the cool hours,
Shuffled their sandals o'er the pavement white,
Companion'd or alone; while many a light
Flared, here and there, from wealthy festivals,
And threw their moving shadows on the walls,
Or found them cluster'd in the corniced shade   360
Of some arch'd temple door, or dusky colonnade.

    Muffling his face, of greeting friends in fear,
Her fingers he press'd hard, as one came near
With curl'd gray beard, sharp eyes, and smooth bald crown,
Slow-stepp'd, and robed in philosophic gown:
Lycius shrank closer, as they met and past,
Into his mantle, adding wings to haste,
While hurried Lamia trembled: 'Ah,' said he,
'Why do you shudder, love, so ruefully?
Why does your tender palm dissolve in dew?'—   370
'I'm wearied,' said fair Lamia: 'tell me who
Is that old man? I cannot bring to mind
His features:—Lycius! wherefore did you blind
Yourself from his quick eyes?' Lycius replied,
''Tis Apollonius sage, my trusty guide
And good instructor; but to-night he seems
The ghost of folly haunting my sweet dreams.'

    While yet he spake they had arrived before
A pillar'd porch, with lofty portal door,
Where hung a silver lamp, whose phosphor glow   380
Reflected in the slabbed steps below,
Mild as a star in water; for so new,
And so unsullied was the marble hue,
So through the crystal polish, liquid fine,
Ran the dark veins, that none but feet divine
Could e'er have touch'd there. Sounds Æolian
Breath'd from the hinges, as the ample span
Of the wide doors disclos'd a place unknown
Some time to any, but those two alone,
And a few Persian mutes, who that same year   390
Were seen about the markets: none knew where

They could inhabit; the most curious
Were foil'd, who watch'd to trace them to their house:
And but the flitter-winged verse must tell,
For truth's sake, what woe afterwards befel,
'Twould humour many a heart to leave them thus,
Shut from the busy world, of more incredulous.

Part II

Love in a hut, with water and a crust,
Is—Love, forgive us!—cinders, ashes, dust;
Love in a palace is perhaps at last
More grievous torment that a hermit's fast:—
That is a doubtful tale from faery land,
Hard for the non-elect to understand.
Had Lycius liv'd to hand his story down,
He might have given the moral a fresh frown,
Or clench'd it quite: but too short was their bliss
To breed distrust and hate, that make the soft voice hiss.   10
Besides, there, nightly, with terrific glare,
Love, jealous grown of so complete a pair,
Hover'd and buzz'd his wings, with fearful roar,
Above the lintel of their chamber door,
And down the passage cast a glow upon the floor.

For all this came a ruin: side by side
They were enthroned, in the even tide,
Upon a couch, near to a curtaining
Whose airy texture, from a golden string,
Floated into the room, and let appear   20
Unveil'd the summer heaven, blue and clear,
Betwixt two marble shafts:—there they reposed,
Where use had made it sweet, with eyelids closed,
Saving a tythe which love still open kept,
That they might see each other while they almost slept;
When from the slope side of a surburb hill,
Deafening the swallow's twitter, came a thrill
Of trumpets—Lycius started—the sounds fled,
But left a thought, a buzzing in his head.
For the first time, since first he harbour'd in   30
That purple-lined palace of sweet sin,
His spirit pass'd beyond its golden bourn

Into the noisy world almost forsworn.
The lady, ever watchful, penetrant,
Saw this with pain, so arguing a want
Of something more, more than her empery
Of joys; and she began to moan and sigh
Because he mused beyond her, knowing well
That but a moment's thought is passion's passing bell.
'Why do you sigh, fair creature?' whisper'd he: 40
'Why do you think?' return'd she tenderly:
'You have deserted me;—where am I now?
Not in your heart while care weighs on your brow:
No, no, you have dismiss'd me; and I go
From your breast houseless: ay, it must be so.'
He answer'd, bending to her open eyes,
Where he was mirror'd small in paradise,
'My silver planet, both of eve and morn!
Why will you plead yourself so sad forlorn,
While I am striving how to fill my heart   50
With deeper crimson, and a double smart?
How to entangle, trammel up and snare
Your soul in mine, and labyrinth you there
Like the hid scent in an unbudded rose?
Ay, a sweet kiss–you see your mighty woes.
My thoughts! shall I unveil them? Listen then!
What mortal hath a prize, that other men
May be confounded and abash'd withal,
But lets it sometimes pace abroad majestical,
And triumph, as in thee I should rejoice   60
Amid the hoarse alarm of Corinth's voice.
Let my foes choke, and my friends shout afar,
While through the thronged streets your bridal car
Wheels round its dazzling spokes.'—The lady's cheek
Trembled; she nothing said, but, pale and meek,
Arose and knelt before him, wept a rain
Of sorrows at his words; at last with pain
Beseeching him, the while his hand she wrung,
To change his purpose. He thereat was stung,
Perverse, with stronger fancy to reclaim   70
Her wild and timid nature to his aim:
Besides, for all his love, in self despite,
Against his better self, he took delight

Luxurious in her sorrows, soft and new.
His passion, cruel grown, took on a hue
Fierce and sanguineous as 'twas possible
In one whose brow had no dark veins to swell.
Fine was the mitigated fury, like
Apollo's presence when in act to strike
The serpent—Ha, the serpent! certes, she   80
Was none. She burnt, she lov'd the tyranny,
And, all subdued, consented to the hour
When to the bridal he should lead his paramour.
Whispering in midnight silence, said the youth,
'Sure some sweet name thou hast, though, by my truth,
I have not ask'd it, ever thinking thee
Not mortal, but of heavenly progeny,
As still I do. Hast any mortal name,
Fit appellation for this dazzling frame?
Or friends or kinsfolk on the citied earth,   90
To share our marriage feast and nuptial mirth?'
'I have no friends,' said Lamia, 'no, not one;
My presence in wide Corinth hardly known:
My parents' bones are in their dusty urns
Sepulchred, where no kindled incense burns,
Seeing all their luckless race are dead, save me,
And I neglect the holy rite for thee.
Even as you list invite your many guests;
But if, as now it seems, your vision rests
With any pleasure on me, do not bid   100
Old Apollonius—from him keep me hid.'
Lycius, perplex'd at words so blind and blank,
Made close inquiry; from whose touch she shrank,
Feigning a sleep; and he to the dull shade
Of deep sleep in a moment was betray'd.

It was the custom then to bring away
The bride from home at blushing shut of day,
Veil'd, in a chariot, heralded along
By strewn flowers, torches, and a marriage song,
With other pageants: but this fair unknown   110
Had not a friend. So being left alone,
(Lycius was gone to summon all his kin)
And knowing surely she could never win
His foolish heart from its mad pompousness,

She set herself, high-thoughted, how to dress
The misery in fit magnificence.
She did so, but 'tis doubtful how and whence
Came, and who were her subtle servitors.
About the halls, and to and from the doors,
There was a noise of wings, till in short space   120
The glowing banquet-room shone with wide-arched grace.
A haunting music, sole perhaps and lone
Supportress of the faery-roof, made moan
Throughout, as fearful the whole charm might fade.
Fresh carved cedar, mimicking a glade
Of palm and plantain, met from either side,
High in the midst, in honour of the bride:
Two palms and then two plantains, and so on,
From either side their stems branch'd one to one
All down the aisled place; and beneath all   130
There ran a stream of lamps straight on from wall to wall.
So canopied, lay an untasted feast
Teeming with odours. Lamia, regal drest,
Silently paced about, and as she went,
In pale contented sort of discontent,
Mission'd her viewless servants to enrich
The fretted splendour of each nook and niche.
Between the tree-stems, marbled plain at first,
Came jasper pannels; then, anon, there burst
Forth creeping imagery of slighter trees,   140
And with the larger wove in small intricacies.
Approving all, she faded at self-will,
And shut the chamber up, close, hush'd and still,
Complete and ready for the revels rude,
When dreadful guests would come to spoil her solitude.

     The day appear'd and all the gossip rout.
O senseless Lycius! Madman! wherefore flout
The silent-blessing fate, warm cloister'd hours,
And show to common eyes these secret bowers?
The herd approach'd; each guest, with busy brain,   150
Arriving at the portal, gaz'd amain,
And enter'd marveling: for they knew the street,
Remember'd it from childhood all complete
Without a gap, yet ne'er before had seen

That royal porch, that high-built fair demesne;
So in they hurried all, maz'd, curious and keen;
Save one, who look'd thereon with eye severe,
And with calm-planted steps walk'd in austere;
'Twas Apollonius: something too he laugh'd,
As though some knotty problem, that had daft   160
His patient thought, had now begun to thaw,
And solve and melt:—'twas just as he foresaw.

He met within the murmurous vestibule
His young disciple. "Tis no common rule,
Lycius,' said he, 'for uninvited guest
To force himself upon you, and infest
With an unbidden presence the bright throng
Of younger friends; yet must I do this wrong,
And you forgive me.' Lycius blush'd, and led
The old man through the inner doors broad-spread;   170
With reconciling words and courteous mien
Turning into sweet milk the sophist's spleen.

Of wealthy lustre was the banquet-room,
Fill'd with pervading brilliance and perfume:
Before each lucid pannel fuming stood
A censer fed with myrrh and spiced wood,
Each by a sacred tripod held aloft,
Whose slender feet wide-swerv'd upon the soft
Wool-woofed carpets: fifty wreaths of smoke
From fifty censers their light voyage took   180
To the high roof, still mimick'd as they rose
Along the mirror'd walls by twin-clouds odorous.
Twelve sphered tables, by silk seats insphered,
High as the level of a man's breast rear'd
On libbard's paws, upheld the heavy gold
Of cups and goblets, and the store thrice told
Of Ceres' horn, and, in huge vessels, wine
Come from the gloomy tun with merry shine.
Thus loaded with a feast the tables stood,
Each shrining in the midst the image of a God.   190

When in an antichamber every guest
Had felt the cold full sponge to pleasure press'd,

By minist'ring slaves, upon his hands and feet,
And fragrant oils with ceremony meet
Pour'd on his hair, they all mov'd to the feast
In white robes, and themselves in order placed
Around the silken couches, wondering
Whence all this mighty cost and blaze of wealth could spring.

Soft went the music the soft air along,
While fluent Greek a vowel'd undersong   200
Kept up among the guests, discoursing low
At first, for scarcely was the wine at flow;
But when the happy vintage touch'd their brains,
Louder they talk, and louder come the strains
Of powerful instruments:—the gorgeous dyes,
The space, the splendour of the draperies,
The roof of awful richness, nectarous cheer,
Beautiful slaves, and Lamia's self, appear,
Now, when the wine has done its rosy deed,
And every soul from human trammels freed,   210
No more so strange; for merry wine, sweet wine,
Will make Elysian shades not too fair, too divine.

Soon was God Bacchus at meridian height;
Flush'd were their cheeks, and bright eyes double bright:
Garlands of every green, and every scent
From vales of deflower'd, or forest-trees branch-rent,
In baskets of bright osier'd gold were brought
High as the handles heap'd, to suit the thought
Of every guest; that each, as he did please,
Might fancy-fit his brows, silk-pillow'd at his ease.   220

What wreath for Lamia? What for Lycius?
What for the sage, old Apollonius?
Upon her aching forehead be there hung
The leaves of willow and of adder's tongue;
And for the youth, quick, let us strip for him
The thyrsus, that his watching eyes may swim
Into forgetfulness; and, for the sage,
Let spear-grass and the spiteful thistle wage
War on his temples. Do not all charms fly
At the mere touch of cold philosophy?   230

There was an awful rainbow once in heaven:
We know her woof, her texture; she is given
In the dull catalogue of common things.
Philosophy will clip an Angel's wings,
Conquer all mysteries by rule and line,
Empty the haunted air, and gnomed mine—
Unweave a rainbow, as it erewhile made
The tender-person'd Lamia melt into a shade.

By her glad Lycius sitting, in chief place,
Scarce saw in all the room another face,   240
Till, checking his love trance, a cup he took
Full brimm'd, and opposite sent forth a look
'Cross the broad table, to beseech a glance
From his old teacher's wrinkled countenance,
And pledge him. The bald-head philosopher
Had fix'd his eye, without a twinkle or stir
Full on the alarmed beauty of the bride,
Brow-beating her fair form, and troubling her sweet pride.
Lycius then press'd her hand, with devout touch,
As pale it lay upon the rosy couch: 250
'Twas icy, and the cold ran through his veins;
Then sudden it grew hot, and all the pains
Of an unnatural heat shot to his heart.
'Lamia, what means this? Wherefore dost thou start?
Know'st thou that man?' Poor Lamia answer'd not.
He gaz'd into her eyes, and not a jot
Own'd they the lovelorn piteous appeal:
More, more he gaz'd: his human senses reel:
Some hungry spell that loveliness absorbs;
There was no recognition in those orbs.   260
'Lamia!' he cried—and no soft-toned reply.
The many heard, and the loud revelry
Grew hush; the stately music no more breathes;
The myrtle sicken'd in a thousand wreaths.
By faint degrees, voice, lute, and pleasure ceased;
A deadly silence step by step increased,
Until it seem'd a horrid presence there,
And not a man but felt the terror in his hair.
'Lamia!' he shriek'd; and nothing but the shriek
With its sad echo did the silence break.   270

'Begone, foul dream!' he cried, gazing again
In the bride's face, where now no azure vein
Wander'd on fair-spaced temples; no soft bloom
Misted the cheek; no passion to illume
The deep-recessed vision:—all was blight;
Lamia, no longer fair, there sat a deadly white.
'Shut, shut those juggling eyes, thou ruthless man!
Turn them aside, wretch! or the righteous ban
Of all the Gods, whose dreadful images
Here represent their shadowy presences,   280
May pierce them on the sudden with the thorn
Of painful blindness; leaving thee forlorn,
In trembling dotage to the feeblest fright
Of conscience, for their long offended might,
For all thine impious proud-heart sophistries,
Unlawful magic, and enticing lies.
Corinthians! look upon that gray-beard wretch!
Mark how, possess'd, his lashless eyelids stretch
Around his demon eyes! Corinthians, see!
My sweet bride withers at their potency.'   290
'Fool!' said the sophist, in an under-tone
Gruff with contempt; which a death-nighing moan
From Lycius answer'd, as heart-struck and lost,
He sank supine beside the aching ghost.
'Fool! Fool!' repeated he, while his eyes still
Relented not, nor mov'd; 'from every ill
Of life have I preserv'd thee to this day,
And shall I see thee made a serpent's prey?'
Then Lamia breath'd death breath; the sophist's eye,
Like a sharp spear, went through her utterly,   300
Keen, cruel, perceant, stinging: she, as well
As her weak hand could any meaning tell,
Motion'd him to be silent; vainly so,
He look'd and look'd again a level—No!
'A Serpent!' echoed he; no sooner said,
Than with a frightful scream she vanished:
And Lycius' arms were empty of delight,
As were his limbs of life, from that same night.
On the high couch he lay!—his friends came round—

Supported him—no pulse, or breath they found,   310
And, in its marriage robe, the heavy body wound.*

*'Philostratus, in his fourth book *de Vita Apollonii*, hath a memorable instance in this kind, which I may not omit, of one Menippus Lycius, a young man twenty-five years of age, that going betwixt Cenchreas and Corinth, met such a phantasm in the habit of a fair gentlewoman, which taking him by the hand, carried him home to her house, in the suburbs of Corinth, and told him she was a Phœnician by birth, and if he would tarry with her, he should hear her sing and play, and drink such wine as never any drank, and no man should molest him; but she, being fair and lovely, would live and die with him, that was fair and lovely to behold. The young man, a philosopher, otherwise staid and discreet, able to moderate his passions, though not this of love, tarried with her a while to his great content, and at last married her, to whose wedding, amongst other guests, came Apollonius; who, by some probable conjectures, found her out to be a serpent, a lamia; and that all her furniture was, like Tantalus' gold, described by Homer, no substance but mere illusions. When she saw herself descried, she wept, and desired Apollonius to be silent, but he would not be moved, and thereupon she, plate, house, and all that was in it, vanished in an instant: many thousands took notice of this fact, for it was done in the midst of Greece.'
Burton's 'Anatomy of Melancholy.' Part 3. Sect. 2. Memb. 1. Subs. 1.

'Pensive they sit, and roll their languid eyes'

Pensive they sit, and roll their languid eyes
Nibble their tosts, and cool their tea with sighs,
Or else forget the purpose of the night
Forget their tea—forget their appetite.
See with cross'd arms they sit—ah hapless crew
The fire is going out, and no one rings
For coals, and therefore no coals Betty brings.
A Fly is in the milk pot—must he die
Circled by a humane society?
No no there Mr. Werter takes his spoon   10
Inverts it—dips the handle and lo, soon
The little struggler sav'd from perils dark
Across the teaboard draws a long wet mark.
Romeo! Arise! take Snuffers by the handle

There's a large Cauliflower in each candle.
A winding-sheet—Ah me! I must away
To No. 7 just beyond the Circus gay.
'Alas my friend! your Coat sits very well:
Where may your Taylor live?' 'I may not tell—
O pardon me—I'm absent now and then.   20
Where *might* my Taylor live?—I say again
I cannot tell. Let me no more be teas'd—
He lives in Wapping *might* live where he pleas'd.'

To Autumn

I

Season of mists and mellow fruitfulness,
   Close bosom-friend of the maturing sun;
Conspiring with him how to load and bless
   With fruit the vines that round the thatch-eves run;
To bend with apples the moss'd cottage-trees,
    And fill all fruit with ripeness to the core;
      To swell the gourd, and plump the hazel shells
With a sweet kernel; to set budding more,
    And still more, later flowers for the bees,
    Until they think warm days will never cease,   10
      For Summer has o'er-brimm'd their clammy cells.

2

Who hath not seen thee oft amid thy store?
   Sometimes whoever seeks abroad may find
Thee sitting careless on a granary floor,
   Thy hair soft-lifted by the winnowing wind;
Or on a half-reap'd furrow sound asleep,
    Drows'd with the fume of poppies while thy hook
      Spares the next swath and all its twined flowers:
And sometimes like a gleaner thou dost keep
    Steady thy laiden head across a brook;   20
    Or by a cyder-press, with patient look,
      Thou watchest the last oozings hours by hours.

3

Where are the songs of Spring? Ay, where are they?
　　Think not of them, thou hast thy music too,—
While barred clouds bloom the soft-dying day,
　　And touch the stubble-plains with rosy hue;
Then in a wailful choir the small gnats mourn
　　Among the river sallows, borne aloft
　　　Or sinking as the light wind lives or dies;
And full-grown lambs loud bleat from hilly bourn;　　30
　　Hedge-crickets sing; and now with treble soft
　　The red-breast whistles from a garden-croft;
　　　And gathering swallows twitter in the skies.

'Bright Star, would I were stedfast as thou art'

Bright Star, would I were stedfast as thou art—
　　Not in lone splendor hung aloft the night,
And watching, with eternal lids apart,
　　Like nature's patient, sleepless Eremite,
The moving waters at their priestlike task
　　Of pure ablution round earth's human shores,
Or gazing on the new soft-fallen masque
　　Of snow upon the mountains and the moors—
No—yet still stedfast, still unchangeable
　　Pillow'd upon my fair love's ripening breast,　　10
To feel for ever its soft swell and fall,
　　Awake for ever in a sweet unrest,
Still, still to hear her tender-taken breath,
And so live ever—or else swoon to death—

On Coaches

From 'The Jealousies'

1

Eban, untempted by the Pastry-Cooks,
(Of Pastry he got store within the Palace)
With hasty steps, wrapp'd cloak, and solemn looks,
Incognito upon his errand sallies,
His smelling-bottle ready for the allies;
He pass'd the Hurdy-gurdies with disdain,
Vowing he'd have them sent on board the gallies;
Just as he made his vow, it 'gan to rain,
Therefore he call'd a coach, and bade it drive amain.

2

'I'll pull the string,' said he, and further said,   10
'Polluted Jarvey! Ah thou filthy hack!
Whose springs of life are all dried up and dead,
Whose linsey-wolsey lining hangs all slack,
Whose rug is straw, whose wholeness is a crack:
And evermore thy steps go clatter-clitter;
Whose glass once up can never be got back,
Who prov'st, with jolting arguments and bitter,
That 'tis of vile no-use to travel in a litter.

3

'Thou inconvenience! thou hungry crop
For all corn! thou snail-creeper to and fro,   20
Who while thou goest ever seem'st to stop,
And fiddle-faddle standest while you go;
I' the morning, freighted with a weight of woe,
Unto some Lazar-house thou journiest,
And in the evening tak'st a double row
Of dowdies, for some dance or party drest,
Besides the goods meanwhile thou movest east and west.

4

'By thy ungallant bearing and sad mien,
An inch appears the utmost thou couldst budge;
Yet at the slightest nod, or hint, or sign,　　　　30
Round to the curb-stone patient does thou trudge,
School'd in a beckon, learned in a nudge,
A dull-eyed Argus watching for a fare;
Quiet and plodding thou dost bear no grudge
To whisking Tilburies, or Phaetons rare,
Curricles, or Mail-coaches, swift beyond compare.'

5

Philosophising thus, he pull'd the check,
And bade the Coachman wheel to such a street,
Who turning much his body, more his neck,
Louted full low, and hoarsely did him greet.　　　　40

'What can I do to drive away'

What can I do to drive away
Remembrance from my eyes? for they have seen,
Aye, an hour ago, my brilliant Queen!
Touch has a memory. O say, love, say,
What can I do to kill it and be free
In my old liberty?
When every fair one that I saw was fair,
Enough to catch me in but half a snare,
Not keep me there:
When, howe'er poor or particolour'd things,　　　　10
My muse had wings,
And ever ready was to take her course
Whither I bent her force,
Unintellectual, yet divine to me;—
Divine, I say!—What sea-bird o'er the sea
Is a philosopher the while he goes
Winging along where the great water throes?

How shall I do
To get anew

Those moulted feathers, and so mount once more   20
Above, above
The reach of fluttering Love,
And make him cower lowly while I soar?
Shall I gulp wine? No, that is vulgarism.
A heresy and schism,
Foisted into the canon law of love;—
No,—wine is only sweet to happy men;
More dismal cares
Seize on me unawares,—
Where shall I learn to ge my peace again?   30
To banish thoughts of that most hateful land,
Dungeoner of my friends, that wicked strand
Where they were wreck'd and live a wrecked life;
That monstrous region, whose dull rivers pour,
Ever from their sordid urns unto the shore,
Unown'd of any weedy-haired gods;
Whose winds, all zephyrless, hold scourging rods,
Iced in the great lakes, to afflict mankind;
Whose rank-grown forests, frosted, black, and blind,
Would fright a Dryad; whose harsh herbaged meads   40
Make lean and lank the starv'd ox while he feeds;
There flowers have no scent, birds no sweet song,
And great unerring Nature once seems wrong.

    O, for some sunny spell
To dissipate the shadows of this hell!
Say they are gone,—with the new dawning light
Steps forth my lady bright!
O, let me once more rest
My soul upon that dazzling breast!
Let once again these aching arms be placed,   50
The tender gaolers of thy waist!
And let me feel that warm breath here and there
To spread a rapture in my very hair,—
O, the sweetness of the pain!
Give me those lips again!
Enough! Enough! it is enough for me
To dream of thee!

To Fanny

Physician Nature! let my spirit blood!
  O ease my heart of verse and let me rest;
Throw me upon thy Tripod, till the flood
  Of stifling numbers ebbs from my full breast.
A Theme! a Theme! Great Nature! give a theme;
     Let me begin my dream.
I come—I see Thee, as Thou standest there,
Beckon me out into the wintry air.

Ah! dearest Love, sweet home of all my fears
  And hopes and joys and panting miseries,—   10
To-night, if I may guess, thy beauty wears
     A smile of such delight,
     As brilliant and as bright,
As when with ravished, aching, vassal eyes,
     Lost, in a soft amaze,
     I gaze, I gaze!

Who now, with greedy looks, eats up my feast?
  What stare outfaces now my silver moon!
Ah! keep that hand unravished at the least;
     Let, let the amorous burn—   20
     But, prithee, do not turn
The current of your Heart from me so soon:
     O save, in charity,
     The quickest pulse for me.

Save it for me, sweet love! though music breathe
  Voluptuous visions into the warm air,
Though swimming through the dance's dangerous wreath;
     Be like an April day,
     Smiling and cold and gay,
A temperate lily, temperate as fair;   30
     Then, Heaven! there will be
     A warmer June for me.

Why this—you'll say—my Fanny!—is not true;
  Put your soft hand upon your snowy side,

Where the heart beats: confess—'tis nothing new—
  Must not a woman be
  A feather on the sea,
Swayed to and fro by every wind and tide?
  Of as uncertain speed
  As blow-ball from the mead?   40

I know it—and to know it is despair
 To one who loves you as I love sweet Fanny,
Whose heart goes fluttering for you every where,
  Nor when away you roam,
  Dare keep its wretched home:
 Love, Love alone, has pains severe and many;
  Then, Loveliest! keep me free,
  From torturing jealousy.

Ah! if you prize my subdued soul above
 The poor, the fading, brief, pride of an hour: 50
Let none profane my Holy See of Love,
  Or with a rude hand break
  The sacramental cake:
 Let none else touch the just new-budded flower;
  If not—may my eyes close
  Love on their last repose!

'This living hand, now warm and capable'

This living hand, now warm and capable
Of earnest grasping, would, if it were cold
And in the icy silence of the tomb,
So haunt thy days and chill thy dreaming nights
That thou would wish thine own heart dry of blood
So in my veins red life might stream again,
And thou be conscience-calm'd—see here it is
I hold it towards you—

'In after time a Sage of mickle lore'

In after time a Sage of mickle lore,
Yclep'd Typographus, the Giant took
And did refit his limbs as heretofore,
And made him read in many a learned book,
And into many a lively legend look;
Thereby in goodly themes so training him,
That all his brutishness he quite forsook,
When meeting Artegall and Talus grim,
The one he struck stone blind, the other's eyes wox dim.

Notes

ABBREVIATIONS

The three volumes of poetry published by Keats during his lifetime are referred to as *1817*, *Endymion*, and *1820*.

FQ   Edmund Spenser, *The Faerie Queene*.

Hazlitt, *Works* P. P. Howe (ed.), *The Complete Works of William Hazlitt*, 21 vols. (London, 1930–4).

PL   John Milton, *Paradise Lost*.

1 *Imitation of Spenser*. Composed probably early in 1814; published in *1817*. Brown calls this Keats's 'earliest attempt'.

2 *Written on the Day That Mr. Leigh Hunt Left Prison*. Composed 2 Feb. 1815; published in *1817*. Hunt (whom Keats had not met at this point) had been imprisoned for two years for libelling the Prince Regent in the *Examiner* (22 Mar. 1812, p. 179).

To Hope. Composed Feb. 1815; published in *1817*.

ll. 19–20. The Keats family had been broken up on the death of their grandmother in December 1814.

4 *Ode to Apollo*. Composed Feb. 1815; not published during Keats's life.

l. 12. Homer was traditionally blind.

l. 14. *Maro*: Virgil (Publius Virgilius Maro).

l. 17. *Aeneid* vi. 212–35.

5 l. 33. *FQ* iii tells the legend of Chastity and the whole work is dedicated to Elizabeth, the Virgin Queen.

l. 34. *Æolian lyre*: wind-harp.

l. 36. *Tasso*. Author of *Gerusalemme Liberata* ('Jerusalem Delivered').

Lines Written on 29 *May, the Anniversary of Charles's Restoration, on Hearing the Bells Ringing*. Composed 29 May 1815; not published during Keats's life.

l. 5. Algernon Sidney (1622–83), Lord William Russell (1639–83), and Sir Henry Vane (1613–62) were executed for treason against Charles II and so were icons of republicanism to 19th-c. liberals.

6 *'O Solitude! if I must with thee dwell'*. Composed late 1815 or early 1816; published in the *Examiner* 5 May 1816, and in *1817*. This was Keats's first published poem and was written shortly after his move from Edmonton to London to study medicine.

'Give me women wine and snuff'. Composed late 1815 or early 1816; not published during Keats's life.

l. 4. *resurrection*. This may be a medical student's joke since the men who dug up corpses for anatomies were known as 'resurrection men'.

'*I am as brisk*'. Composed probably Feb. 1816; not published during Keats's life.

7 '*O grant that like to Peter I*'. Date of composition unknown; not published during Keats's life.

To My Brother George. Composed Aug. 1816 as a verse letter from Margate; published in *1817*.

l. 19. *the bay*: poetry (rewarded by a laurel crown).

8 l. 66. *spell*: enchant.

10 l. 130. Red-jacketed soldiers.

l. 141. *westward*: towards London (where George was).

11 *To Charles Cowden Clarke*. Composed Sept. 1816 as a verse letter from Margate; published in 1817. Charles Cowden Clarke had taught at his father's school at Enfield, which Keats attended. As teacher and friend he was a greatly formative influence on Keats, introducing him to liberal politics, feeding his love of literature, and introducing him to practising writers (including Hunt and Lamb). This poem gratefully acknowledges the mental worlds which he had opened for Keats.

ll. 29–31. *Baiæ's shore*: the Bay of Naples, home of Torquato Tasso, whose work Cowden Clarke had introduced to Keats.   *Armida*: the heroine of *Gerusalemme Liberata*.

ll. 33–7. Allusions to Spenser: *Mulla's stream* is the river near Spenser's home in Kilcolman, Ireland.   *Belphoebe . . . Una . . . Archimago*: figures from *FQ* i and ii.

12 l. 44. *Libertas*: Leigh Hunt.

13 ll. 110–12. Cowden Clarke was a good pianist and introduced Keats to much of the music that he loved.   *Arne*: Thomas Arne (1710–1778), an English composer who set many of Shakespeare's songs to music.   *song of Erin*: probably a reference to Thomas Moore's *Irish Melodies* (published in London and Dublin between 1808 and 1834).

14 l. 122. *bland*: smooth (without pejorative sense).

On First Looking into Chapman's Homer. Composed Oct. 1816; published in the *Examiner*, 1 Dec. 1816 and in *1817*. Hunt's view was that this sonnet 'which terminates with so energetic a calmness . . . completely announced the new poet taking possession'. George Chapman's *The Whole Works of Homer* was published in 1614. It is significant that Keats and most of his contemporaries (though not

Byron) should have favoured this translation and not the more recent one by Pope.

14 l. 7. *serene*. A substantive, as in the Latin *serenum* ('a clear, bright, or serene sky').

l. 11. *Cortez*. In fact Balboa was the first European to sight the Pacific.

Sleep and Poetry. Composed between Oct. and Nov. 1816; published in *1817* as the final poem in the volume.

Motto 'The Floure and the Leafe' 17-21; this poem is no longer attributed to Chaucer.

15 l. 33. *lymning*: painting, drawing

16 l. 74. *Meander*: a river in Asia Minor notorious for its windings.

17 l. 89. *Montmorenci*: a river in Quebec with a sheer waterfall.

ll. 96-154. Keats's programme for poetic and spiritual development owes much to Wordsworth's 'Lines written a few miles above Tintern Abbey'.

ll. 102-21. The visual details of this passage may owe something to Nicholas Poussin's *L'Empire de Flore*. This is the world of pagan pastoral.

18 l. 126. *car*: chariot.

19 l. 168. *ether*: the clear sky (OED). In Keats's account of English poetry the fullness of Elizabethan and Jacobean writing (ll. 171-180) was wilfully betrayed by the neoclassicists (ll. 181-206).

l. 172. *paragon*: a verb (so used by Shakespeare and Milton).

ll. 186-7. *rocking horse . . . Pegasus*. Keats is attacking the mechanical evenness of the heroic couplet.

20 l. 198. *certain wands of Jacob's wit*: Gen. 30: 37-42 (Jacob uses wands of poplar, hazel, and chestnut to control the breeding of his cattle at the expense of Laban).

l. 202. *the bright Lyrist*: Phoebus Apollo.

l. 206. *Boileau*: (1636-1711), author of the neoclassicist *Art Poétique*.

l. 209. *boundly*: a coinage (on analogy with (e.g.) 'goodly').

l. 218. *lone spirits*. According to Woodhouse, an 'allusion to H[enry] Kirke White [1785-1806], Chatterton—& other poets of great promise neglected by the age, who died young'. Later allusions are to Wordsworth (ll. 224-6), Leigh Hunt (ll. 226-8), and possibly Coleridge or Byron (ll. 230-5).

21 l. 257. *Yeaned*: brought forth, born (used of lambs and kids).

22 l. 303. *Dedalian wings*: see Glossary q.v. *Daedalus*.

23 l. 322. *rout*: Usually a disorderly crowd, but here in the (not necessarily contradictory) sense of 'fashionable gathering'.

l. 338. Hunt introduced Keats to many examples of visual art through his portfolio collections of engravings (the 19th-c. alternative to photographic plates). Keats describes some of the contents of Hunt's cottage in ll. 354–91.

24 l. 379. *unshent*: not disfigured.

l. 381. A bust of Sappho (b. Lesbos *c.*620 BC), woman poet and first great lyrist.

l. 387. *Kosciusko*. See note to 'To Kosciusko' (below, note to p. 26).

25 *To My Brothers*. Composed 18 Nov. 1816 (Tom Keats's seventeenth birthday); published in *1817*.

l. 8. *condoles*. Used transitively ('lore' is the subject, 'care' the object).

Addressed to [*Haydon*]. Composed 19 or 20 Nov. 1816 and enclosed in a letter of 20 Nov. to Haydon as apropos the previous evening; published *1817*. Keats had met Benjamin Robert Haydon (a painter of huge works on epic themes) at Hunt's during Oct. 1816. Haydon sent a copy of this poem to Wordsworth.

ll. 2–8. 2–4 refer to Wordsworth (Helvellyn is a mountain near his home in Grasmere), 5–6 to Leigh Hunt, and 7–8 to Haydon. Hunt had proclaimed Haydon the successor to Michelangelo and Raphael so *Raphael* is probably the painter (but he might possibly be the archangel who in *PL* explains the works of God to Adam and Eve).

l. 13. The mute half line seems to have been Haydon's suggestion.

26 *To Kosciusko*. Composed Dec. 1816; published in the *Examiner*, 16 Feb. 1817 and in *1817*. Tadeusz Kosciusko (1746–1817) was a Polish patriot. Having fought with Washington in the American Army in 1776 (and been made an honorary American citizen) he returned to Europe to find his native Poland's independence compromised and threatened. In 1794 he led a patriot insurrection against the Russians and defeated the Russian army at Raclawice. Later in the same year he was defeated and taken as a prisoner to Russia. In 1798 he settled in France where he resisted Napoleon's attempts to make Poland a pawn whilst enlisting his support for the cause of independence. Kosciusko was a hero to many English liberals.

27 *'I stood tip-toe upon a little hill'*. Completed Dec. 1816; published in 1817 as the first poem in the volume. The poem was originally titled, and referred to in letters as, 'Endymion' (ll. 113–24 and 181 210 explain why).
Motto: Leigh Hunt, *The Story of Rimini* iii. 430.

29 l. 89. *sleek*: a verb.

30 l. 134. *vases*: to rhyme with *faces*.

30 l. 147. *lamp*. by which Psyche illicitly glimpsed, and thereby forfeited, her divine lover.

31 ll. 181–204. See *Endymion*; these lines show that Keats understood this myth as a key to the nature of poetry and go far to explain his very extensive treatment of it in *Endymion*.

33 *Written in Disgust of Vulgar Superstition*. 'Written in 15 minutes' on 22 Dec. 1816; not published during Keats's life.

'*After dark vapors have oppress'd our plains*'. Composed 31 Jan. 1817; published in the *Examiner*, 23 Feb. 1817.

34 l. 14. *a poet's death*. Keats later wrote to Reynolds, 'I always somehow associate Chatterton with autumn'.

On seeing the Elgin Marbles. Composed 1 or 2 Mar. 1817 after visiting the British Museum with Haydon to see the Parthenon frieze which Lord Elgin had recently acquired for the nation. According to the painter, Joseph Severn, Keats went 'again and again to see the Elgin Marbles, and would sit for an hour or more at a time beside them rapt in revery'. Published in both the *Champion* and the *Examiner* on 9 Mar. 1817, and in *Annals of the Fine Arts*, 3 (Apr. 1818).

On a Leander which Miss Reynolds my kind friend gave me. Composed probably during Mar. 1817; not published during Keats's life. A 'Leander' was one of James Tassie's paste reproductions of gems engraved with classical scenes. This one depicted Leander swimming across the Hellespont to Hero. At some point in 1819 Keats gave his sister a set of Tassie's cameo gems.

35 *On the Sea*. Composed probably on 17 Apr. 1817 while Keats was lodging at Carisbrooke on the Isle of Wight. Published in the *Champion*, 17 Aug. 1817.

l. 3. Hecate's 'spell' is her influence over the tides.

l. 9. *vex'd*: a latinate use (from *vexare* to shake, agitate).

'*Hither hither Love*'. Date of composition unknown; not published during Keats's life.

36 *Endymion*. Composed between late Apr. 1817 and 28 Nov. 1818; published, as a separate volume, in 1818. Keats began work on the poem while at Carisbrooke with a clear, workmanlike programme for its completion: see i 39–77 and the spring letter to George in which the poem is described as 'a test, a trial of my Powers of Imagination and chiefly of my invention . . . by which I must make 4000 Lines of one bare circumstance and fill them with Poetry'. In a preface to the poem (later rejected in favour of the published preface) Keats describes *Endymion* rather as 'an endeavour than a thing accomplished', seeing the poem as a necessary but flawed apprentice piece. The reviews in the Tory press were not favourable. It is they that are

alluded to in the sentimental myth that hostile criticism was the cause of Keats's early death. The 'bare circumstance' of which Keats was to make 4000 lines is the legend of Endymion (see Glossary) which he had adumbrated in 'I stood tip-toe' 181–94.

Motto to Preface: misquoted from Shakespeare, *Sonnets* xvii. 12.

41 ll. 141–4. Apollo spent a period of exile living as a Thessalonian shepherd (Ovid, *Metamorphoses* ii. 677–82).

l. 158. *Leda's love*: Jupiter disguised as a swan.

42 l. 208. *scrip*: satchel.

43 ll. 232–306. This stanzaic 'Hymn to Pan' is a working towards the form of the later odes. Shelley saw in it a 'promise of ultimate excellence'.

l. 248, *Passion*: a verb.

46 l. 334. *raft*: an archaic form of 'reft' (torn); useful for the rhyme.

47 l. 392. *famish'd scrips*: depleted lunch-boxes.

ll. 405–6. Probably 'The History of the Young King of the Black Isles' in the *Arabian Nights*, in which a young man appears whose lower half is marble.

50 l. 510. *Paphian*: from Venus' temple at Paphos.

51 l. 555. *ditamy, and poppies*: plants sacred to Diana.

53 l. 614. *gordian'd*: knotted—Keats's own coinage; cf. iii. 494.

54 l. 683. *ouzel*: blackbird.

55 l. 726. *bard*: a metonym for what the bards will sing?

57 ll. 776–81. See Introduction p. xvi for Keats's comments on this passage.

l. 786. *Eolian*: as in the music of an 'Aeolian' wind-harp.

l. 792. The war between the Titans and the Olympians—the starting-point of *Hyperion*.

58 l. 815. *pelican*. The pelican was fabled to wound its breast in order to feed its young with its own blood. As such it is a type of Christ.

ll. 832–42. According to T. Medwin, Byron's summary of what 'Keats somewhere says' was 'that "flowers would not blow, leaves but" &c, if man and woman did not kiss. How sentimental!'

60 l. 907. *sloth*. Sloths are in fact herbivorous, but Keats puns on the sense of 'idleness' to make sloth a deadly predator.

In Book ii Endymion begins his quest in the underworld. He suffers from loneliness until he prays to Diana and his aspiration transforms his experience. He encounters Adonis (another mortal loved by a divinity) being roused from his half-year sleep by Venus, and later

Alpheus and Arethusa whose sadness moves Endymion to pray to Diana for their happiness.

62 *Book* iii. Composed during Sept. 1817—mostly while staying with Bailey at Magdalen Hall, Oxford. This book follows Endymion under water.

ll. 1–21. Described as a 'jacobinical apostrophe' by one reviewer. Woodhouse notes that Keats said, 'It will easily be seen what I think of the present Ministers by the beginning of the 3rd book'.

ll. 7–8. *fire-branded foxes*: Judg. 15: 4–5.

ll. 16–18. Perhaps recalling the loud festivities after Napoleon's abdication (6 Apr. 1814).

64 ll. 97–9. Each braved a hostile element for love's sake (Leander water, Orpheus the underworld, Pluto the upper air).

66 l. 192. *an old man*: Glaucus.

67 l. 234. *Thou art the man*: 2 Sam. 12: 7.

l. 243. *that giant*: Typhon.

68 ll. 281–end; Endymion soon comes to pity the old man. Glaucus tells the story of his love for Scylla and of how the witch Circe seduced him away from his beloved in order to enthrall and degrade him. When he learns the truth and plans escape it is too late: Scylla is dead and he is doomed to live and age 1000 years. During this time his own compassion earns him a hopeful prophecy: if he fulfils certain obligations, the chief of which is to tend the bodies of all lovers drowned in the sea, he will ultimately be rescued by a pre-elected youth. Endymion is he. The rescue is accomplished, Scylla and all the other dead lovers are revived. Venus tells Endymion it will not be long before he is reunited with his own beloved. Swooning, he is carried by nereids to dry land.

Book iv. Composed between *c.*5 Oct. and 28 Nov. 1817.

ll. 1–29 Keats's recent reading of *PL* may have inspired the invocation to the Muse. The Muse is shown to have bided her time before flowering in England. In this brief history of world poetry the Muse's achievements are instanced as the Old Testament (l. 10), Classical Greek poetry (ll. 11–14), the Latin/Italian poetry of Virgil and Dante (ll. 14–16), and, at last, the English flowering in Shakespeare and the Elizabethans (ll. 17–18); but Keats laments a subsequent falling off of poetic genius.

l. 15. *Ausonia*: ancient name for Italy.

69 l. 26. *shrives*: confesses (by metonymy from its proper meaning of 'grants absolution').

l. 27. *poets gone*: Burns and Chatterton?

71 l. 129. *gorgon*: petrifying.

72 l. 157. *spry*: spray.

76 ll. 291–end. After the song Endymion dreams he is carried up to heaven where his perplexity is increased by meeting Diana, his heavenly love. He wakes to find the dream is true but is then carried back to earth where he swears no longer to be duped by apparitions but to be content with his human love, the Indian Maid. She however, says that she is forbidden to be his love. His sister Peona appears and Endymion vows a life of chastity. The Indian Maid then reveals herself to be a form of Phoebe/Diana with whom he is at last united.

On Oxford. Composed during Keats's stay with Bailey at Magdalen Hall, Sept. 1817; not published during Keats's life.

ll. 10 and 11 may contain references to Magdalen College, which then, as now, supported a boys' choir and had a deer park in its grounds. Keats included the poem in a letter to Reynolds of Sept. 1817 with this introduction: 'Wordsworth sometimes, though in a fine way, gives us sentences in the Style of School exercises—for Instance

> The lake doth glitter
> Small birds twitter &c.

Now I think this is an excellent method of giving a very clear description of an interesting place such as Oxford is—'

l. 9. A 'trencher' is a mortar-board; a 'common hat' might mean a commoner's hat (noblemen wore gold tassels), but, since this would be the same as the trencher, the meaning here is probably 'the hat of an ordinary citizen'.

77 *'In drear nighted December'.* Composed Dec. 1817; not published during Keats's life.

'Before he went to live with owls and bats'. Date of composition uncertain, but probably 1817; not published during Keats's life. The poem is an act of solidarity with William Hone, the bookseller who had been tried for writing political parodies of the Creed, Catechism, and Litany. Nebuchadnezzar's dream is in Dan. 2–4. Daniel (here probably a type of Hone) interprets the king's nightmares as foreseeing the overthrow of his kingdom (or Tory rule).

l. 4. *Naumachia*: miniature mock sea-battle (an item in the peace celebrations of 1814).

l. 5. Quoted from *Romeo and Juliet* III. i. 77.

78 *To Mrs Reynoldse's Cat.* Composed 16 Jan. 1818; not published during Keats's life.

78 l. 1. *Grand Climacteric*. 63 years for a man so, if one cat year is equal to seven human years, this cat must have reached nine.

l. 14. In the 19th c. garden walls were often topped with broken glass bottles to deter intruders.

Lines on seeing a Lock of Milton's hair. Composed 21 Jan. 1818; not published during Keats's life. A 'real authenticated Lock of Milton's hair' had been shown to Keats by Hunt.

79 l. 18. *delian*: from Delos (Apollo's birthplace).

l. 35. *the simplest vassal of thy power*: the lock of hair, subject ('vassal') to Milton's vital force.

On Sitting Down to Read King Lear *Once Again*. Composed 22 Jan. 1818; not published during Keats's life. The poem is written inside Keats's folio Shakespeare.

80 *'When I have fears that I may cease to be'*. Composed Jan. 1818; not published during Keats's life. The form of this sonnet, and the way in which the form structures the argument, in Shakespearian. Keats was to favour this form from this point on.

'O blush not so, O blush not so'. Composed probably on 31 Jan. 1818; not published during Keats's life. The poem is written in the manner of an Elizabethan song. Swinburne, in a letter to Rossetti of 23 May 1870, called it 'a short bawdy song which was unfit for publication'.

81 *Lines on the Mermaid Tavern*. Composed towards the end of Jan. 1818 after an evening spent at the Mermaid Tavern, Cheapside, famous meeting-place of poets such as Shakespeare, Jonson, Beaumont, and Fletcher; published in *1820*.

82 l. 12. *sup and bowse*. Both mean 'drink' ('sip' and 'booze').

Robin Hood. Composed *c.*3 Feb. 1818 'in a Spirit of Outlawry'. Robin Hood, in his defiance of the Norman barons, was a patriot hero to early 19th-c. liberals. Published in *1820*.

83 l. 34. *The Tale of Gamelyn* was a 14th-c. metrical romance about a band of forest outlaws.

l. 36. *'grenè shawe'*: green wood; the phrase is Chaucerian.

84 l. 55. *tight*: clever, neat, skilful.

'O thou whose face hath felt the Winter's wind'. Composed 19 Feb. 1818; not published during Keats's life. Keats sent this poem in a letter to Reynolds saying, 'I have not read any Books—the Morning said I was right—I had no idea but of the Morning and the Thrush said I was right.' The sonnet is what the thrush seemed to say.

The Human Seasons. Composed at Teignmouth between 7 and 13 Mar. 1818; published in Leigh Hunt's *Literary Pocket Book* for 1819 where it is signed simply 'I' (for Iohannes?).

85 *'For there's Bishop's Teign'*. Composed *c.*21 Mar. 1818 at Teignmouth; not published during Keats's life.

ll. 1–25. Bishopsteignton, Kingsteignton, and Combeinteignhead are all villages near Teignmouth.

86 l. 35. *plight*: fold or (more generally, as used by Spenser) dress.

l. 38. *Soho*: an area of central London.

l. 39. *dack'd-haired*: short-haired (i.e. docked).

l. 42. *Prickets*: technically, buck deer in their second year; here a sexual pun.

'Where be ye going you Devon maid'. Composition as for previous poem; not published during Keats's life.

87 l. 6. *junkets*: milk dishes traditional to Devon, where they are served with clotted cream. 'Junkets' was Hunt's punning nickname for John Keats.

ll. 13–14. Keats's underlinings suggest sexual meanings.

'Over the hill and over the dale'. Either drafted or copied in a letter of 24 Mar. 1818 (Dawlish fair had taken place on 23 Mar. which was Easter Monday); not published during Keats's life.

l. 2. Dawlish is about three miles from Teignmouth.

l. 5. *Rantipole*: wild, rakish.

88 l. 16. *venus*: prostitute.

To J. H. Reynolds Esq. Composed 25 Mar. 1818 and sent from Teignmouth on that date as a verse letter to Reynolds who was unwell in London; not published during Keats's life.

ll. 7–10. Types of the world upside down: the contemplative Voltaire is seen as a man of action; the active soldier Alexander as a slugabed; the great unworldly philosopher as a mere social creature; Hazlitt disliked the novelist Maria Edgeworth (1767–1849) and would presumably have avoided her cat too.

l. 11. Junius Brutus Booth (1796–1852), the actor; 'so so' means drunk.

l. 16. *wild boar tushes*: such as those that puncture Venus's joy in Adonis.

l. 21. *Gloams*: darkens (a Scots verb).

ll. 26–66. The reference is to Claude's *Enchanted Castle* now in the National Gallery; probably known to Keats through an engraving.

89 l. 29. *Urganda*: the enchantress Urganda the Unknown in the 16th-c. romance *Amadis of Gaul*.

l. 42. *santon*: a Mohammedan monk or hermit.

90 l. 88. *Lampit*: limpit (a Scots spelling).

91 l. 108. The Kamschatka peninsula is on the east coast of Russia.

    l. 112. *Centaine*: 100 lines.

    l. 113. 'Soft! here follows prose' (*Twelfth Night* II. v. 142).

    Isabella. Composed between Feb. and Apr. 1818 (completed by 27 Apr.); published in *1820*. The story of Isabella comprises the Fifth Novel of the Fourth Day in *The Novels and Tales of the Renowned John Boccaccio* (i.e. *The Decameron*). Charles Lamb, in his review of *1820*, was to call 'Isabella' 'the finest thing in the volume', but Keats came to be dissatisfied with the poem and uneasy about its tone, which he was to describe as 'too smokeable'.

92 l. 44. *ruddy tide*. blood engorging his vocal chords.

93 l. 62. *fear*: frighten.

94 l. 95. *Theseus' spouse*: Ariadne.

    ll. 105–20. Bernard Shaw wrote that these two stanzas 'contain all the Factory Commission Reports that Marx read, and that Keats did not read because they were not yet written in his time'.

    l. 107. *swelt*: swelter.

95 l. 113. *Ceylon diver*: diving for pearls to enrich the brothers.

    l. 123. *orange-mounts*: plantations of orange trees (or, possibly, heaps of gold).

    l. 124. *lazar stairs*: stairs in a lazar house, occupied by the poor and the sick.

    l. 125. *red-lin'd accounts*: account books showing income, expenditure, and profit.

    l. 131. *that land inspired*: Palestine; Keats is succumbing to an anti-Semitic cliché in this line. The 'ducats' of l. 134 suggest that Shylock may be behind this.

    l. 140. *pest*: Exod. 10: 21.

96 l. 150. *ghittern*: a kind of guitar.

98 l. 209. *murder'd man*. Charles Lamb was the first to admire this prolepsis in print: 'The anticipation of the assassination is wonderfully conceived in one epithet'.

99 l. 262. '[Ahaz] burnt incense in the valley of the son of Hinnom, and burnt his children in the fire, after the abhominations of the heathen' (2 Chron. 28: 3).

103 l. 370. She had embroidered a design on it.

    l. 374. Her breasts.

    l. 381. *horrid*. The Latin *horridus* means 'bristling'. Keats uses the word etymologically.

l. 393. *Perséan sword*: given to Perseus by Mercury for decapitating Medusa.

l. 396. *harps*: bards, minstrels.

105 l. 451. *Baälites of pelf*: worshippers of the false god money.

107 *Old Meg she was a Gipsey*. Written for Fanny Keats and enclosed in a letter to her of 3 July 1818; not published during Keats's life. During their walk through Kirkudbrightshire, the setting of Scott's novel *Guy Mannering* (1815)—which Keats had not read—Brown described to Keats the charcter of Meg Merrilies who appears in that novel.

l. 25. *Margaret Queen*: probably referring to the wife of Henry VI as portrayed by Shakespeare.

108 l. 28. *chip hat*: hat made of thin strips of wood.

'*There was a naughty Boy*'. Composed 3 July 1818 at Kirkudbright and included in a letter to Fanny Keats of 2–5 July where it is introduced as 'a song about myself'; not published during Keats's life.

l. 20. *revetted*: rivetted.

110 l. 76. *Miller's thumb*: a small freshwater fish, like the stickleback (childishly pronounced 'Tittle bat') of the following line.

111 *Sonnet to Ailsa Rock*. Composed on 10 July 1818 at Girvan, Ayrshire; published in Leigh Hunt's *Literary Pocket Book* for 1819 (1818) where, like 'The Human Seasons', it is signed simply 'J'.

'*There is a joy in footing slow across a silent plain*'. Composed before 22 July 1818 after a visit to Burns's country. Published in the *Examiner*, 14 July 1822. Keats's use of rhyming fourteeners reflects his reading of Renaissance literature, such as Chapman's Homer.

113 '*Not Aladin magian*'. Composed late July 1818 after a visit to Fingal's Cave on Staffa; not published during Keats's life.

l. 3. *wizard of the Dee*: Merlin.

l. 5. Cf. Rev. I: 9–12 for St John's description of his vision on Patmos.

l. 24. *thrice*. Trice—Keats's spelling may reflect the incorrect belief that the word means 'a third of a second'.

114 l. 32. *Finny palmers*: fish, who are palmers (pilgrims) because they swim to a shrine.

l. 39. *Pontif priest*: high priest.

l. 51. *cutters*: small passenger boats.

'*Upon my Life Sir Nevis I am piqued*'. Composed 3 Aug. 1818 at Letterfinlay, Inverness-shire in a letter to Tom; not published during Keats's life. Keats tells Tom about: 'one Mrs. Cameron of 50 years

of age and the fattest woman in all inverness shire who got up this
Mountain some few years ago—true she had her servants but then
she had her self—She ought to have hired Sysiphus . . . 'T is said a
little conversation took place between the mountain and the Lady—
After taking a glass of Wiskey as she was tolerably seated at ease she
thus begun' [the poem follows].

114 l. 2. *reek'd*: sweated.

   l. 4. *bate*: rest.

115 l. 30. *how the gemini*: a tacit pun on 'how the deuce' (gemini-twins-
   dual—deuce).

   l. 32. As humans quake, so mountains earthquake.

116 l. 43. *Buss*: kiss.

   l. 52. *gust*: both 'blast' and 'taste' ('gusto' was a fashionable concept;
   see Hazlitt, *Works*, iv 77–80).

117 *Nature withheld Cassandra in the Skies*. A 'free translation of a Sonnet
   of Ronsard' done at some point in Sept. 1818; not published during
   Keats's life. The Ronsard original is the second sonnet of *Le Premier
   Livre des amours* (1587).

   '*'Tis "the witching time of night"*'. Composed in a letter to George and
   Georgiana, 14 Oct. 1818 where it is introduced as a prophecy 'that
   one of your Children should be the first American poet'; not
   published during Keats's life. The first line is from *Hamlet* (III. ii. 388).

119 '*And what is Love?—It is a doll dress'd up*' Composed during 1818; not
   published during Keats's life.

   l. 8. *Wellingtons*: boots—not then made of rubber—named after the
   Duke of Wellington *c.* 1817; modish at the time of writing.

   ll. 15–16. Cleopatra was fabled to have dissolved and drunk a pearl
   in a toast to Antony.

   l. 17. *beaver hats*: hats made of beaver fur. Keats's guardian, Abbey,
   wanted Keats to consider a career as a hatter.

   Fragment: 'Welcome joy, and welcome sorrow'. Composed during 1818;
   not published during Keats's life. The motto misquotes *PL* ii 898–90
   'For Hot, Cold, Moist, and Dry, four champions fierce | Strive here
   for mastery, and to battle bring | Their embryon atoms; they around
   the flag | Of each his faction'.

   l. 2. The contrast is between dull obliviousness and mercurial
   sharpness.

120 *Fragment: 'Where's the Poet? Show him! show him!'* Composed during
   1818; not published during Keats's life.

121 *To Homer*. Composed during 1818; not published during Keats's life.

l. 1. Keats compares his own 'giant ignorance' to the traditional blindness of Homer, the inward seer.

l. 12. *triple sight*. Making three worlds visible: Jove's heaven, Neptune's ocean, and Pan's earth.

Hyperion. Composed between late 1818 and Apr. 1819 when it was abandoned unfinished. Published as 'A Fragment' in *1820*. The subject of the poem—the overthrow of the Titans by the Olympian gods and the establishment of Apollo as god of the sun, music and healing, in the place of the Titan sun-god Hyperion—had been on Keats's mind for some time and was certainly part of the plan for future work at the time he was completing *Endymion*. Keats's reading of Dante and Milton strongly inform the poem while Shakespeare's *King Lear* influences the portrayal of Saturn. The writing of the poem was so bound up with the period of Tom's illness and death that Keats may have lacked heart to complete it—though he was to revive the project in 'The Fall of Hyperion' later. The poem was greatly admired by contemporaries. Even Byron, who on the whole disliked Keats's work, wrote that 'His fragment on *Hyperion* seems actually inspired by the Titans and is as sublime as Aeschylus'.

l. 1. Keats, annotating *PL* i 321, writes: 'There is a cool pleasure in the very sound of vale—The english word is of the happiest chance.'

122 l. 31. *Memphian sphinx*. Memphis was a major city in ancient Egypt.

124 l. 129. *gold clouds metropolitan*. Miltonic word order; the clouds form a metropolis for the gods.

125 l. 147. *The rebel three*: Saturn's sons Jupiter, Neptune, and Pluto.

128 l. 274. *colure*: an astrological term for 'each of two great circles which intersect each other at right angles at the poles, and divide the equinoctial and the ecliptic into four equal parts' (*OED*); Keats found the word in *PL*.

129 l. 323. *first born*: Saturn.

Book ii

130 ll. 7–12. This description is informed by Keats's experience of the Lake District through his own travels and through his reading of Wordsworth.

131 ll. 39 ff. The description of the Titans' suffering reflects Keats's recent reading of Dante's *Inferno*.

134 l. 161. *engine*: mobilize.

ll. 168–9. Oceanus is self-taught.

136 l. 232. *young God of the Seas*: Neptune.

139 l. 341. *winged thing*. Victory was traditionally represented with wings.

139 ll. 374–6. The statue erected to Memnon near Thebes was reputed to utter sounds at dawn and at sunset as if saluting the day and lamenting its passing.

Book iii

140 l. 12 *Dorian flute*. The Dorian mode is one of the ancient musical modes. Here the Delphic harp and Dorian flute usher in another era than that of shell music (i. 131, ii. 270).

l. 13. Apollo.

141 l. 29. Hyperion.

ll. 31–2. *mother . . . twin-sister*: Latona and Diana.

l. 46. *awful Goddess*: Mnemosyne.

142 ll. 77–9. Mnemosyne has staked her future on Apollo and abandoned the Titans, once her peers.

ll. 82–120. Keats told Woodhouse that Apollo's speech 'seemed to come by chance or magic—as if it were something given to him'.

143 l. 136. Woodhouse noted (in his copy of *Endymion*) that 'The poem, if completed, would have treated of the dethronement of Hyperion, the former God of the Sun, by Apollo—and incidentally of Oceanus by Neptune, of Saturn by Jupiter &c and of the war of the Giants for Saturn's reestablishment—with other events, of which we have but very dark hints in the Mythological poets of Greece & Rome. In fact, the incidents would have been pure creations of the Poet's brain'.

Fancy. Composed late 1818; published in *1820*.

144 l. 21. *shoon*: shoes.

145 l. 81. *Ceres' daughter*: Proserpine, or Persephone, captured by Pluto, the 'God of Torment'.

146 *Ode: 'Bards of Passion and of Mirth'*. Composed late 1818; published in *1820*. Keats describes this as 'on the double immortality of Poets'.

147 *'I had a dove and the sweet dove died'*. Composed during Dec. 1818 or the very beginning of Jan. 1819; not published during Keats's life.

Song: 'Hush, hush, tread softly, hush hush my dear'. Composed during 1818; not published during Keats's life. It has been suggested that the poem echoes Keats's flirtation with Isabella Jones. If so it is strange that he should have given the poem to Fanny Brawne to transcribe.

148 *The Eve of St. Agnes*. Drafted during the last two weeks of Jan.—and perhaps the first few days of Feb.—1819 while Keats was at Chichester and Bedhampton; significantly revised at Winchester during early Sept. 1819; published in *1820*. Keats subsequently revised the poem making it clear that sexual union takes place between the lovers. His

friend, Woodhouse, and his publisher, Taylor, strenuously objected to these changes which would render the poem 'unfit for ladies'. Keats countered 'that he writes for men—& that if in the former poem there was an opening for doubt what took place, it was his fault for not writing clearly & comprehensibly.' Eventually, however, he left it to his publishers to decide on which version they pleased. For a complete text of 'St. Agnes Eve' which includes the contested stanzas see *John Keats*. ed. Elizabeth Cook (Oxford, 1990), 544–54.

The poem takes as its starting-point the popular superstition that if a virgin observes certain disciplines on St. Agnes's Eve she will dream of her future husband.

150 l. 70. *amort*: dead.

l. 71. *lambs unshorn*. St Agnes appeared to her parents in a vision after her death in the company of a white lamb—thereafter her emblem. On her day lambs'-wool was offered on the altar to be spun and woven by nuns (see l. 117).

154 l. 173. *cates*: edible delicacies (Elizabethan); there is a semantic link with 'catering' (l. 177).

155 l. 206. *tongueless nightingale*: evokes the myth of Procne and Philomel in Ovid, *Metamorphoses vi*. The presence of this myth is a reminder that the events in this poem could be construed as rape.

156 l. 257. A sleep-inducing charm.

l. 261. Keats told Cowden Clarke that this line 'came into my head when I remembered how I used to listen in bed to your music at school'.

l. 266. *soother*: Keats's compound of 'smoother' and 'more soothing'.

157 l. 280. *unnerved*: weak, slack.

l. 292. *'La belle dame sans mercy'*. Title of a poem written by Alain Chartier in 1424; Keats's own poem of this title had not yet been composed.

159 l. 344. *haggard*: a haggard is a hawk that has refused training; so, 'wild', 'intractable'.

l. 355. *darkling*: an Elizabethanism for 'dark', 'obscure', which Keats made his own.

160 *The Eve of St. Mark*. Composed between 13 and 17 Feb. 1819, shortly after Keats's return from Chichester and Bedhampton; not published during Keats's life. St Mark's eve is on 24 Apr. The practice attached to it is described in John Brand's *Observations on Popular Antiquities* (London, 1813), i. 166: 'It is customary in Yorkshire ... for the common people to sit and watch in the church porch on St. Mark's Eve, from eleven o'clock at night till one in the morning. The third year (for this must be done thrice), they are supposed to see the ghosts of all those who are to die the next year, pass by into the church.

When any one sickens that is thought to have been seen in this manner, it is whispered about that he will not recover, for that such, or such an one, who watched St. Mark's Eve, says so.' The poem as it stands contains no reference to this custom, but the following poem—a fragment almost certainly intended to be part of the present poem—does. The poem's Middle English pastiche recalls Chatterton, though Keats's manner is more parodic and light-hearted. Cf. 'He is to weet a melancholy Carle' (above, p. 164).

161 l. 28. *golden broideries*: the gold illuminations of the volume; the patterns of these are often intricately intertwined.

l. 33. *Aaron's breastplate*: Exod. 28: 15–30, Lev. 8: 8.

ll. 33–4. *seven Candlesticks*: Rev. 1: 13–20.

l. 38. *golden Mice*: 1 Sam. 6: 4, 11, 18.

162 l. 79. *Lima Mice*: phonetic spelling of 'lemur mice'.

l. 80. *legless*. Traditionally, birds of Paradise are always in the air and never alight.

l. 81. *av'davat*: the amadavat, an Indian song-bird.

163 l. 98. In copying the fragment in a letter to George and Georgiana Keats breaks off at the end of this line to introduce the remainder: 'What follows is an imitation of the Authors in Chaucer's time—'t is more ancient than Chaucer himself and perhaps between him and Gower.'

l. 117. *holy shrine*: St Mark's basilica at Venice.

'*Gif ye wol stonden hardie wight*'. Date of composition uncertain but probably close to the date of the previous poem; not published during Keats's life.

164 '*Why did I laugh tonight? No voice will tell*'. Composed Mar. 1819; not published during Keats's life.

ll. 9–12. The figure of Marlowe's Doctor Faustus, who dies at midnight having made 'a deed of gift of body and soul' to Mephostophilis, is behind these lines and the imagery of the whole poem.

'*He is to weet a melancholy Carle*'. Composed 16 Apr. 1819 in Keats's journal-letter to George and Georgiana as an extempore portrait of Charles Brown 'in the manner of Spenser'; not published during Keats's life.

165 l. 10. *half and half*: 'a mixture of ale and beer, or beer and porter, in equal quantities' E. B. Partridge, *A Dictionary of Slang and Unconventional English* (rev. edn., London, 1949).

l. 14. *lewd ribbalds*: *FQ* II. i. 10.

l. 15. *lemans*. Lovers.

ll. 16–17. Ps. 13: 1.

l. 21. *olden Tom or ruin blue*. Two terms for gin—Blue Ruin was cheap gin.

ll. 22. *nantz*: cherry brandy (originally from Nantes).

ll. 26–7. 'The daughters of Zion are haughty . . . walking and mincing as they go, and making a tinkling with their feet' (Isa. 3: 16).

A dream, after reading Dante's Episode of Paolo and Francesca. Composed Apr. 1819; published in the *Indicator*, 28 June 1820, p. 304, where it is signed 'Caviare'—a reference to *Hamlet* II. ii. 457 possibly suggested by the review of *Endymion* in the *Chester Guardian* which deemed it 'caviar to the general'.

166 *La belle dame sans merci.* Composed 21 Apr. 1819 in Keats's journal-letter to George and Georgiana (the present text); published (in a different version) in the *Indicator*, 10 May 1820 where it, like the previous poem, is signed 'Caviare'. The title of the poem is that of a medieval ballad written by Alain Chartier in 1424.

167 *Sonnet to Sleep.* Composed late Apr. 1819; not published during Keats's life. This and the 4 poems which follow represent a period of concentrated technical endeavour and experiment with patterns of rhyme and consonance to bind a stanza.

168 *Ode to Psyche.* Composed late Apr. 1819; published in *1820*. Keats's treatment of the legend of Cupid and Psyche is based on the episode in Apuleius' *Golden Ass* in William Adlington's translation (1566).

l. 14. *Tyrian*: purple (a dye that comes from Tyre).

l. 21. *winged boy*: Cupid (not named *because* the speaker knew him).

169 l. 41. *lucent fans*: gleaming wings.

On Fame ('*Fame like a wayward girl will still be coy*'). Composed 30 Apr. 1819; not published during Keats's life.

170 l. 10. *Potiphar*: Gen. 39.

On Fame ('*How fever'd is that Man who cannot look*'). Composed 30 Apr. 1819 as an extempore in Keats's journal-letter to George and Georgiana; not published during Keats's life.

'*If by dull rhymes our English must be chain'd*'. Composed late Apr. or early May 1819 and enclosed in Keats's journal-letter to George and Georgiana; not published during Keats's life.

ll. 3, 5. *Fetter'd . . . Sandals.* Plays on the idea of metrical feet.

171 *Two or three Posies.* Composed probably on 1 May 1819 in a letter to Fanny Keats; not published during Keats's life.

l. 20. *Mrs.—mum!* The self-censored name is, as the rhyme suggests, 'Abbeys'. Fanny was still living under the restrictive care of her guardian Richard Abbey and his wife at the date of this letter. In a letter to George and Georgiana of 17–27 Sept. 1819 Keats writes 'Does not the word mum! go for ones finger beside the nose—I hope it does'.

172 *Ode on Indolence*. Composed during spring 1819; not published during Keats's life. A prose description of the mood which this poem treats occurs in the 19 Mar. passage of Keats's journal-letter to George and Georgiana: 'Neither Poetry, nor Ambition, nor Love have any alertness of countenance as they pass by me: they seem rather like three figures on a greek vase'. The mood of the poem is linked, reactively, to the pressure which Keats was under to make himself financially eligible to be Mrs Brawne's son-in-law.

Motto: Matt. 6: 28.

l. 10. *Phidian lore*. The mysteries of plastic art; Phidias (5th c. BC) was the creator of the Elgin Marbles.

173 l. 43. *lawn*: both fabric (picking up on 'embroider'd', l. 42) and grass.

l. 54. *pet-lamb*. In a letter to Mary-Ann Jeffery of 9 June 1819 Keats writes 'I hope I am a little more of a Philosopher than I was, consequently a little less of a versifying Pet-lamb.'

174 *'Shed no tear—O shed no tear'*. Date of composition uncertain, but probably some time in 1819; not published during Keats's life. The song was written to be included in Brown's unfinished 'The Fairies' Triumph'. The princes Elury and Azameth have heedlessly plucked a flower and seen it shrivel to dust. In their grief they 'heard a most enchanting melody breathed forth; and looking up they saw, perched on a slender bough, a bird of lovely form, and brilliant plumage, and it gazed down on them with its mild dove-like eyes, and warbled its song to cheer them'. That song is the poem.

Ode to a Nightingale. Composed May, 1819; published in *Annals of the Fine Arts*, July, 1819 and in *1820*. Brown described the circumstances of the poem's composition in his 'Life' of Keats (written 17 years after the event): 'In the spring of 1819 a nightingale had built her nest near my house. Keats felt a tranquil and continual joy in her song; and one morning he took his chair from the breakfast-table to the grass-plot under the plum-tree, where he sat for two or three hours. When he came into the house, I perceived he had some scraps of paper in his hand, and these he was quietly thrusting behind the books. On inquiry, I found those scraps, four or five in number, contained his poetic feeling on the song of our nightingale. The writing was not well legible; and it was difficult to arrange the stanzas on so many scraps. With his assistance I succeeded, and this was his "Ode to a Nightingale", a poem which has been the delight of every one'

l. 2. *hemlock*: a sedative or poison.

175 l. 15. *warm South*: southern wine.

l. 26. Tom Keats had died of tuberculosis on 1 Dec. 1818. In a letter to Bailey (10 June 1818) Keats writes: 'were it my choice I would reject a petrarchal coronation—on account of my dying day, and because women have Cancers'.

176 l. 60. *requiem*: prolepsis, anticipating the speaker's death.

ll. 65–7. Ruth was driven from her native Moab by famine and worked in Bethlehem as a gleaner (Ruth 2: 1–3). Hazlitt, in his lecture 'On Poetry in General', writes that 'The story of Ruth . . . is as if all the depth of natural affection in the human race was involved in her breast' (*Works*, v. 16).

177 *Ode on a Grecian Urn*. Composed during 1819; published in *Annals of the Fine Arts*, 15 (Jan. 1820), and in *1820*. The Keats-Shelley Memorial House in Rome has a drawing, or tracing, made by Keats of the Sosibios Vase taken from the Musée Napoléon. The 'heifer lowing at the skies' (l. 33) is, however, almost certainly inspired not by an image on an urn but by the heifer being led to sacrifice in the south frieze of the Elgin Marbles.

178 l. 41. *brede . . . overwrought*. The principal meanings are concerned with decoration and embroidery, but the biological and emotional senses of the homophones are played on.

l. 48. *friend to man*. In a letter to Rice (24 Mar. 1818) Keats remarks that Milton was 'an active friend to Man all his Life and . . . since his death'.

Ode on Melancholy. Composed during 1819; published in *1820*.

179 ll. 6–7. Psyche (the soul) was often represented as a butterfly; the death's head moth, whose markings resemble the human skull, is presented as a deathly antitype.

The Fall of Hyperion. Begun as a revision of 'Hyperion' probably during July, 1819 while Keats was at Shanklin, Ise of Wight; 'given up' *c.*21 Sept. 1819; not published during Keats's life. The poem attempts a reconstruction of the abandoned 'Hyperion' and retains many passages from the earlier poem. Here Keats casts the narrative in the form of a dream vision (a genre with medieval precedents, such as Chaucer's *The Book of the Duchess*). Keats's professed reason for abandoning the poem was his dislike of its 'Miltonic inversions'. He felt Milton's influence to be creatively suffocating and it was clearly so pervasive in this poem as to be ineradicable. (This is equally, if not more, true of 'Hyperion'.) Keats's rapidly deteriorating health may also have contributed to his abandonment of the poem which had reached a position of impasse. His friends tended to prefer the earlier 'Hyperion' and Keats decided against including the new poem in *1820*.

179 *Canto i*

181 l. 48. *Caliphat*. Keats probably meant an individual caliph (Muslim ruler) rather than his abstract office (caliphate); the line smacks of Gothic melodrama.

l. 70. *faulture*: weakness (the letter draft has 'failing'); the word carries a sense of geological fault.

l. 74. *asbestus*: 'the unquenchable stone' (*OED*).

l. 75. Matt. 6: 20.

183 l. 144–5. *Dated on | Thy doom*: postponed your death.

l. 157. Cf. 'Sleep and Poetry' 122–5.

184 ll. 187–210. Woodhouse records 'Keats seems to have intended to erase this.' The lines to some extent conflict with the rest of the poem.

l. 205. *Iliad* i. 9–12 (Apollo spreads a plague among the Greeks).

ll. 207–8: perhaps Hunt (or Thomas Moore), Wordsworth, and Byron.

185 l. 222. *war*: the war of the Titans against the rebel Olympians.

l. 226. *Moneta*: another name for Mnemosyne (the name used in 'Hyperion').

187 l. 294. 'Hyperion' began here.

190 l. 411. Pan is solitary because the Golden Age has passed.

191 *Canto ii*

192 l. 50. *Mnemosyne*: Moneta.

193 *Lamia*. Begun late June or early July 1819 while at Shanklin, and completed at Winchester during late Aug. or early Sept. Revised Mar. 1820; published in *1820*. Keats wrote the poem with an eye to its reception, wishing to create a poem less 'weak-sided' and 'smokeable' than his other two narrative poems. He placed the poem first in *1820*. The prime source for the story is the passage from Burton's *Anatomy of Melancholy* (III. 2. i. 1), which was printed at the end of the poem in *1820*, as it is here. The character of Lamia owes something to that of Geraldine in Coleridge's 'Christabel'.

Part i

ll. 1–145. The episode of Hermes and the nymph derives from Ovid, *Metamorphoses* ii. 708f.

l. 11. *his great summoner*: i.e. Jove, whose cup he bears.

194 l. 46. *cirque-couchant*: lying coiled—a neologism disguised as an archaic heraldic term.

l. 55. *penanced*: transformed from her former shape as penance or punishment.

195 l. 81. *star of Lethe*. One of Hermes' roles is that of *psychopomp* (conductor of the souls of the dead).

196 l. 114. *psalterian*: like the music of the psaltery.

l. 115. *Circean*: dangerously enchanting (like Circe); or, perhaps, 'transformed' (like one of Circe's victims).

ll. 126–7. The idea of realising dreams is a favourite one with Keats (cf. *Endymion*, 'The Eve of St. Agnes'). In a letter to Bailey (22 Nov. 1817) he writes: 'The Imagination may be compared to Adam's dream—he awoke and found it truth.'

197 l. 163. *rubious-argent*: reddish silver—another pseudo-heraldic coinage (Shakespeare uses 'rubious').

l. 174. *Cenchreas*: Cenchrea was a Corinthian port.

l. 179. *Cleone*: a village south of Corinth.

199 l. 256. He is her captive.

200 l. 279. Scholars were reputedly versed in spirit lore.

201 l. 329. *Peris*: Persian genii—familiar through pantomime.

l. 347. *comprized*: absorbed.

202 l. 375. *Apollonius*: Apollonius of Tyana, Pythagorean philosopher b. *c*.1 AD credited with occult knowledge.

203 *Part ii*

205 l. 80. *The serpent*: python.

206 l. 136. *viewless*: invisible (cf. 'Ode to a Nightingale' (above, p. 175) 33).

207 l. 160. *daft*: bemused, foxed.

208 ll. 199–220. A draft of these lines makes the contrast between the gross guests and the ethereal banquet the source of social satire:

> 'Where is that Music?' cries a Lady fair,
> 'Aye, where is it my dear? Up in the air'?
> Another whispers 'Poo!' saith Glutton 'Mum!'
> Then makes his shiny mouth a napkin for his thumb.

ll. 226. Bacchus' wand ('thyrsus') is wound with vine and ivy.

ll. 229–37. Hazlitt, in his 1818 lecture 'On Poetry in General' had said that 'the progress of knowledge and refinement has a tendency to circumscribe the limits of the imagination, and to clip the wings of poetry' (*Works*, v. 9). Haydon recorded in his diary that during a dinner-party at his house on 28 Dec. 1817 Keats had agreed with

Lamb that Newton had 'destroyed all the Poetry of the rainbow by reducing it to a prism'.

211 '*Pensive they sit, and roll their languid eyes*'. Composed at Winchester in a letter to George and Georgiana on 17 Sept. 1819; not published during Keats's life. In spite of having by this time declared his love for Fanny Brawne Keats, wilfully preserving his integrity and ill able to provide for himself, let alone a wife, was resistant to romantic love during his stay in Winchester.

l. 9. *humane society*. The Royal Humane Society was founded in 1774.

l. 10. *Mr. Werter*: sensitive hero of Goethe's cult novel *Die Leiden des jungen Werther* (1773), trans. Richard Graves as *The Sorrows of Young Werter: A German story* (London, 1783). Werter is conscious that 'Every moment I am myself a destroyer. The most innocent walk deprives of life thousands of poor insects.'

212 l. 15. *Cauliflower*: the shape of the untrimmed wick.

l. 16. *winding sheet*: 'a mass of solidified drippings or grease clinging to the side of a candle, resembling a sheet folded in creases and regarded as an omen of death or calamity' (*OED*).

l. 23. *Wapping*: a district in East London, near the Thames. East London has long been associated with garment manufacture.

To Autumn. Composed at Winchester on 19 Sept. 1819; published in 1820.

213 l. 25. *bloom*: a transitive verb.

'*Bright Star, would I were stedfast as thou art*'. Composed during 1819; not published during Keats's life. This was once, mistakenly, believed to be Keats's last poem. In a letter to Tom (25–7 June 1818) Keats writes that the views of Lake Windermere 'refine one's sensual vision into a sort of north star which can never cease to be open lidded and stedfast over the wonders of the great Power'.

214 *On Coaches* (from *The Jealousies*). Composed probably during Nov. and Dec. 1819 at Hampstead. This extract, with this title, was published in the *Indicator*, 23 Aug. 1820 (the present text). The (unfinished) whole was published after Keats's death with the title 'The Cap and Bells; Or, the Jealousies. A Faery Tale. Unfinished'.

The poem remained unfinished because of Keats's ill health. The longer poem deals—lightly, for once—with the Keatsian topic of miscegenation between different orders of being; in this case between fairy and mortal. The fairy emperor Elfinan, preferring the substantial embrace of the mortal Bertha to that of his betrothed, the fairy Bellanaine, attempts to evade his arranged marriage by capturing and eloping with his beloved. (The situation has parallels both with the Prince Regent's marriage to the Princess Caroline and with Byron's unhappy marriage. Elfinan summons his page Eban, 'A fay of colour, slave from top to toe', on an errand to Hum the soothsayer whose assistance he requires in planning his elopement. The extract describes Eban's mode of conveyance.

l. 10. *the string*: the check-string which passengers pulled to signal to the driver to stop.

l. 11. Jarvey: the word used for a driver of a hackney coach (like the modern 'cabbie'); here the speaker addresses the coach and driver as one.　　*hack*: a hackney cab and also the horse.

l. 13. *linsey-wolsey*: a mixture of wool and flax; a cheap cloth.

l. 19. *crop*: stomach.

215 ll. 35–6. *Tilburies . . . Phaetons . . . Curricles . . . Mail-coaches*: all forms of light carriage.

l. 40. *Louted*: bowed (Spenserian, like the stanza).

'*What can I do to drive away*'. Composed probably late in 1819; not published during Keats's life.

216 l. 33. *wrecked*: often emended to 'wretched'; Keats was probably playing on a medieval pronounciation of 'wrecched' whose etymology he may have misunderstood.

217 *To Fanny*. Composed late 1819 or early 1820—most probably after 3 Feb. when Keats was confined indoors after a second haemorrhage and suffered agonies of jealousy at the neighbouring Fanny's relative freedom; not published during Keats's life.

l. 1. *let my spirit blood*! Blood-letting was then, as for the previous 3,000 years, a common therapeutic practice and one which Keats was regularly enduring at the time he wrote this poem. The principle was that pressure would thereby be eased.

l. 27. *wreath*: perhaps a conscious or unconscious play on 'reef'.

218 l. 40. *blow-ball*: dandelion clock.

'*This living hand, now warm and capable*'. Composed probably late 1819; not published during Keats's life. The lines may have been written for inclusion in some future play. It is equally possible to read them as expressions of the jealousy afflicting the previous poem and in the manner of Donne's 'The Visitation'.

219 '*In after time a Sage of mickle lore*'. Keats wrote these lines at the end of the *FQ* in the now lost copy of Spenser which he gave to Fanny Brawne. Brown describes this as 'the last stanza of any kind that [Keats] . . . wrote before his lamented death.' Not published during Keats's life.

l. 2. *the Giant*. See *FQ* v. ii. 30–50 where the Giant travesties justice in his revolutionary attempt to make all things equal. In *FQ* Sir Artegall (the knight of Justice) and Talus, his iron squire, oppose and destroy the giant. Here Keats envisages the giant's re-education into a triumphant champion of real freedom. (See Introduction (above, p. x) for Brown's comments on the poem's politics.)

Further Reading

MAJOR EDITIONS

John Keats, *Poems* (London, 1817).
—— *Endymion* (London, 1818).
—— *Lamia, Isabella, The Eve of St. Agnes, and Other Poems* (London, 1820).
R. M. Milnes (ed.), *Life, Letters, and Literary Remains of John Keats*, 2 vols. (London, 1848).
H. B. Forman (ed.), *The Poetry and Prose of John Keats* (London, 1890; rev. edn. by M. B. Forman, 8 vols. (London, 1938–9: the 'Hampstead Keats')).
E. de Selincourt (ed.), *The Poems of John Keats* (London, 1905, rev. edn. 1926).
H. E. Rollins (ed.), *The Letters of John Keats*, 2 vols. (Cambridge, Mass., 1958).
Robert Gittings (ed.), *Letters of John Keats* [selected] (Oxford, 1970, repr. 1975).
Jack Stillinger (ed.), *John Keats: Complete Poems* (Boston, Mass., 1978).
Elizabeth Cook (ed.), *John Keats* (Oxford 1990; repr. 1992).

WORKS OF REFERENCE

An annual bibliography has appeared in the *Keats-Shelley Journal* from 1952 and covers works dating back to July 1950. These bibliographies from July 1950 to June 1962 are reprinted in D. B. Green and E. G. Wilson (eds.), *Keats, Shelley, Byron, Hunt and their Circles: A Bibliography* (Lincoln, Nebr., 1964) and those covering July 1962 to December 1974 in R. A. Harley (ed.), *Keats, Shelley, Byron, Hunt and their Circles: A Bibliography* (Lincoln, Nebr., 1978).

CRITICISM AND BIOGRAPHY

John Bayley, 'Keats and Reality', *Proceedings of the British Academy* (London, 1962).
W. J. Bate,—(ed.), *Keats: a Collection of Critical Essays* (Englewood Cliffs, NJ, 1964).
—— *John Keats* (London, 1979).
Bernard Blackstone, *The Consecrated Urn* (London, 1959).
Harold Bloom, *The Visionary Company* (Garden City, 1961).
Cleanth Brooks, 'History without Footnotes: An Account of Keats's Urn', in Cleanth Brooks, *The Well Wrought Urn* (New York, 1947).
Hermione De Almeida, *Romantic Medicine and John Keats* (New York, 1991).

Morris Dickstein, *Keats and his Poetry: a Study in Development* (Chicago, 1971).

Claude Lee Finney, *The Evolution of Keats's Poetry* (New York, 1936).

Robert Gittings, *The Living Year* (London, 1954).

—— *John Keats* (London, 1968).

Donald C. Goellnicht, *The Poet-Physician: Keats and Medical Science* (Pittsburgh, 1984).

Ian Jack, *Keats and the Mirror of Art* (Oxford, 1967).

John Jones, *John Keats's Dream of Truth* (Oxford, 1969).

G. Matthews (ed.), *Keats: the Critical Heritage* (London, 1971).

Christopher Ricks, *Keats and Embarrassment* (Oxford, 1984).

M. R. Ridley, *Keats's Craftsmanship* (Oxford, 1933, repr. London, 1963).

Stuart M. Sperry, *Keats the Poet* (Princeton, NJ, 1973).

Jack Stillinger, *The Hoodwinking of Madeline* (Urbana, Ill., 1971).

Helen Vendler, *The Odes of John Keats* (Cambridge, Mass., 1983).

Aileen Ward, *John Keats: The Making of a Poet* (New York, 1963).

Susan Wolfson, Introduction to 'Keats and Politics: A Forum', *Studies in Romanticism*, 25 (1986), 171–81. This includes Morris Dickstein's 1983 Modern Language Association paper 'Keats and Politics' (pp. 175–81) and essays by William Keach (pp. 182–96), David Bromwich (pp. 197–210), Paul H. Fry (pp. 211–19), and Alan J. Bewell (pp. 220–8).

HISTORICAL CONTEXT

Marilyn Butler, *Romantics, Rebels and Reactionaries* (Oxford, 1981).

S. Macoby, *English Radicalism 1786–1832* (London, 1955).

E. P. Thompson, *The Making of the English Working Class* (London, 1963, rev. edn. Harmondsworth, 1968).

W. H. Wickwar, *The Struggle for the Freedom of the Press 1819–1832* (London, 1928).

Glossary of Classical Names

Actaeon: a huntsman who came across Diana bathing naked with her attendants. The goddess transformed him into a stag and he was pursued and devoured by his own hounds.

Adonis: a beautiful huntsman loved by Venus, against whose advice he hunted a boar who impaled and killed him. Venus, in sorrow at his death, changed him into an anemone. Proserpine restored him to life so that he might spend half the year in the underworld with her, the other half above ground with Venus. The myth of Adonis is consequently involved with regeneration and renewal (as in Spenser's 'Garden of Adonis', *FQ* III. vi). The 'Adonian feast' referred to in *Lamia* (i. 320) was an annual fertility rite, held in Venus' temple. Shakespeare's *Venus and Adonis* tells the first part of the story.

Aeolus: king of storms and winds.

Aeothon: one of the horses that drew the chariot of the sun.

Alpheus: a river in Arcadia who fell in love with the nymph Arethusa when she bathed in him. Diana changed her into a fountain which the river Alpheus pursued under the sea as far as the land of Ortygia where the fountain Arethusa rose.

Amphion: son of Jupiter; lyrist of such power that the walls of Thebes were constructed by the sound of his lyre. Keats conflates him with Arion whose music drew helpful dolphins.

Amphitrite: wife of Neptune; mother of Triton.

Andromeda: tied to a rock jutting over the sea to be devoured by a monster in sacrifice to Neptune, she was rescued by Perseus who petrified the monster with Medusa's head.

Apollo: son of Jupiter and Latona, brother of Diana. He took over the role of sun-god from the Titan Hyperion and, as such, drives his chariot daily through the heavens. He is also the god of music and poetry (and often represented with a lyre), a prophet, and the god of medicine.

Arcady: Arcadia; home of poet shepherds and of Pan, their god.

Arethusa: *see* Alpheus.

Argonauts: heroes who sailed with Jason in search of the Golden Fleece.

Argus: a king of Argos. He had one hundred eyes, only two of which slept at any time. Mercury lulled him to sleep with his lyre and slew him (on Jupiter's orders) while he was supposed to be watching over Io on Juno's behalf.

Ariadne: lover of Theseus (who left her) and of Bacchus who crowned her with seven stars which became a constellation at her death.

Atlas: one of the Titans who fought against the Apollonian gods; later changed by Perseus into a mountain in north Africa so high it was said to bear the heavens.

Aurora: goddess of dawn; dawn itself.

Bacchus: son of Jupiter and Semele; god of the vine. He is represented as a young man, crowned with ivy and vine leaves and carrying a thyrsus (a pine-staff twined round with ivy and vine leaves). The panther is sacred to him. He is associated with (and paralleled to) the Egyptian god Osiris. He is represented at the head of his rout, drawn in a chariot by a lion and a tiger, accompanied by Pan, Silenus (his foster-father), satyrs, and Bacchantes (followers inspired by divine fury).

Boreas: god of the North Wind.

Briareus: son of Coelus and Terra; one of the Titans who fought the Apollonians. He had a hundred hands and fifty heads.

Caf: Keats makes him a Titan, father to Asia. Keats found the name of Kaf, a mountain which surrounds the world, in H. Weber's *Tales of the East* (1812) and S. Beckford's *Vathek* (1816).

Caria: home of Endymion.

Ceres: daughter of Saturn and Vesta; goddess of corn and harvest; mother (by Jupiter) of Proserpine.

Circe: daughter of Sol and Perseis. A powerful witch, she lived in Aeaea where, after feasting men as guests, she transformed them into beasts. She did this to all Odysseus' men, but not to Odysseus who became her lover and stayed away from Penelope for another year.

Clio: daughter of Jupiter and Mnemosyne; Muse of history.

Coelus: son (and later husband) of Tellus. His sons were Titans. He is also called Uranus.

Cupid: son of Venus and Jupiter; Eros, the god of love. He is usually represented as a child with a quiverful of arrows with which to wound mortals with love. But as Psyche's lover he should be thought of as a young man.

Cybele: sister and wife of Saturn, daughter of Coelus and Tellus. She is often taken for her mother and invoked as mother earth and mother of the gods.

Cynthia: another name for Diana.

Cytherea: Cyprus, Venus' birthplace.

Daedalus: a great artificer and inventor. He created the Cretan labyrinth and, in order that he and his son Icarus might escape King Minos, wings of wax and feathers.

Diana: daughter of Jupiter and Latona, sister of Apollo (and Moon to his Sun). She has several offices, all associated with her role of moon-goddess, and is goddess of childbirth, chastity, and hunting. As Diana she is represented as a hunter attended by nymphs. In the heavens she is known as Luna, and in hell as Hecate where she is associated with magic and enchantment.

Dido: Queen and founder of Carthage; lover of Aeneas who deserted her under divine compulsion. Dido burned herself to death.

Dis: Pluto.

Dolor: a Titan to Keats (though not to Hesiod or Hyginus). In Hyginus is the phrase 'ex Aethere et Terra, Dolor' ('from Air and Earth, Grief').

Doris: daughter of Oceanus and Tethys; married to her brother Nereus. Their fifty daughters are the Nereides.

Dryad: wood-nymph.

Dryope: there are several nymphs of this name, two of them invoked in *Endymion*. One is mother of Pan by Mercury; the other a nymph raped by Apollo and, along with her son Amphisus, changed into a lotus.

Echo: daughter of Air and Tellus, formerly attendant to Juno who punished her indiscretion by limiting her speech to answers. She fell in love with Narcissus and turned to stone in her grief at his lack of response. The stone retained her voice.

Elysium: paradisal home of the virtuous dead.

Enceladus: son of Titan and Tellus; the most powerful of the Titans who fought the Apollonians. He was eventually overwhelmed under Mount Aetna whose flames are thought to be his breath.

Endymion: a Carian shepherd with whom Diana fell in love when she saw him naked on the top of Mount Latmos. Diana visited him nightly while he slept.

Erebus: son of Chaos and Darkness; an infernal deity used by Keats and others to signify hell itself.

Eurydice: wife of Orpheus, who entered the underworld to recover her at her death. She was allowed to follow him on the condition that he did not turn back during the ascent to earth. Orpheus failed and lost.

Flora: the Roman goddess of flowers and gardens.

Ganymede: a beautiful boy, snatched to heaven by Jupiter who made him cupbearer to the gods.

Glaucus: sea deity who fell in love with the Nereid Scylla and applied to Circe for help (*see* Scylla).

Hamadryads: female deities of particular trees. Their lives are coextensive with those of their trees.

Hecate: Diana's infernal name.

Helicon: a mountain in Boeotia sacred to the Muses.

Hermes: Mercury.

Hesperus: son of Iapetus; the name given to the planet Venus when it appears after sunset.

Hippocrene: fountain that flows from Mount Helicon. According to Baldwin the waters are 'violet-coloured, and are represented as endowed with voice and articulate sound'.

Hyacinthus: a boy loved by Apollo and Zephyrus. Jealous of Apollo, whom Hyacinthus loved, Zephyrus killed the boy with a quoit. Apollo changed the boy's blood into a flower and inscribed it with his own lament.

Hybla: mountain in Sicily; site of odoriferous flowers and a good place for honey.

Hyperion: son of Coelus and Tellus; a Titan. God of the sun until supplanted by Apollo.

Iapetus: a Titan; son of Coelus and Tellus.

Ida: mountain near Troy where Paris gave Venus the prize as the most beautiful. Hence a synonym for Venus.

Iris: goddess of the rainbow.

Ixion: banished from heaven by Jupiter and eternally tied to a revolving wheel in hell.

Jove: Jupiter.

Jupiter: son of Saturn and Ops (who saved him when Saturn devoured all his sons); educated on Mount Ida. After defeating Saturn he divided the world between himself and his brothers and became ruler of heaven.

Latmos: a mountain in Caria where Endymion encountered the moon.

Latona: mother of Diana and Apollo.

Leander: lover of Hero, he swam the Hellespont to spend the night with her and was drowned. Marlowe tells their story in *Hero and Leander*.

Leda: wife of Tyndarus, King of Sparta. She was impregnated by Jupiter (who came to her as a swan) and bore two eggs, one of which contained Helen of Troy.

Lethe: a river in hell; the drinking of its waters induces forgetfulness of all that went before.

Lucifer: the name of the planet Venus when it appears before dawn.

Lycaeus: a mountain in Arcadia sacred to Jupiter and Pan.

Maia: goddess of the month of May; mother of Mercury.

Mars: god of war; lover of Venus (with whom he was caught *in flagrante* by Vulcan).

Mercury: the Roman name for Hermes, son of Maia and Jupiter. He is the messenger of the gods and wears a winged hat (the *petasus*) and has wings (*talaria*) on his heels; he also carries a wand (the *caduceus*) with wings at the top and two intertwined serpents on the stem. He is noted for his nimbleness and wit (he is the god of eloquence) and also for his magical powers. As 'psychopomp' he conducts the souls of the dead.

Midas: King of Phrygia. In recompense for the hospitality he had shown towards Silenus, Bacchus undertook to grant whatever he wished. Midas asked that all he touched should turn to gold. This he regretted when he was unable to eat.

Minos: one of the three judges of hell.

Mnemosyne: originally a Titan; daughter of Coelus and Tellus. By Jupiter she is mother of the nine Muses. Her name means 'memory'.

Momus: son of Nox; god of satire.

Moneta: although this is a name given to Juno, (daughter of Saturn and wife of Jupiter), Keats's Moneta is identified with Mnemosyne on the authority of Hyginus.

Morpheus: son and minister of Somnus, god of sleep.

Mulciber: Vulcan.

Naiad: female deity of woods and streams.

Nais: sea nymph; mother of Glaucus.

Narcissus: beautiful boy who fell in love with his own reflected image and pined to death.

Neptune: son of Saturn after conquering whom he took over the rule of the sea. He wields a trident.

Nereids: sea nymphs; daughters of Nereus and Doris.

Nereus: son of Oceanus and Tellus; a sea deity resident in the Aegean sea. He is a prophet and is usually represented as an old man.

Niobe: mother by Amphion of ten sons and ten daughters. All but one of these were killed by Diana and Apollo on behalf of their mother Latona whom Niobe had insulted. In her grief she turned to stone and is almost an emblem of sorrow ('like Niobe, all tears' (*Hamlet* 1, ii. 149)).

Nox: daughter of Chaos; one of the most ancient deities.

Oceanus: son of Coelus and Tellus; he presided over every part of the sea. According to Homer he was the father of all gods.

Olympians: members of Jupiter's court on the top of Mount Olympus.

Ops: daughter of Coelus and Tellus: often identified with Cybele.

Oread: a mountain nymph, such as one of those who attend Diana.

Orpheus: son of Calliope and Apollo; a Thracian shepherd whose lyric music had the power to move animals and stones as well as Pluto, who allowed him to attempt the recovery of Eurydice.

Osiris: son of Jupiter and Niobe; husband of Isis. He is a great Egyptian deity and often identified with Bacchus.

Pan: the Greek πᾶν means 'all' or 'everything'. Pan is the son of Mercury and Dryope. He is the god of shepherds; a satyr—goat from the waist down and with horns on his head. His chief home is Arcadia. He attempted to rape the nymph Syrinx, and when she eluded him by changing into a reed, he made the reed into a 'pan-pipe' and played it.

Paphos: Venus' birthplace in Cyprus.

Pegasus: a winged horse born of Medusa's blood. He lives on Mount Helicon and is an emblem of the soaring imagination.

Philomel: the name often refers to any nightingale. The original Philomel was raped by her brother-in-law Tereus who cut out her tongue to keep her quiet. She conveyed her history to her sister Procne by weaving a tapestry. Procne punished Tereus by serving their son, Itylus, to him as meat. Before Tereus could stab them Procne was turned into a swallow and Philomel into a nightingale.

Phoebe: another name for Diana (though, properly, her Titan mother).

Phoebus: Apollo; the sun.

Phorcus: son of Pontus and Tellus; father (with his sister Ceto) of the Gorgons and the dragon who guarded the apples of the Hesperides. Keats thought of him as a Titan.

Pleiad: one of the Pleiades, Atlas' seven daughters who were constellated at their deaths.

Pluto: son of Saturn and Ops; ruler of the infernal kingdom after the division of Saturn's realm. His wife is Proserpine.

Polyphemus: King of the Cyclops (one-eyed shepherd giants); he was outsmarted by Odysseus who blinded him and escaped with those of his men whom Polyphemus had not already eaten.

Porphyrion: son of Coelus and Tellus: a Titan.

Proserpine: daughter of Ceres and Jupiter; resident of Sicily until Pluto carried her down to the underworld and made her his queen. Ceres sought her everywhere in vain. To comfort her Jupiter arranged for Proserpine to spend half the year above ground with her mother.

Proteus: a sea deity with prophetic gifts. He seldom uses these because of his ability to change shape and elude those who would consult him.

Psyche: a nymph with whom Cupid fell in love and whom he visited unseen at night. Psyche, incited by the suggestion that her lover was a serpent, hid a lamp in order to see him. A drop of hot oil fell from his lamp and woke the god who, once seen, fled. After a period of expiatory suffering Psyche was reunited with Cupid and granted immortality by Jupiter. Consequently she is a recent addition to the Olympian hierarchy. The Greek ψυχή means 'soul' and also 'butterfly' (the latter an emblem of the former).

Pyrrha: *see* Deucalion.

Pythia: priestess of Apollo at Delphi and a prophetic medium. When divinely inspired she would often seem possessed by furies and was fearful to witness.

Saturn: son of Coelus (or Uranus) and Tellus; leader of the Titans, with whom he was overthrown by his sons under Jupiter's leadership. According to traditional accounts the banished Saturn fled to Italy where his civilizing and beneficent rule came to be known as the Golden Age. Keats antedates this Golden Age to before the overthrow of the Titans.

Scylla: a Nereid with whom Glaucus fell in love. Circe, to whom Glaucus had applied for help, wanted Glaucus for herself and transformed Scylla into a monster. In her terror Scylla threw herself into the sea and was changed into the rock which bears her name.

Silenus: tutor and companion to Bacchus. He is usually represented as fat, jolly, and drunk, riding on an ass.

Syrinx: a nymph who was transformed into a reed in her flight from Pan.

Tartarus: 'the abode of woe'; the part of the underworld that is not Elysium.

Tellus: the earth; mother of the Titans. Only Chaos is older.

Tempe: a valley in Thessaly celebrated for its cool shades and pleasant landscape.

Tethys: daughter of Uranus and Tellus; wife of Oceanus and mother of the great rivers and the Oceanides.

Thalia: the Muse of festivals and of pastoral and comic poetry; she is one of the three Graces.

Themis: for Keats, following Hesiod, one of the Titans.

Thetis: a sea goddess; daughter of Nereus and Doris; mother of Achilles.

Titans: the forty-five sons of Coelus and Tellus. They include Saturn, Hyperion, Oceanus, Iapetus, Briareus, and Cottus. They were giants of enormous strength.

Triton: son of Neptune and Amphitrite; a sea deity. He is usually represented blowing a conch shell.

Typhon: for Keats, a Titan.

Urania: daughter of Jupiter and Mnemosyne; Muse of astronomy. She is usually represented in an azure robe and crowned with stars.

Uranus: another name for Coelus.

Venus: sea-born goddess of beauty; mother of Cupid (by Mars). Her girdle (or 'zone') has the power to impart beauty and excite love. Among the many she has loved is Adonis. Venus is also the name of the evening star.

Vesper: another name for Venus, the evening star.

Zephyrus: the West Wind, son of Atreus and Aurora. He is able to generate fruit and flowers with his sweet breath and is represented as a delicate winged youth.

Index of Titles and First Lines

The Oxford World's Classics Website

www.worldsclassics.co.uk

- Information about new titles
- Explore the full range of Oxford World's Classics
- Links to other literary sites and the main OUP webpage
- Imaginative competitions, with bookish prizes
- Peruse *Compass*, the Oxford World's Classics magazine
- Articles by editors
- Extracts from Introductions
- A forum for discussion and feedback on the series
- Special information for teachers and lecturers

www.worldsclassics.co.uk

American Literature

British and Irish Literature

Children's Literature

Classics and Ancient Literature

Colonial Literature

Eastern Literature

European Literature

History

Medieval Literature

Oxford English Drama

Poetry

Philosophy

Politics

Religion

The Oxford Shakespeare